'And *then* I met...'

'And *then* I met...'

STORIES OF GROWING UP, MEETING FAMOUS PEOPLE,
AND ANNOYING THE HELL OUT OF THEM

JAMES ROGAN

SHENANDOAH
PRESS

'And *then* I met....'

Copyright © 2014, 2021 by James Rogan

Library of Congress Control Number: 2021940329

Hardcover ISBN: 978-1-7369334-3-5
Paperback ISBN: 978-1-7369334-2-8
eBook ISBN: 978-1-7369334-4-2

Book designed by Mark Karis
Printed in the United States of America

For my mother Alice,
who forgave all the times that I ditched school to meet politicians,

And for my kid brother Pat,
who always handled the dirty work.

CONTENTS

INTRODUCTION

Six degrees of separation, a theory developed in the 1960s, holds that everyone in the world connects to everyone else by no more than six people. For example, even though we have never met, I once met someone who met someone who met someone who met you. The chain connects everyone by no more than six people.

I don't know if this notion has any validity, but it intrigues me because, according to it, I am only one degree away from Marilyn Monroe and Rudolph Valentino; from Winston Churchill and Theodore Roosevelt; from Babe Ruth and Charles Lindbergh; from Buffalo Bill and Chief Crazy Horse. On the darker side, just one person stands between me and Charles Manson, Al Capone, and Adolf Hitler. When it comes to "no degree of separation," meaning the people I've met whose stories once populated the headlines, the list is endless. Their ranks include presidents and the men that they vanquished to win the White House, great statesmen of their day, movie stars, astronauts, and sports legends. I had one friend who costarred in *Gone with the Wind,* and another who danced with Judy Garland in *The Wizard of Oz.* I was "attacked" by an Indian who witnessed General Custer's massacre at Little Big Horn. I've "sparred" with Muhammad Ali, and I played practical jokes on both Pope John Paul II and the first man on the Moon.

A congressman meeting famous people is no big deal; in fact, it goes with the turf. The difference between me and the other legislators with whom I served is that I met most of the ones in this book when I was a boy, and I did it under very unlikely circumstances. No, they weren't the friends of my wealthy or connected parents. I was the illegitimate son of a convicted felon mother who later raised four children on welfare and food stamps. My high school principal expelled me when I was in the tenth grade and I never returned to earn a diploma. I spent my teens hanging around car thieves and drug users. I sold vacuum cleaners to the local brothels and I bartended in Hollywood stripper clubs. During these roughhouse years, I carried a gun (and sometimes I used it). How I went from this background to university graduate, lawyer, gang murder prosecutor, state court judge, legislator, congressman, author, husband, and father instead of ending up on a police blotter or on a morgue slab is a great story, but it's not one for this journey. Dig up a copy of my first book, *Rough Edges: My Unlikely Road from Welfare to Washington*, to learn about that early and wild ride.

So, how did I stay out of prison? The short answer is that as a young boy, and despite all the swirling dysfunction around me, I developed an insatiable appetite for history, government, and politics. I worked hard to get my education, and I spent 30 years working even harder to reach Washington as a congressman. Once I got there, I became something of a Capitol Hill nuisance for demanding respect for the rule of law over fidelity to the latest polling data. It's funny how the voters always say they want politicians who will do what is right rather than what is popular—until they get one, and then they get mad at the guy who didn't do what was popular. That's another great story, and you'll find it in my second book, *Catching Our Flag: Behind the Scenes of a Presidential Impeachment.*

• • •

Readers of my earlier books know that I am at heart a political aficionado, a lifelong collector of campaign memorabilia, and (mostly) a wannabe historian. I started meeting famous people to ask for autographs and advice when I was 12. Although my interest centered on politicians, these encounters covered the gamut of fame-dom. I brought along my camera and notebook to memorialize my adventures. These photo albums and diaries remained buried in storage until early 2013 when I began working on this book. As I read my old entries (most unseen since first written some 40 years earlier), I noticed that my contemporary memories had more color than the hastily scrawled, bland, and ancient notebook jottings of a young boy.

The dilemma: how to harmonize the dull written source with my vivid recollections? The 1962 film, *The Man Who Shot Liberty Valance,* helped resolve the question. The movie opened with aging U.S. Senator Ransom Stoddard (who built his career on the reputation he earned as a young lawyer in the Old West for killing outlaw Liberty Valance) returning to the small town of Shinbone for the funeral of the town drunk. When the reporter from the *Shinbone Star* demanded to know why America's most distinguished statesman had come back for the burial of a ne'er-do-well, the movie fades to the past for the story. Near the film's end, the plot returns to the present and the senator confesses to the reporter that it was the drunk, and not he, that had killed Liberty Valance. Senator Stoddard had built his entire career by taking credit for another man's act. After hearing the confession, the reporter tore up his notes. When the senator asked why the reporter refused to write the true story, the reporter replied, "Senator, this here's the West. And in the West, when truth conflicts with legend, we print the legend."

Finally, a word to anyone present with me at any of the stories recounted herein: If your version conflicts with mine, I recommend to you President Harry Truman's account of growing up on a Missouri farm during the late nineteenth century. His father brought young Harry to the annual county picnic, where Colonel Crisp (Truman described him as a colonel "by agreement") ended the affair each year by standing on a buffet table and orating on his Civil War experience at the Battle of Lone Jack. After the colonel finished his tale at one such shindig, a soldier who had actually fought at Lone Jack rose and gave a point-by-point contradiction of the colonel's account. At the conclusion of the soldier's narrative, Colonel Crisp spat out a reply to this attack on his veracity: "Goddamn an eyewitness. He always spoils a good story."[1]

Like old Colonel Crisp, when invited to share recollections of famous people that I have met or known, it takes little coaxing to get me to climb atop the picnic table. And unlike that *Shinbone Star* reporter, I've done my best to be faithful to the truth over the legend.

---

1   David McCullough, *Truman* (1992), 63.

1

Homework Assignment

When I was in the seventh grade in 1969, I spent untold hours at the Daly City Public Library looking up the addresses of retired government leaders so I could write them for both autographs and advice on entering politics. Getting former President Harry Truman's address came in handy for one particular middle-school project, although not without causing distress along the way.

That year my teacher, Mr. Puhr, assigned us to write a biography of a famous person. This was my first long-term homework assignment. Our paper had to be researched, single-space typed, and at least seven pages long. In the pre–personal computer era, very few 12 year-olds were keyboard literate, so he gave us three months to complete this monumental task. "But you'd better have it ready to turn in on the due date," he warned us ominously, "or there will be consequences."

For my subject, I picked the 86-year old Truman. Born in 1884, he saw combat in France during World War I before returning home and winning election in 1922 as a Missouri county judge. Twelve years later he advanced to the U.S. Senate. Tapped by Franklin Roosevelt as his 1944 running mate, Truman became president less than three months into his vice presidential term when FDR died suddenly in April 1945. As the new commander in chief, he oversaw the final months of World War II, and he ordered the atomic bombs dropped on Japan to end the conflict. During his second term he sent U.S. troops to Korea, where the fighting continued until after he retired from the presidency in 1953. He spent the next two decades speaking, writing, and overseeing the construction of his presidential library.

I dove into my Truman project. Instead of spending three months on it, I finished it in three days. With so much time to spare, and having once read that the ex-president answered personally every letter written to him by young people, I decided to mail him my report and get his opinion on it. Long before the ubiquity of copying machines (and decades before the invention of hard drives), I had no duplicate copy when I mailed it to his home at 219 North Delaware Street in Independence, Missouri. It never dawned on me that he wouldn't return it.

The three months elapsed. On the project's due date, I remained empty-handed. Mr. Puhr rejected my explanation, called me a liar in front of the class, and he accused me of never doing the report. "Besides," he announced, "Truman's dead. I watched his funeral on television 20 years ago."

"Actually, Mr. Puhr, he's not dead. He's alive, he has my paper, and when he gives it back to me I'll be happy to turn it in."

My class project grade: F.

More months went by and I forgot about the incident. Then one afternoon I returned home from school and found a large white envelope bearing Truman's return address, and his bold franking signature in the upper right corner.[1] The envelope contained my report, an autographed portrait of the great man, and a personal letter to me that read as follows:

---

[1] A former president of the United States may send free mail (without using postage stamps) by placing his signature in the upper right corner of the envelope. See U.S. Postal Regulation Special Eligibility Standards E050, https://pe.usps.com/Archive/HTML/DMMArchive20030810/E050.htm (accessed August 23, 2020).

April 29, 1970

Dear Jim:

I was very pleased to have your letter and manuscript. I am sorry I cannot help you with it, because I have a rule against working on another author's paper. It is clear, however, that you did your homework well.

With best wishes for success in your life.

Sincerely,

Harry S Truman

At the beginning of history class the next day, I walked up to Mr. Puhr's desk and placed my proof in front of him. His face reddened as he read over the documents silently. When he finished, he handed them back to me and said sternly, "Take your seat."

"Is that all you have to say to me, Mr. Puhr?"

"I said to take your seat." After humiliating me earlier and calling me a liar, he refused to

President Harry Truman's letter to me, April 29, 1970. (Author's collection)

acknowledge his mistake.

I fumed over this injustice for the rest of class. When the recess bell rang I jumped from my desk, rushed to the classroom door, and blocked the exit. Holding aloft my treasures, I yelled to my classmates, "Hey, if anybody wants to see the letter and autographed picture I got yesterday from the *late* President Harry Truman, I'll show it to you on the playground."

Despite my protests, Mr. Puhr wouldn't accept my paper. I went to the principal, Mrs. Zenovich, and presented my case. Marching me back to class, she confronted Mr. Puhr and cajoled him into accepting it.

Later, Mr. Puhr handed back my paper in front of the entire class and announced that he marked me down for "repeated punctuation errors" because I kept failing to put a period after Truman's middle initial "S." I told him the omission was intentional: the "S" didn't get a period because "S" was his middle name. He grabbed Volume T of the *Encyclopedia Britannica*, turned to Truman's entry, and pronounced, "Aha! The encyclopedia lists him as Harry *S-With-A-Period* Truman! What do you say to that, Mr. Rogan?"

"The encyclopedia's wrong."

"So!" he chortled, "the encyclopedia is wrong and Mr. Rogan is right! My, aren't we lucky to have such a brilliant student in our midst!" Students laughed as he mocked me for the rest of class. For days afterward, he called on me to "confirm" facts such as George Washington was our first president ("Or was it Benjamin Franklin, Mr. Rogan?"), or that Columbus discovered America in 1492 ("Or was it in 1493, Mr. Rogan?").

Growing tired of the ridicule, I took matters into my own hands: "Dear President Truman," my new letter began, "You won't believe this teacher of mine." I asked him to settle the issue.

The school year ended without a reply and again I forgot about it. One day near the end of summer vacation another letter with the black signature and no postage stamps arrived:

4

August 19, 1970

Dear Mr. Rogan:

... The "S" in my middle name stands for the first letter of the first name of each of my grandfathers. In order to be strictly impartial in naming me for one or the other, I was given the letter "S" as a middle name. It can be used with or without a period after it.

I appreciate your very kind comments and send you best wishes.

Sincerely yours,

Harry S Truman

Now, for the first time, I noticed Truman's engraved letterhead: it bore the name *Harry S Truman* with no period after the middle initial. The proof had been in my hands all along.

On the first day of eighth grade, I arrived at school early and tracked down my seventh grade teacher. Mr. Puhr looked baffled when I entered his classroom as if I had made another mistake. I walked to his desk and

In this second letter to me, Truman settled a lingering historical question. (Author's collection)

showed him the second Truman letter. Again, he refused to re-grade my report, but he changed his mind when I threatened him with more Mrs. Zenovich therapy.

As I walked away, he called to me sharply:

"Rogan," he said, "I'm very glad you won't be in my class this year."

• • •

Former President Harry S Truman died at age 88 on December 26, 1972.

In the early 1990s, *American Heritage* magazine first published my story of how Harry Truman helped me with my homework assignment from Mr. Puhr. A few years later, I gave *Readers Digest* permission to republish it in its April 1995 issue, which commemorated the fiftieth anniversary of Truman's presidential inauguration.

A couple of weeks later, while on a trip to Missouri, I toured Truman's house in Independence (now a national historic site). The guide led about 20 of us to the rear porch and said, "Here's where Mr. Truman sat each morning answering his mail. In fact, in this month's *Readers Digest* there is a story of how he helped a young boy with his homework. This porch is where he would have read the boy's letter and dictated his reply to his secretary, Rose Conway."

When the tour ended, I mentioned to the guide that I was the story's author. He asked me to wait while he called his wife working at the nearby Truman Presidential Library. A few minutes later, cars arrived with library staff and docents. They led me back to the porch and had me recount the entire story for them.

Some years later, I attended a legislative retreat with fellow members of Congress. The guest speaker was one of my generation's preeminent historians, David McCullough, who wrote a Pulitzer Prize–winning biography on Truman. When I asked him to autograph my copy of his book, I mentioned with a grin that I was pleased to meet "a fellow Truman scholar." He asked if I had written a Truman book, too. I laughed and told him no, and then I explained about my little story of Truman helping with my homework.

McCullough's eyes brightened. "The 'homework' story in *American Heritage!*" he said. "Truman wrote to you and explained about the *S* in his middle name! I not only read it, but it helped me win a bet on that issue!"

It seems that when Harry Truman took the time to help a young admirer with his research assignment long ago, both David McCullough and I came out as winners.

From the tomb: Engraved portrait autographed for me by President and Mrs. Harry S Truman, signed 20 years after Mr. Puhr claimed that he watched Truman's funeral on television! (Author's collection)

2

KGO's Gift

In 1960s and 1970s San Francisco, newsman Jim Dunbar's *AM Show* on station KGO was a staple of local morning television. From 6:30 to 8:30 a.m., Dunbar hosted a live call-in program with newsmakers. While watching the station one Saturday in 1971, I heard an announcement that Senators Hubert H. Humphrey (D-MN) and Edward "Ted" Kennedy (D-MA), two of the most recognizable political titans of their generation, would appear with Dunbar the following Monday morning. I called my classmates and fellow political junkies Dan Swanson and Roger Mahan. Together we concocted a plan to cut eighth grade classes and try to meet Kennedy and Humphrey when they arrived at the studio.

Writing this story five decades later, I am mindful that with each passing year Hubert Humphrey's name registers with fewer people. That was not true when I was young. A Washington heavyweight for decades, the former pharmacist and Minneapolis mayor first won election to the U.S. Senate in 1948. He ran unsuccessfully against John F. Kennedy for the 1960 Democrat presidential nomination, but four years later President Lyndon Johnson tapped him as his running mate. As the 1968 Democrat presidential nominee, Humphrey lost the White House to Richard Nixon by a whisker. After recapturing his old Senate seat two years later, and with the 1972 presidential campaign around the corner, he itched for a rematch with the Republican president.

Humphrey was more than a politician to me. He was an early inspiration. As a fifth grade boy during his 1968 presidential run, I read a *Life* magazine profile on him. It told of his experience as a young Midwestern pharmacist making his first visit to 1930s Washington and the newfound passion for politics he found there. One night, after an exhilarating tour of the monuments, he rushed off an excited letter to his fiancée back home. After pleading with her not to laugh at him, he wrote that if he applied himself then maybe he could return one day as a congressman. She didn't laugh, they married, and along the way he helped shape almost every landmark law of his era. That magazine profile on HHH showed me that if an ordinary Midwestern druggist could accomplish such great things through politics, then maybe one day I could do the same. Once I connected those dots, I set my compass.

Senator Edward Kennedy, the youngest sibling of President John F. Kennedy and Senator Robert F. Kennedy, was the last surviving brother of America's most famous political dynasty. Perhaps the most popular politician in the 1970s, he topped all presidential preference polls despite his reluctance to bid for national office after losing two brothers to assassination. To party activists, however, his hesitation was of no moment. Most Democrats viewed his future presidency as inevitable.

• • •

Well before daybreak that Monday morning, Dan, Roger, and I caught the trolley to downtown San Francisco. To get to KGO, we walked many long blocks down dark streets while passing hobos sleeping in doorways and winos urinating in the gutter. It was a spooky journey for three boys, but we arrived safely. A friendly studio doorman told us that if we waited by the front entrance we would encounter the senators coming into the building.

Whenever I saw television coverage of famous political leaders making public appearances, they always had Secret Service, police motorcycle escorts, and photographers wedged between them and their throngs of fans. Expecting this setting for Kennedy's and Humphrey's arrival, I assumed that every distant siren signaled their approaching motorcade. When an unassuming blue sedan pulled up to the curb at 6:30 a.m., I paid no immediate attention to it or the man reading the morning newspaper in the front passenger seat. A second, closer look at his familiar features prompted a shock of recognition. I drove an elbow into Dan's ribs and whispered, "There's Kennedy."

Ted Kennedy exited the car and walked down the empty street toward the entrance. We were so nervous that we almost let him pass by. When he spied us holding cameras and staring at him anxiously, he surmised our purpose and greeted us.

After signing autographs, he suggested that we take a group picture. He took my camera, conscripted a companion, and then gave him stage directions: "Cock it—cock it," he told his aide fumbling with my camera. When the photographer was ready, Kennedy told us, "Come on boys, move in a bit *closah*." He gathered us about him and his assistant snapped the shot.

While standing next to him, I studied his gold *PT-109* tie bar. I knew from reading history that President Kennedy gave these out as souvenirs commemorating his World War II service on that ship. Until now, I had only read about these tie clasps. Seeing a genuine one worn by the martyred president's brother left me awed.

He shook our hands, thanked us for coming to see him, and then he entered the studio for his interview. We were so ecstatic at succeeding in our plan that we almost forgot there was more to come.

• • •

Despite Kennedy's stealth arrival, I still expected a motorcade scenario for former Vice President Humphrey, but to play it safe I watched for him while I studied people riding in every passing car. Thankfully, I was ready when another plain sedan double-parked in front of the studio and dropped off its passenger. I raised my camera and snapped a picture of Humphrey as he stepped unescorted from the car.

He bounded toward us with a broad smile and a friendly greeting. While signing autographs, he showed a genuine and unhurried interest in each us. He asked our names and he wanted to know where we came from. When Dan told him that we lived and went to school in nearby Daly City, Humphrey chuckled, *"Daly City—that sounds like Chicago!"*[1]

I snapped this photo of former Vice President Hubert H. Humphrey as he stepped from his car at KGO Studio, May 16, 1971. He autographed it for me later that year. (Author's collection)

When he heard that we liked politics, he beamed with enthusiasm. While the KGO doorman tried to hurry him along, he stood on the sidewalk and spoke of his love of public service. He encouraged us to work hard in school, and he expressed the hope that we would one day join him in Washington. He wished us luck, waved goodbye, and then he headed inside the studio.

Here was my first political hero in the flesh—a man who almost became president—now encouraging me to keep up my interest in

---

1   Humphrey's joke about Daly City referred to Richard J. Daly (1902-1976), Chicago's longtime mayor from 1955 to 1976. Daly hosted Chicago's 1968 Democratic National Convention where Humphrey won his Party's presidential nomination less than three years earlier.

government. He left me so tongue-tied that I could only mumble thanks. I don't think I had a bigger thrill as a boy. Half a century later, the memory of that excitement remains undiminished.

• • •

Back at our junior high school Advanced Government class, our chutzpah in meeting Humphrey and Kennedy became the stuff of classroom legend. It so impressed our teacher Mr. Lasley that he ran interference with the principal to help clear our unexcused truancy.

• • •

Over the next few years, Dan, Roger, and I became regular fixtures outside KGO. Whenever newsman Jim Dunbar scheduled an interview with any national political figure, we rode the predawn trolley into town, ran the gauntlet of street derelicts, and waited outside to get autographs, take pictures, and seek advice on politics. Thanks to the studio staff, we met many notables making their way through San Francisco in the early to mid-1970s. We became so familiar to Dunbar and his crew that they sometimes let us watch his interviews from inside the control booth.

Each visit there proved memorable, and making these connections with famous leaders at an early age taught me an important lesson beyond autograph collecting. In sizing up so many of them personally, I developed the confidence that someday—*someday*—I could do this, too.

• • •

Almost three decades after our KGO encounter, Ted Kennedy and I served together in Congress. One day while we chatted on the Senate floor at the end of President Clinton's impeachment trial, I showed him our 1971 photograph. It so amazed him that he grabbed my arm and dragged me around the chamber as he showed it to every Senate colleague he could find.

Senator Edward Kennedy with (from left) Dan Swanson, Roger Mahan, and me outside KGO Studio, May 16, 1971. (Author's collection)

During that same period, when I served on the House Judiciary Committee during President Bill Clinton's impeachment and Senate trial, I repaid the KGO debt whenever I could. My press secretary, Jeff Solsby, fended off scores of media requests each day. Despite my backbreaking schedule and my very limited time to accommodate the press, Jeff was under orders to put through every interview request from Jim Dunbar (still broadcasting at KGO almost 30 years later) or any other reporter at the station.

• • •

After an assassin's bullet ended Senator Robert Kennedy's 1968 presidential campaign, Ted Kennedy remained an emotional Democrat presidential favorite, but, like Humphrey, it was not to be. He ran for the White House only once, but he lost a bitter struggle for the presidential nomination to Jimmy Carter in 1980. Resuming his Senate duties, he died of brain cancer at age 77 on August 25, 2009. At his death, he was the fourth-longest serving senator in U.S. history.

Jim Dunbar broadcast at KGO for almost 40 years before he retired in 2004. San Francisco's first inductee into the Radio Broadcasters Hall of Fame, he died of natural causes at age 89 on April 22, 2019.

As for Hubert Humphrey, I'll have more stories about him later in the book.

3

The Indian and the Preacher

Excepting the Apostles, Billy Graham may have been the best-known evangelist of all time. Born in 1918, the ordained pastor accepted an invitation to lead a revival meeting under a large tent in Los Angeles in 1949. The media attention he garnered from that event made him famous. Over the next 60 years his ministry grew worldwide, and he led untold millions of people to faith in Jesus Christ.

When he came to the Bay Area in July 1971 for a five day crusade at the Oakland Coliseum, classmate Roger Mahan and I again braved the early-morning streets of San Francisco to meet "the world's pastor" when he came to KGO to promote his upcoming rallies. Just as when we met former Vice President Hubert Humphrey and Senator Edward Kennedy at that studio a few months earlier, we waited on the sidewalk for him to arrive.

Shortly after dawn, a car turned onto Golden Gate Avenue and parked by the entrance. Six men jumped out and moved together as a tight group toward the door. All of them dressed identically: dark sunglasses, tweed hats, and trench coats—quite a bizarre ensemble for a balmy mid-summer California morning. We didn't recognize Graham until he and his entourage removed their disguises, but by then they were inside the lobby behind locked doors and boarding the elevator.

Having missed meeting him on the way in, we waited around

to try again when he left. It was during this lull that I experienced a curious encounter.

Soon after Graham's incognito entrance, the lobby door opened and out shuffled a grizzled old man wearing ceremonial Native American clothes and headdress. Impulsive curiosity led me to raise my camera and take his picture. My flash bulb caught his attention. His face contorted in anger as he shuffled toward me. When he came within reach, he lunged for my hand. "Give me that camera!" he shouted. "My image is copyrighted by Congress! You cannot take my picture! Give me that camera so I can destroy your film!" Startled by his response, I kept backing away from this apparent lunatic as he continued advancing, shouting, and grasping for my Kodak Instamatic.

After a few passes, he abandoning his attempted seizure. He leaned forward and brought his face close to mine. His pale yellow-red eyes glared, and I felt his breath on my face. I stood frozen, bewildered, and too frightened to say anything.

Straightening up, the old Indian grunted before turning away and shuffling down Golden Gate Avenue toward Hyde Street. Roger and I looked at each other in disbelief. We didn't know what to make of the bizarre situation.

Mike, the KGO doorman, walked over to us. "Hey, don't you know who that was?" he asked. "That's Chief Red Fox. He was born in 1870 and he's in town promoting his autobiography." Mike explained that the chief, now 101 years old and a nephew of Crazy Horse, was the last surviving witness to both the massacres of General Custer and his troops at Little Bighorn (1876), and of the Lakotas at the Battle of Wounded Knee (1890).

At the end of the nineteenth century, Chief Red Fox joined Buffalo Bill's *Wild West Show* and remained with it for many years. During one performance in 1905, he jumped from his horse and faux "scalped" Great Britain's King Edward VII during an exhibition show in England. He also claimed to be the original model for the old Indian

Head-Buffalo nickels first struck by the U.S. Mint in 1913 (that explained his claim that Congress copy-righted his image).

Having a confronta-tion with the last living witness to Custer's Last Stand—how many 13 year-old boys can top that? Still, the experi-ence left me rattled for the remainder of the day. After all, if the chief tried scalping the King of England, I could only imagine what he might have done to me if given the opportunity.

I watched the old Indian as he continued lumbering in the dis-tance down Golden Gate Avenue. Curiously, dozens

The offending snapshot that I took of Chief Red Fox as he left KGO, July 20, 1971. (Author's collection)

of pedestrians on their way to work passed him while walking in the opposite direction. Nobody gave him a second look.

Only in San Francisco.

• • •

Chief Red Fox died at age 105 on March 1, 1976.

By the time Billy Graham died at age 99 on February 21, 2018, he had preached the Gospel of Jesus Christ to over 2 billion

Evangelist Billy Graham, San Francisco, July 20, 1971. (Author's collection)

people during his 70-year ministry, and with an estimated 215 million attending his live events. Had Chief Red Fox succeeded in snatching my camera that morning, I wouldn't have had Billy Graham pose for this photograph when I met him inside KGO's lobby:

4

The Happy Warrior

As I mentioned in an earlier chapter, during my youth former Vice President Hubert Humphrey, the 1968 Democrat presidential nominee, was a dominant actor on the political stage in the 1960s and 1970s. He also remained a personal favorite of mine. Only Ronald Reagan matched him in kindness when encountering fans too young to vote for him.

Vice President and Mrs. Hubert Humphrey with Senator and Mrs. Edmund S. Muskie after accepting the Democrat presidential and vice presidential nominations, 1968 Democrat National Convention, Chicago. The Humphreys and the Muskies autographed this photograph for me in the early 1970s. (Author's collection)

I met Humphrey many times during his campaign swings through San Francisco in the 1970s. For you old-time political aficionados out there, here are a few more of my memories of the man dubbed "The Happy Warrior."

• • •

Since my classmate Dan Swanson and I had succeeded in meeting Humphrey the morning we cut eighth grade classes and traipsed to KGO in May 1971, we tried again later that year when he paid a return visit there shortly before declaring his presidential candidacy for the third and final time.

We stood outside the studio shivering in the cold while awaiting his early morning arrival when a late 1950s-style limousine pulled up to the building. Humphrey looked dour as he stepped out of the car and hurried by us toward the entrance. I held out a card and asked him to autograph it. "No," he said brusquely while waving me away. "I'm in a hurry."

As he rushed by, I saw his eyes fix on the "Humphrey for President" badge pinned to my sweater. He stopped in his tracks. A broad smile crossed his face. "Well," he declared, "of course I have time to sign an autograph! Come with me, boys." With that, he grabbed Dan and me by the arms and escorted us inside the warm studio lobby.

I handed him a small White House card signed previously by Richard Nixon, the man who defeated him in 1968. As he signed his name to it with a flourish, he asked where I got it. "I wrote him a letter," I replied. "When you're president, I'll write you a letter." His face lit up. Suddenly, the candidate in a hurry now became the candidate with time on his hands.

"Now," he asked us, "what else can I sign for you boys?" Dan and I looked at each other as if we'd just discovered an unattended cookie jar. We started passing him all of the 1968 campaign mementos we had brought along just in case he proved a generous signer. As he

Good answer! White House card signed (eventually) by 1968's major party presidential and vice presidential nominees: Republicans Richard Nixon and Spiro Agnew, and Democrats Hubert Humphrey and Edmund Muskie. (Author's collection)

penned his signature on each, he kept repeating, "Such fine young boys! Fine young boys!"

When he finished signing, he told us both, "I'm mighty proud of you boys." Then he threw his arm around my shoulder and instructed Dan to take our photo. Dan followed orders, and then HHH called out, "Let's have another—I wasn't smiling in that one." Dan took a second snapshot, and then he handed the camera to me so that I could return the favor.

Humphrey continued ignoring an aide's plea to keep on schedule. "Now," he asked us after we posed with him, "is there anything else I can do for you?" There wasn't, since Dan and I had no more autograph-able items. He pumped our hands heartily, thanked us for coming to see him, and then he stepped into the lobby elevator.

Just as the doors closed, he thrust out his arm and caused them to pop back open. "Are you boys *sure* I can't sign anything else for you?" he called out. When we assured him that we were covered, he again waved goodbye. As the doors closed a second time, we could hear him telling the doorman, "I am so proud of those boys! What

Hubert Humphrey and me at KGO Studio, September 27, 1971. Note the very helpful HHH campaign button pinned to my sweater. (Author's collection)

fine young boys!"

If America had enfranchised 12 year-olds back then, Hubert Humphrey would have had my vote. By the time those elevator doors had closed, I began to think that Dan and I had his.

• • •

After becoming a presidential candidate for the 1972 Democrat presidential nomination, I next saw him during a San Francisco campaign swing in March 1972. My younger brother Pat and I grabbed our cameras and waited for the candidate outside station KPIX, located at 2655 Van Ness Avenue, a busy street that cut through downtown. Remembering the positive response my little Humphrey campaign button had generated at KGO six months earlier, I doubled down on that strategy. Pat and I each had pinned to our jackets two jumbo-sized Humphrey for president badges.

Humphrey exited the studio and waved to the small cheering crowd waiting for him. When he saw Pat and me wearing the oversized badges, he made a beeline straight for us while exclaiming, "Oh, boy! Am I for you!" I had brought a typescript quotation from one of his major 1968 campaign speeches for him to sign, but he went one better. Ignoring the increasingly frantic pleas of his Secret Service detail to return to the safety of his car, he led Pat and me (along with a parade of security agents and reporters) down to Filbert Street so that he could use the mailbox at the northwest corner as his writing desk.

He took several minutes to write out the quote in slow and careful longhand strokes. Unhappy and fidgety agents nervously watched the nearby rooftops, passing cars, and gathering spectators with good reason: Two weeks earlier, a would-be assassin pumped four bullets into Alabama Governor George Wallace as he campaigned for the presidency. Tossing aside safety concerns, HHH created what remains one of the sentimental favorites in my political memorabilia collection.

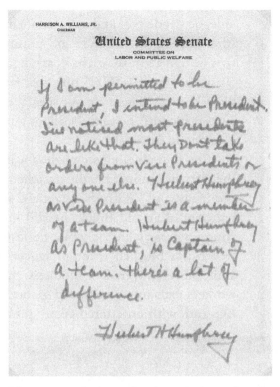

"If I am permitted to be president, I intend to be president. I've noticed most presidents are like that. They don't take orders from vice presidents or anyone else. Hubert Humphrey as vice president is a member of a team. Hubert Humphrey as president is captain of a team. There's a lot of difference. —Hubert H. Humphrey." HHH wrote out this quotation for me using a mailbox on a busy street corner while agitated Secret Service agents tried to hurry him along, March 24, 1972. (Author's collection)

Later that evening, Pat and I snuck into Humphrey's private reception for his California Democrat National Convention delegation slate in the Fairmont Hotel's Crystal Room. Near the end of his brief campaign speech, a group of young and pretty stewardesses staying at the hotel peeked inside the room and recognized him. Sheepishly, one of them asked a campaign aide if they could come in and meet the candidate. When Humphrey saw them talking to his aide, he strode over and escorted them personally into his reception. After shaking their hands and posing for a photo, he announced that he had a gift for each. Reaching into his pocket, he pulled out a fistful of brass "HHH" pins that fastened in the back with a butterfly clutch. "These are our special campaign pins that we give to special friends," he told the flight attendants, "and I would like to give one to each of you."

The first giggling stewardess reached out her hand to receive the gift. He ignored her outstretched palm and said, "Here, let me pin it on you!" With the practiced speed of a teenage boy in the backseat of an old Buick, he slid his hand down and inside the young woman's blouse while he fastened the clasp. The startled stewardess blushed through saucer-sized eyes, but her giggling smile never wavered. Onlookers chuckled while two campaign workers exchanged awkward glances as HHH moved down the line and, with unfettered gusto, pinned one to each woman's top.

I took this snapshot of HHH in the Fairmont Hotel's Crystal Room before the stewardesses distracted him, March 24, 1972. He autographed it for me ("H.H. Humphrey") a couple of months later at another campaign event. (Author's collection)

As he fastened the last pin, someone in the crowd called out, "Muriel [Mrs. Humphrey] will give you hell for this!" He ignored the crack and completed the task. As the last flushed attendant straightened her disheveled blouse and thanked him, he looked over at Pat and me and gave us a wink. "Ahh," he exclaimed with a grin, "the joys of running for president!"

• • •

Not everyone in San Francisco was glad to see Hubert Humphrey's campaign come to town. In late May, just days before the 1972 California Democrat primary, he made an outdoor campaign appearance. His motorcade pulled up to the world-famous cable car turntable at Powell and Market Streets, where he leaped from his car and plunged into the sizable crowd. He crisscrossed busy Powell Street trying to shake every extended hand as he made his way to Union Square.

I learned from attending previous campaign events like this that TV cameramen will do whatever it takes to get their shot, and they have no remorse when banging their heavy equipment into innocent bystanders in their way. While trying to take pictures at earlier events like this, sometimes I came away bruised from these aggressive photojournalists. In the now-huge crowd pressing forward to meet Humphrey, it became difficult for anyone with a camera to get a decent photo. Looking for an assist, I spied a tall concrete tree planter on the sidewalk. Climbing atop it quickly, I now had a great view of the approaching candidate.

The view proved too perfect. A cameraman from station KTVU decided he wanted my spot and tried to yank me off the planter. I kicked at him when he grabbed me.

The sudden shouting of an irate and horn-honking motorist stuck in this street gridlock interrupted our struggle. "Damn you, Humphrey!" the driver screamed out the window while leaning on his horn. "Get out of my way! I'm late for an appointment! Get out of my way, you damn Humphrey! Move, you bastard reporters!" My attacker and another nearby TV cameraman exchanged knowing glances, and then they rushed toward the angry driver's car. Clambering atop it with their equipment, they trained their lenses on Humphrey from this elevated perch. When the driver saw the photographers mount his car, and with its hood and trunk starting to dent from their weight, his banshee screams reached such a pitch that I thought he might have a stroke. The sounds of the cheering crowds mixed with his horn blasts nearly drowned out the trapped motorist's profane screams.

As the parade moved on, the cameramen jumped off the car and chased their quarry toward Union Square. As I followed the entourage up the street, I could hear a faint, distant cry above the din: "Hummmmm-phrey! Damn you, bastard! Hummmmm-phrey . . . !"

• • •

I had just turned 18 when I visited Washington for the first time in 1975. While in town, Humphrey invited me to visit him in his Senate office. I showed up for our afternoon appointment, and his aide apologized for a late-scheduled legislative luncheon that had delayed the boss. While waiting for his return, she gave me a tour of the vast collection of photographs and memorabilia decorating his walls. A large color photograph of him and his running mate Ed Muskie acknowledging the cheers of the delegates at the 1968 Democrat Convention hung in a prominent location.

After 45 minutes, she answered a phone call. She hung up and grabbed my hand. "Come on, Jim," she said. "Let's go find the senator." We took the subway to the Capitol and then walked to the private Senate Dining Room. On the way there, I tried to beg off by saying that I didn't want to disturb his luncheon meeting. She brushed off my concern and said that he told her to bring me over.

I waited in the foyer, pacing nervously, while she fetched him. A few minutes later, he exited the dining room and approached me with a warm smile. I apologized for interrupting his lunch but he dismissed my concern. "Oh, nonsense to that lunch, Jim," he exclaimed as he gripped my hand, "I'm glad to see you."

He handed my camera to his aide with directions to take an updated picture of us. As we posed, he pointed to her and said to me, "We've got the prettiest photographer on Capitol Hill."

After she took a couple of photos, I urged him to return to his

"Nonsense to that lunch": Senator Hubert H. Humphrey and me, U.S. Capitol, September 12, 1975. (Author's collection)

lunch. He put off my suggestion, and instead he questioned me about my first impressions of Washington and all of my activities since arriving. No wonder I loved him. He treated me like an old friend instead of a young pest.

When I told him that I would begin classes at a community college next week and hoped to go on to law school and (someday) politics, he beamed. "That's wonderful!" he exclaimed. "That's just wonderful. I know exactly how you feel." He closed his eyes and rubbed his temples as if conjuring a distant memory, and then he shared with me this recollection: "My first trip to Washington was in 1935, and I spent a week here on the Hill, like you, just looking all around. As I sat in the Senate gallery, I decided that's what I wanted to do in my life. I composed all my thoughts and feelings, and then I sat outside and wrote a letter to my wife Muriel back in Minnesota. I told her that I wanted to set my sights on one day running for Congress." How well I knew that story. I told him that I had read that very letter in *Life* magazine as a fifth grade schoolboy in 1968, and that it had motivated me to do the same.

"Well, Jim," he said with a parting smile, "if you do come back here as a congressman, bring honor to the place. That's the obligation of all who serve here."

I returned home to California a few days later and found a letter from him awaiting. In it he thanked me for visiting and he referenced the story he had told me of his first Washington visit. After encouraging me in my future endeavors, he closed with this line: "Just remember that you always have a friend here in the Humphrey office."

I knew that already.

• • •

For Humphrey fans, 1976 looked to be his year—finally. As former Georgia Jimmy Carter, the frontrunner for the Democrat presidential nomination, stumbled in the polls, support for a fourth Humphrey presidential candidacy surged. In every preference poll he beat all comers including delegate-leader Carter. For the first time in his public life, he resisted the seduction and announced to a shocked political world he would not be a candidate. "I am available for a draft, but I will not run," he stated. "If my party wants me and needs me, I will answer the call."

The call never came.

After the convention nominated Carter, the Happy Warrior stumped the nation for the Democrat ticket. His mid-August campaign visit to San Francisco coincided with the publication of his recently published autobiography, *The Education of a Public Man.* When I heard a last-minute announcement that he would drop by KGO that afternoon to discuss his book, I drove to the studio with friends Dan Swanson and Alex Pava to say hello and to have him sign copies that we planned to buy on our way there. Unfortunately, the nearby bookstore had not yet stocked it, so we had only congratulations to offer the author.[1]

When Humphrey arrived and saw us waiting outside for him, he invited us to join him in the studio. Dressed in a jaunty green plaid sport jacket, he wore a small peanut pin on his lapel (Carter's campaign symbol). A bout with cancer in 1974 had caused some health concerns, but he had beat back the disease and doctors gave him a clean bill of health. His appearance at KGO confirmed their findings. He looked hearty and sounded exuberant.

Our visit was brief. He needed to start his

A jaunty and hearty Hubert Humphrey posed for me as he signed a book for a fan, KGO Studio, San Francisco, August 16, 1976. (Author's collection)

---

1   It had been more than five years since Dan Swanson, Roger Mahan, and I made our first trip to KGO. During those years, our visits there provided us the rare boyhood opportunity to meet dozens of national leaders as well as fuel our growing interest in government and politics. This trip to see Hubert Humphrey at KGO marked the last time we ever visited the station. Appropriately, we met Humphrey there on our first trip to the studio in 1971. After this final visit, we channeled our energies toward college.

     KGO moved to a new location in 1985. Almost 30 years later, I attended a judicial conference in San Francisco, which was a couple of blocks from the site of the old studio. During a break I wandered over and stood on the sidewalk outside 277 Golden Gate Avenue where, as a boy, I had met so many leaders. Now the building remained vacant and the windows boarded. Scheduled for demolition in 2012, the structure received a last-minute reprieve from the wrecking ball. Investors converted it into a modern apartment building. Given the history that I saw inside and outside that building so long ago, I am delighted that it survives.

interview and I needed to return home for my after-school job. He thanked us for stopping by, and he told us to mail our books to him for an autograph once the bookstore stocked them. He entered the studio elevator, smiled as he saluted us, and then the doors closed.

I never saw him again.

• • •

Humphrey's hale appearance at that last KGO visit gave no indication of the undetected cancer spreading silently through his bladder. Two weeks after our meeting, he entered the hospital for a routine checkup. Doctors found the tumor and diagnosed it as terminal. Later news photos of him shocked me. I hardly recognized the cadaver-like shell as the same buoyant person who had saluted me on a KGO elevator only weeks earlier.

He refused to surrender. "Life was not meant to be endured," he said. "Life was meant to be enjoyed." He gamely resumed his duties in the Senate and helped lead the battle for President Carter's legislative agenda. Despite this brave determination, news clips throughout 1977 depicted a progressively haggard and dying man.

He spent his final days calling old friends and political enemies to say goodbye. He made one such call to the man who had vanquished his dream in 1968, Richard Nixon, and invited him to attend his funeral.

Hubert H. Humphrey died at age 66 on January 13, 1978.

In the final letter he sent me a few months before the end, he encouraged me to press on with my goals for the future. He closed with this advice: "We need good, progressive, honorable young people in government and politics. So, go to it. Work hard; study hard; fight the good fight; and, my friend, be of good cheer."

Even though our political philosophies parted long before I returned to Washington as a congressman, I always tried to live by Hubert Humphrey's advice—and by his example.

5

George Who?

On January 18, 1971, Senator George McGovern (D-SD) announced his candidacy for the 1972 Democrat presidential nomination. These days, White House contenders start running many years before the contest, but back then a candidate announcing almost two years before Election Day was unprecedented. The unknown McGovern needed the time. With heavyweight opponents lining up to run, the press mocked his quixotic effort. At the starting gate he registered only 2 percent in the Gallup poll, earning him the nickname, "George Who?"

Born in 1922, McGovern flew 35 combat missions as a bomber pilot during World War II. Returning home, he earned a Ph.D. and taught history and political science. Elected in 1956 to the U.S. House of Representatives from South Dakota, he gave up his seat to run unsuccessfully for the Senate in 1960. He served for two years as director of Food for Peace, and then he won a close Senate race in 1962. In 1972, he captured the Democrat presidential nomination, only to go on and lose the White House to Richard Nixon in one of America's most lopsided landslides.

McGovern brought his fledgling campaign to San Francisco in August 1971 for a $3 per person fundraising reception at the Rodeway Inn.[1] His presidential viability appeared so remote that

---

1   Now the Best Western Plus Airport Hotel, 380 Airport Blvd., South San Francisco.

RODEWAY INN
380 AIRPORT BLVD.
SAN FRANCISCO, CALIFORNIA 94080

We invite you to meet Senator

George McGovern

Sunday, August 29, 1971

3 to 6 PM

Rodeway Inn's La Paz Room

Nominal Charge
$3.00 per person
$5.00 per couple
Proceeds to McGovern Campaign and the
San Mateo County United Democratic Fund

For the San Mateo County McGovern Committee

Rich Meagher   Urban Whitaker   Dave Larson

For the San Mateo County Democratic Party

Senator Arlen Gregorio   Charlotte Schultz
Hon. Tony Governale   Melvin C. Kerwin
Al Kochman, Chairman   Audrey Ohlson
  County Central Committee   Jim Madison

R.S.V.P.   873-6300

You do the Traveling...Leave the REST to us.

Invitation to meet Senator George McGovern at the Rodeway
Inn reception, August 29, 1971, signed for me by the candidate.
(Author's collection)

none of my political collector buddies wanted to attend it with me, so I conscripted my little brother Pat to come along. Even at that absurdly low price we couldn't afford tickets, so we snuck into the event.

We stood outside the hotel's front door hoping to see McGovern when he arrived. While waiting we met his lone aide staffing the event, who spoke freely about the problems of running a campaign that most considered a joke and with no money in the bank. He said McGovern usually stayed in private homes during these trips because his campaign couldn't afford hotel rooms.

As we spoke, a banged-up 1960s station wagon pulled forward at the entrance. The aide whispered to us, "If I tell you something, can you keep a secret? There he is now."

McGovern climbed out of the car, combed his thinning hair, put on his suit jacket, and then he greeted Pat and me. There was no danger of breaching the aide's secret because as McGovern walked through the lobby nodding and smiling at people, nobody recognized him. It fell upon Pat to hold the elevator for the understaffed candidate, who rode it upstairs to freshen up in a room that a sympathetic supporter rented for him.

The aide we befriended kept riding up and down the elevator to check on the reception turnout and then reporting upstairs to McGovern. On one of these revolving trips he offered to get an autograph for me. He returned a few minutes later with a signed card. I asked what McGovern was doing when he signed it. "Truthfully," he replied with a smile, "he was standing naked in the bathroom shaving."

About 50 people attended McGovern's reception in the La Paz Room. When he arrived, the woman at the door collecting the entrance fee grew distracted, which enabled Pat and me to slip inside.

McGovern gave an impromptu talk that

Snapshot I took of presidential candidate George McGovern as he walked unrecognized through the Rodeway Inn motel lobby, San Francisco, August 29, 1971. He signed it for me at a later event. (Author's collection)

focused on his commitment to ending the Vietnam War, which was the cause motivating his entry into the race. His style was low key and casual, and he took questions from the audience for half an hour.

The affair ended with him leaving as he had arrived—walking through the lobby in anonymity to his waiting station wagon. But when he returned to campaign in San Francisco eight months later, the dynamic had changed dramatically.

• • •

Question: *When is the winner the loser and the loser the winner?*
Answer: *When the winners and losers are presidential candidates.*

The above riddle is a phenomenon of politics, where expectations often count more than votes. The 1972 Democrat presidential primaries are an example of this conundrum. As the gun sounded for the nomination race, Senator Edmund Muskie (D-ME) remained the heavily favored frontrunner for the three years leading up to 1972.

Universal expectations had Muskie wining New Hampshire's first-in-the-nation primary. George McGovern, still largely unknown after over a year of campaigning, straggled far behind in the polls. On primary night, Muskie did very well. He won almost 50 percent of the vote in a field of five contenders. McGovern lost, but his grass-roots campaign did better than expected with a second-place finish at 37 percent. Immediately the pundits and network anchors proclaimed the meaning of the New Hampshire results in their peculiar version of political algebra:

Muskie won

+

McGovern lost, but he did much better than the pundits expected

=

Muskie lost; McGovern won

The following morning, McGovern's name, and not Muskie's, splashed across the headlines. In the upcoming Wisconsin primary, McGovern parlayed his New Hampshire momentum into a stunning first-place victory. This catapulted the near-anonymous candidate only days earlier into the frontrunner position.

The day after his Wisconsin win, McGovern brought his now-energized campaign back to San Francisco. For weeks his local headquarters couldn't give away tickets to his scheduled $25 per person fundraising dinner at the Hilton Hotel. Within minutes of Wisconsin's vote tabulation, the event sold out.

Today, we live in an era where tickets to political events cost thousands of dollars. It's hard to conceive that in 1972 the price tag for admission to a sit-down dinner for the leading presidential candidate at a major venue cost $25. Yet, for my brother Pat and me, the price might as well have been $25,000. We had no money for a ticket, but that didn't dissuade us from trying to get inside.

We took the Greyhound bus from the East Bay (where we now lived) to San Francisco and arrived at the Hilton three hours before the dinner began. We sat in the lobby hoping to see McGovern when he arrived. Not long after we parked ourselves, I saw a chunky man with a buzz haircut and wearing a Hilton blazer staring at us from across the room. He approached, identified himself as hotel security, and he asked what we were doing there. I explained that we had taken the bus from Pinole to see McGovern. Once he learned that we had no dinner ticket, his already unpleasant attitude grew nasty. "Let me give you boys some advice," he said sarcastically. "Get back on your bus to Pinole and get the hell out of here. You aren't meeting anybody in this hotel tonight." Before we knew it, we found ourselves outside on the sidewalk.

Pat and I didn't surrender easily. We snuck back inside at another entrance, but the same guard nabbed us. Tossing us out once again, he warned that any further entry would result in our arrest.

I had an idea. Finding a pay telephone, I called the hotel switchboard, dropped my voice to the deepest baritone a 14 year-old could muster, and I told the operator that I was Senator McGovern's speech writer. I commanded her to put me through to his suite. To my surprise, she routed the call.

Dick Dougherty, McGovern's national campaign press secretary, answered. I explained our situation and he proved sympathetic. He arranged for us to get freelance photographer passes and complimentary dinner tickets at the press table. Dougherty told us to have the hotel security guard call him directly if he gave us any more problems.

We returned to the hotel and waited. It didn't take long for Inspector Javert to find us. He grabbed our arms and started yanking us across the lobby while saying that the police were on the way to arrest us for trespassing. When I told him to call Dougherty to confirm that we had tickets, he refused. Amid the yelling and the tugging, the hotel manager rushed over to investigate the disturbance. After hearing our explanation, the manager picked up a courtesy phone in the foyer and called McGovern's suite. A few moments later, the manager summoned the guard to join him over in the corner. I couldn't hear their discussion, but I saw the guard's face redden as the manager spoke with him harshly while poking an index finger into his chest. The guard stalked away.

The manager returned to where we waited. "Personal guests of Senator McGovern are always welcome in this hotel," he said.

With the event still two hours away, and while we continued our lobby stakeout, I saw McGovern alone and unrecognized strolling from the elevator bank. Pat and I introduced ourselves, and the candidate (in no apparent hurry) settled into a high-backed lobby chair and invited us to visit with him for a few minutes. "I was just going to take a walk around the block," he said with a chuckle, "so I've got some time to kill." When we told him the story of the guard and Dick Dougherty, he laughed. "So—*you're* the boys, eh? Dick told me about your enterprising effort to join us tonight. We're glad to have you."

I asked how he felt about his sudden vault to the front of the presidential pack. He said he felt reluctant to claim frontrunner status just yet, but yesterday's Wisconsin result gratified him, and he hoped to continue his momentum.

Before resuming his walk, he obliged an autograph request. On an index card he wrote out in longhand and signed his campaign slogan for me: "For Jim, I make one pledge above all others—to seek and speak the truth. With kindest regards, George McGovern."

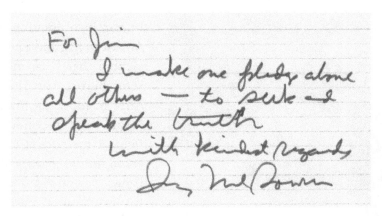

Presidential candidate George McGovern put his campaign pledge in writing for me, April 5, 1972. (Author's collection)

After thanking him and wishing him luck, we watched as McGovern rode the escalator down to O'Farrell Street for his constitutional.

Later that evening, and shortly before the dinner began, two couples chatting nearby came over to talk to Pat and me. One man in the group said they saw us in the lobby with McGovern earlier and he asked if we had gotten his autograph. I showed him the quotation, and they passed it around and congratulated me on the acquisition. It wasn't until they introduced themselves that we realized with whom we were speaking—movie stars Jack Nicholson, Warren Beatty and Julie Christie, along with pop singer Michelle Phillips from the 1960s rock group *The Mamas and the Papas*.

Following dinner, Congressman Don Edwards (D-CA) introduced McGovern to the packed and enthusiastic ballroom. I moved from the press table to the stage to snap a few photographs as the candidate urged his supporters to help him win the California primary and clinch the nomination.

At the end of the dinner, and as the crowd departed, I saw California State Assemblyman (later Congressman) John Burton standing nearby. He wore on his lapel a type of McGovern campaign

Presidential candidate George McGovern, the San Francisco Hilton, April 5, 1972. (Photograph by the author)

Assemblyman John Burton's 1972 memento of "The Good Old Days" that he gave me at the McGovern for president dinner, Hilton Hotel, April 5, 1972. (Author's collection)

button incorporating the American flag and a peace symbol that I had never seen before (or since). After introducing myself, I told him I collected political memorabilia and asked him to give me the badge. Burton didn't want to part with it, but my zeal wore him down and he relented.

Twenty-four years after he gave me the badge, John Burton and I served together in the State Assembly as colleagues. One day I wore his old McGovern button in my lapel and struck up a conversation with him in the chamber while waiting to see if he recognized my vintage treasure. Sure enough, after a few moments he asked about it. I recounted the story for him. "Those were the good old days," he sighed.

I sought to draw him out: "You mean the good old days when liberalism was on the rise? You mean the days when liberals believed they could solve the ills of the world, and when idealistic antiwar activists marched for world peace?"

He looked at me dismissively. "No," he said. "I don't mean any of that shit. I mean *the good old days*—when we could take money out of the Assembly Rules Committee budget and use it to pay for our fuckin' campaign buttons!"

• • •

In writing this memoir over 40 years after Dick Dougherty helped create a fond memory for two grateful boys crashing the San Francisco Hilton, I thought he might enjoy this story. I wanted to send him a copy of it to renew my thanks for his help. I looked for his address on the Internet and found this entry, dated January 2, 1987: "Richard Dougherty, former New York bureau chief of the *Los Angeles Times* and press secretary for Senator George McGovern, died of lung cancer Tuesday. He was 65."

Thanks again, Dick. I never forgot your kindness.

• • •

A few years after McGovern's presidential campaign ended, I attended his speech on Cuban-American relations before the San Francisco Commonwealth Club. To a sold-out audience, he called for lifting the longstanding embargo against Cuba, describing it as a "foolish sanction that has weakened [Cuban president Fidel] Castro, but forced a stronger Cuban reliance on the Soviet Union." He also described his recent visit to Cuba by saying that he and Castro made an impromptu visit to the local marketplace: "The warmth of the reception given Castro was enough to bring envy to the heart of every American politician," he said.

Following his prepared remarks, he took a few questions from the floor. When asked if he might seek the presidency again in 1976, he smiled and said, "I knew that question was coming. The chances are 100-to-1 against my running. In all candor, I have

Senator George McGovern later admired this photograph that I took of him at the Sheraton Palace Hotel, San Francisco, July 2, 1975. (Author's collection)

no plans to run. I have sought the advice of a few close friends as to what role I should play in the 1976 elections, whether I should speak on behalf of other candidates or whatever, but I will not be a candidate again."

Another questioner noted that Alabama Governor George Wallace, a former segregationist, led most polls for the 1976 Democrat presidential nomination. When asked if he would support Wallace if he won the nomination, his response was emphatic and brief: "No."

At the end of the lunch, he spoke with me about his 1976 decision. I asked under what circumstances he might reconsider. "Oh, I don't know," he said with a shrug. "I'll just have to wait and see what these other guys do."

Three years earlier, as the presidential nominee, reporters and security guards had crowded every inch of his path. Now, just as it was back in the early days of his race, when today's event ended, McGovern left the ballroom and walked through the lobby—alone and anonymous.

• • •

Before I began college classes in 1975, I made my first visit to Washington, and McGovern invited me to visit him when I arrived. A delay in floor votes pushed back our scheduled meeting by two hours, so I waited for him in his Senate office. Finally, his secretary told me he had returned. She took me into the public hallway, unlocked an unmarked door, and escorted me into his private quarters.

Senator George McGovern and me, U.S. Capitol, Washington, September 9, 1975. (Author's collection)

McGovern sat behind his desk at the far end of the room. Dressed in a cream-colored suit, he rose from his chair and welcomed me while offering repeated apologies for keeping me waiting so long. "When you do the people's business," he said with a smile, "sometimes the people aren't in a big hurry to get their matters brought to a vote!"

He wanted to know about my trip and my impressions of the Capitol, and he put me at ease with his friendly and unhurried manner. We talked about the upcoming 1976 presidential race as well as his decision not to run again. He said the main reason he had opted out of the race was because his 1972 run had caused deep divisions in the Party and he felt it needed a unifier in 1976. "I'm not sure that my being a candidate and being nominated would do that because several factions of the Party were alienated by my candidacy in 1972," he said. "I do not expect to run for president again."

I mentioned that I had seen a recent Gallup poll (taken after Nixon resigned the presidency). It showed that in a rematch, McGovern would have prevailed over Nixon handily. A wan smile crossed his face. He stepped back and leaned against his desk. "Yes, I saw the poll when it came out," he said. "I was very gratified by it. Do you know why? Because it vindicated me." Then he dropped his voice to a whisper and looked out the window as he said it again: "It vindicated me."

Senator George McGovern in his private Senate office signing a photograph I had taken of him previously (note his reading glasses tossed hastily on his desk), U.S. Capitol, September 9, 1975. (Photograph by the author)

I brought along the photograph I had taken of him at the Commonwealth Club a few months earlier and asked him to autograph it. He took the photo from me, sat behind his desk, slid on his reading glasses, and studied it carefully. "You took this?" he asked with a touch of surprise at my youthful effort. "You know, it's a very, very good picture."

As he began to inscribe it, I raised my camera to take a couple of candid photos while he signed. When he noticed my camera, he quickly slid off his reading glasses and placed them on his desk. Apparently, even with a humble man like McGovern, vanity prevailed over good penmanship.

• • •

I stayed in touch with McGovern over the years. In 1994, after I won a seat in the California legislature, he remembered his old campaign volunteer of long ago and called to congratulate me on my victory.

Later that year we reunited at a couple of conferences hosted by ALEC (the American Legislative Exchange Council), a national forum for conservative state legislators. The liberal McGovern proved an unlikely but very popular speaker before this group.

In August 1994, at one of these conferences, McGovern joined Newt Gingrich (still a relatively unknown Georgia congressman but destined for political superstardom three months later when he led Republicans to seize control of the House of Representatives for the first time in 40 years). More than 1,000 conferees crowded into the breakfast, with many there out of sheer curiosity as to why ALEC had paired this leading American liberal with a black-belt conservative champion.

A Democrat legislator (one of the few at the conference) introduced McGovern, who joked about the dearth of liberals in attendance: "I am pleased to be introduced by one of the select few at this conference who voted right in 1972!" He then related a story about his presidential run:

> One of the joys of running for president is that it gives one the opportunity to visit every state in the Union. In 1972 I carried only one state, but I fell in love with all of them. Pardon me if I say I carry a special place in my heart for Massachusetts [the only state McGovern carried], but I love them all. I remember a time during the 1972 Florida primary when I was to fly in for a large airport rally. When we landed, only a few mechanics were on the tarmac. We later learned that our problem was that we landed in the wrong town. As one of my rivals later noted, "If McGovern can't find the right town, how can he run the country?" America will never know! My parents were old-fashioned conservatives who believed that the least government is the best government. I have often wondered if they had lived to 1972 whether they would have voted for me. I am sure they might have been sympathetic, but it would have been a hard sell!

Alluding to his famous bent for liberalism, he recalled, "When last I spoke at one of your conferences, I had my arm in a sling. I had fallen down on a slippery Washington street outside the Avalon Theater on a rainy day and broke my shoulder. A Republican neighbor asked me what shoulder I broke. I told him it was my left shoulder. He said, 'McGovern, you're so liberal you can't even fall to the right!'"

After the laughter subsided, he shared that after leaving the Senate in 1981 he had taken his life's savings and bought a small hotel in Connecticut. The hotel failed despite his hiring an adept manager:

> The experience taught me that a small businessman faces a plethora of federal, state and local regulations. My manager burned the midnight oil not trying to make the hotel profitable but to keep up with the compliance requirements of regulations. I was also sued over an injury at the hotel. A drunk left the hotel bar and got into a fight in the parking lot. He was hurt and he sued me, saying the hotel should have provided him more security. We did have a security guard and lights outside, but a small business cannot afford to station the Marine Corps in its parking lot. We won the lawsuit, but not without a large expenditure of money. I was later sued when a lady tripped and broke her hip. These fraudulent and frivolous lawsuits are hurting small businesses.

McGovern called for comprehensive tort reform and suggested three ways it might occur: "The first way would be for self-correction by the American Bar Association, but I do not expect that to happen [laughter]. The second alternative would be for Congress to enact it, but I am not optimistic that will happen. The third route is tort reform in the states, and this is where it has to happen. These excessive lawsuits take the civility out of society. When I fell and broke my shoulder, it was an accident. It never occurred to me to sue someone over it."

The conferees greeted McGovern's remarks with a standing ovation. When Gingrich spoke, he shook his head in disbelief and said, "I never thought I would hear myself say this, but I agree with every- thing George McGovern just said!"

Following his speech, McGovern and I visited outside of the hotel bar. He wanted to hear my impressions of life in the

I wanted my State Assembly colleague Curt Pringle in this picture so he couldn't tease me at our GOP caucus meetings about my friendship with George McGovern. From left: Assembly GOP assistant leader Curt Pringle, me, and former Senator George McGovern, Hyatt Regency Hotel, Tampa, Florida, August 6, 1994. (Author's collection)

legislature and how it compared to my years as a trial court judge. He said he took pride in my having started in politics as a boy vol- unteering on his campaign a quarter century earlier. However, when he told my colleague, Assemblyman Curt Pringle (then assistant Republican Assembly leader and later speaker) that I was one of his favorite Republicans, it caused Curt to question my conservative bona fides—then and now.

A few months later, McGovern and Gingrich brought their act on the road to the ALEC winter conference in Washington. This time Gingrich received a reception reserved normally for rock stars. After having delivered a crushing defeat to House Democrats a few weeks earlier, Gingrich prepared to become the first GOP speaker since 1954.

McGovern reiterated to the audience his thoughts on tort reform, and he cited his failed hotel venture in Connecticut as the policy wake-up call he received. Then, shifting his tone, he took Gingrich to task over comments the speaker-designate had made recently: "Newt and I have become good friends," he said, "but I was bothered when he recently called President and Mrs. Clinton a couple of 'counter-culture McGovernites.' Over the years, I have heard people accused of being radical liberals called 'McGovernites' or 'McGoverniks.' I started as a noun, and now I am an adjective! I must confess I never really understood it. I served in World War II and flew 35 bombing missions. I have gone to war, I was the son of a Methodist minister, and I have been married to the same woman for 50 years. I do not feel I am part of any counterculture."

Lightening the mood, he joked about the results of the Republican sweep of Congress a few weeks earlier. "Judging from your broad smiles," he told the conservative audience, "I can tell most of you enjoyed the results of November 8!" Referring to his own presidential loss in 1972, he related this story:

> In 1972 I lost 49 of 50 states. The first Senate colleague I had run into after my defeat was Barry Goldwater, the 1964 Republican presidential nominee, who had also lost in a landslide. Barry later sent over a cartoon to me with the caption "If you must lose, lose big!" I thought it was a joke, but Barry later told me that he was serious. Barry explained what he meant by the cartoon: "In 1960 Dick Nixon lost the presidency to John F. Kennedy by less than 100,000 votes," he said. "Nixon spent the next eight years torturing himself and saying things like, 'If only I had gone to Chicago that last weekend instead of Alaska, I might have won.'
>
> "George," Barry said in comforting me, "in our case, it wouldn't have mattered how many times we went to Chicago!"

At the end of his speech, he remained at the head table signing autographs and posing for pictures. Before leaving, he came to my table and said he had heard that I might be running for Congress in the next cycle. "You know, Jim, if you run, as a Democrat I won't be able to endorse you," he said apologetically. "But the fact I can't endorse you doesn't mean I can't take great pride in you if you win."

That meant much more than an endorsement.

• • •

When I went to Congress in 1997, McGovern and I visited occasionally. I last saw him, of all places, when he spoke at the presidential library of the man who defeated him in 1972. At age 88

"To Jim Rogan, who stood with me in 1972—and still does. With the very best wishes of his friend, George McGovern." George McGovern and me, 1995. (Author's collection)

he gave a talk and did a book signing at the Richard Nixon Library in 2009. As an elegant touch, all the Nixon Library employees and docents wore vintage McGovern campaign buttons to welcome the Democrat Party's elder statesman.

• • •

George McGovern died of natural causes in a South Dakota hospice facility at age 90 on October 21, 2012. I consider it an honor to have known this decent man and devoted public servant.

6

Mr. Conservative

U.S. Senator Barry Goldwater (R-AZ) didn't invent the modern conservative political movement, but his presidential campaign brought it out of the shadows and started its march to the mainstream.

Born in 1909, Goldwater won a seat on the Phoenix City Council in 1949, and then he ran successfully for the U.S. Senate three years later. He brought his brand of aggressive libertarianism to a heavily bureaucratized and power-centralized Washington. In his 1960 bestselling book, *The Conscience of a Conservative*, he set forth his philosophy that still rallies the faithful:

> I have little interest in streamlining government or in making it more efficient, for I mean to reduce its size. I do not undertake to promote welfare, for I propose to extend freedom. My aim is not to pass laws, but to repeal them. It is not to inaugurate new programs, but to cancel old ones that do violence to the Constitution, or have failed in their purpose, or that impose on the people an unwarranted financial burden. I will not attempt to discover whether legislation is "needed" before I have first determined whether it is constitutionally permissible. And if I should later be attacked for neglecting my constituents' "interests," I shall reply that I was informed their main interest is liberty and that in that cause I am doing the very best I can.[1]

---

1   Barry Goldwater, *The Conscience of a Conservative* (1960), 23.

As the 1964 Republican presidential nominee, he railed against socialism, communism, New Deal liberalism, and the welfare state while arguing for a return to constitutional principles of individual liberty and self-government. Although he led the GOP to a landslide defeat against Lyndon B. Johnson, his army of young conservative warriors in that race learned how to organize, fight, and win. The DNA of Barry Goldwater's 1964 loss ran through the 1980 victory of his ideological heir, Ronald Reagan.

As a boy, I met Goldwater several times. The first was at the California Republican Party's two-day "Victory '72" state convention held at San Francisco's St. Francis Hotel in May 1972. He spoke at the two-day event also headlined by California Governor Ronald Reagan, New York Governor Nelson Rockefeller (later vice president), and Senator Bob Dole (R-KS) (later the 1996 GOP presidential nominee). Thanks to a press pass acquired from my high school's radio station, I was (at age 14) the youngest accredited journalist at the conference.

An unexpected treat came when I entered the ballroom for the kickoff dinner and recognized the evening's emcee, Edgar Bergen, seated alone at the head table. Born in 1903, the ventriloquist toured the vaudeville circuits with his dummy, Charlie McCarthy. Moving to radio in the 1930s, he and Charlie starred in one of the top-rated comedy shows for 20 years. His stage, radio, television, and motion picture career stretched over 60 years, and he co-starred alongside Hollywood luminaries ranging from W.C. Fields to Marilyn Monroe.

When I introduced myself to Bergen, he told me that he was surprised to have a fan born long after his heyday had ended. I told him I was a longtime aficionado of the Golden Age of Radio, and I asked if he might share a favorite memory from it.

"Well," he said, "I once caused a national panic by taking a commercial break during a 1938 broadcast." He explained that his top-rated NBC show competed for the 8:00 p.m. time slot with CBS's "Mercury Theatre on the Air" starring Orson Welles. During Bergen's broadcast, he broke for a commercial midway through the program. Many in his radio audience turned the dial during the lull. Those listeners that tuned to CBS heard Welles's adaptation of *The War of the Worlds* already in progress. Because Welles presented the drama in a modern "breaking news" format, thousands believed the fictional news bulletins reporting that an invading army of Martians had landed in New Jersey. As one writer noted, latecomers to the Welles broadcast "greatly misinterpreted what they heard. The next day, newspapers nationwide reported that thousands of people across the country had taken the fake news to be true and fled their homes in terror—grabbing firearms, putting on gas masks, and clogging the highways in a mad rush to escape imaginary Martians."[2] *The War of the Worlds* remains one of the most famous radio broadcasts in history, and by cutting to a scheduled commercial break, Bergen added to his already substantial contribution to radio history.

I was returning to my table when people in the rear of the ballroom began cheering when Barry Goldwater entered. He strode to the head table, greeted Bergen, waved to the crowd, and then signaled everyone to take their seats.

After the waiters had served dinner, Bergen flagged me to his table and introduced me to Goldwater, who said how pleased he was to see a young person attending the GOP conference. I replied that his race created for me my first awareness of the political process. "Well," he laughed, ""I'm sorry *that's* the race that introduced you to politics!"

Taking a sip from his water glass, he continued, "I didn't plan it to go the way it went. In 1964, I had planned to run against Jack Kennedy. Kennedy and I understood each other. We even talked about traveling the country together on the same plane and debating at various cities. We would have run a hell of a campaign."

---

2   A. Brad Schwartz, *Broadcast Hysteria: Orson Welles's War of the Worlds and the Art of Fake News* (2015), 7.

He said that he had known Lyndon Johnson since their days together in the Senate, but his fondness for President Kennedy did not extend to JFK's successor. He called Johnson a contemptable politician who would do whatever it took to win: "He had no principles. He wrapped himself in Kennedy's martyrdom and the voters bought it. I don't think Abe Lincoln could have won in 1964 if he had run against Johnson—especially running less than a year after the assassination. Once Kennedy died, I knew I had no chance of winning."

I asked if he might ever try again for the White House. "No," he said, "I'm too old now."

After savoring these few uninterrupted minutes with Goldwater, I noticed that other people now lined up behind me to meet him. Before saying goodbye, I asked a final question: What was it was like to be the presidential nominee of his Party?

He grinned. "Son," he replied, "the main lesson I learned from the experience is this—you've never been beaten in your life until you've been beaten for the presidency of the United States."

Card signed for me by Senator Barry Goldwater and comedian Edgar Bergen (and Charlie McCarthy), St. Francis Hotel, San Francisco, May 13, 1972. (Author's collection)

• • •

On the tenth anniversary of Barry Goldwater winning the presidential nomination at the 1964 Republican National Convention (held at San Francisco's Cow Palace),[3] he returned to the city of his victory to commemorate this milestone with a speech to the Young Americans for Freedom (YAF). Comprised of youthful conservatives, the group viewed Goldwater's nomination as their political high-water mark to date. Looking to the future, they saw in Ronald Reagan a new champion to carry that banner to the White House. Once organizers announced that both Goldwater and Reagan had accepted invitations to speak, the conference sold out in an hour.

With my ticket in hand, I arrived at the Sheraton Palace Hotel for Goldwater's dinner speech. Concession tables sold vintage 1964 Goldwater campaign trinkets and "YAF Backs Barry" badges. The hottest-selling badge read simply, "Goldwater in 1976." Other big sellers were bumper stickers lambasting current national Democrat Party leaders: Senators Edward Kennedy (*Teddy Kennedy—Unsafe at Any Speed*)[4] and George McGovern (*Acid—Amnesty—Appeasement—Vote McGovern*).[5]

Outside the packed ballroom, I overheard a panicked discussion between two conference officers that a several-hour delay in Goldwater's flight from Washington might require cancellation of his much-anticipated appearance. After dinner ended, an officer announced that the senator was running three hours late. When he put to a

---

3   Technically, the Cow Palace property spreads into both San Francisco and neighboring Daly City. The parking lot is located within San Francisco, and the building sits in Daly City. Since San Francisco served the official host city for the 1964 Republican National Convention, historians usually credit that city as the site of the convention.

4   A reference to Kennedy's 1969 accident where his young female passenger drowned when he drove his automobile off a bridge after leaving a late-night party with her.

5   During his 1972 presidential campaign, George McGovern pledged to legalize marijuana, grant amnesty to Vietnam War draft dodgers, and he stated that as president he would be willing to go before our communist enemies in North Vietnam and "beg" for the release of American prisoners.

vote whether they should adjourn for the evening, a resounding cry rocked the room: "NO!"

Hours after the busboys collected the dirty dinner plates, an excited voice outside the ballroom shouted, "Here he comes!" Klieg lights and flashbulbs went off as Goldwater entered. The YAF'ers jumped to their feet chanting, "WE WANT BARRY! WE WANT BARRY!" Admirers besieged him for a handshake as the escort committee ushered him to the head table.

Senator Barry Goldwater, the Sheraton Palace Hotel, San Francisco, July 18, 1974. (Photograph by the author)

Wasting no time in beginning the program, Congressman Sam Steiger (R-AZ) introduced Goldwater as "the greatest living statesman this country has ever had." With the audience roaring, Goldwater approached the lectern. A YAF'er from Hawaii, dressed in a traditional hula outfit, shimmied up to him, placed a Polynesian lei around his neck, and then she kissed him on the lips. The cheers increased as he laughed and jiggled the lei up and down, which caused water drops from the flowers to splash the front of his light-gray suit jacket.

He thanked everyone for waiting, and he acknowledged the anniversary of the night ten years earlier when "I waited in a small Cow Palace anteroom to be introduced to the convention as the nominee for an office that I knew I could not win."

He focused his brief remarks on the current state of the economy, and especially the need to fight inflation. "Don't let the radicals and liberals get away with kidding you," he declared. "There is only one cause of inflation, and I blame the left-wing Democrats and, yes, the left-wing Republicans for almost four decades of government extravagance—and above all, I blame the Congress of the United States."

With the Nixon Administration collapsing under the weight of its Watergate scandal, he urged the group to fight hard to rebuild and strengthen the Republican Party. "We have been going morally downhill for 30 or 40 years," he lamented. "I thought we'd have something like this, but I thought it would be under someone else's administration—and I won't mention his name! But we'll survive it. Our people are tough. This country is so tough that not even the *New York Times* or the *Washington Post* can hurt it."[6]

After his speech ended and the banquet room cleared, I ran into Goldwater in a hotel corridor. As we chatted, I asked him about conservatism's future as he looked to the post-Nixon years. He expressed the hope that his 1964 effort, although unsuccessful, might pave the way for another conservative candidate to win the White House in 1976 or 1980.

"By the way," he added with a wink, "I understand Ronald Reagan is speaking here tomorrow."

• • •

When Barry Goldwater delivered his presidential nomination acceptance speech, he antagonized the political writers and mainstream media of his day with this declaration: "Extremism in the defense of liberty is no vice... Moderation in the pursuit of justice is no virtue." Democrats jumped on the phrase as proof that he was a reckless "extremist" whose finger on the nuclear trigger might imperil humanity. In fact, the phrase itself was not original. His

6   Richard Nixon resigned the presidency in disgrace three weeks after Goldwater's San Francisco speech to the YAF convention.

speechwriter borrowed it from one of Cicero's ancient addresses to the Roman Senate.

For the rest of his life, Goldwater bristled over any suggestion that he meant the phrase to promote "extremism" in the sinister sense. He later explained that he merely emphasized that "there was nothing wrong in being strong in the defense of freedom and no particular good in being weak toward justice."[7] Despite the ongoing criticism over that phrase, he never backed down from it. When he addressed the Republican National Convention 20 years after his Cow Palace victory, he drew the longest ovation of the night when he repeated it in his speech.

Another treasure from my political memorabilia collection: Presidential candidate Barry Goldwater wrote out and signed for me his famous quotation from his 1964 Republican nomination acceptance speech: "Extremism in the defense of liberty is no vice; moderation in the pursuit of justice is no virtue." (Author's collection)

---

7   Barry Goldwater, *Goldwater* (1988), 186.

• • •

Barry Goldwater retired from the U.S. Senate in 1987. He remained active in politics for another decade until suffering a massive stroke in 1996. He died at age 89 on May 29, 1998.

On September 21, 1978, comedian and ventriloquist Edgar Bergen announced his retirement after 60 years in show business. Nine days later, he played his farewell engagement at Caesar's Palace in Las Vegas and received six standing ovations during his performance. Before taking his final bow, he closed his career by telling the audience, "Every vaudeville act must have an opening and a closing, so I'll pack up my jokes and my little friends and now say goodbye." Later that evening, he died in his sleep at age 75. His wooden sidekick for over five decades, Charlie McCarthy, now sits on display at the Smithsonian Institution.

7

My Governor

I was in the fourth grade when Ronald Reagan became my state's governor. I met him many times before he left Sacramento and charted his course to Washington. Just a few of my recollections from those early encounters follow.

Seeing him in person was my first celebrity experience. On June 26, 1970, hundreds of international dignitaries arrived at San Francisco's Opera House for the 25th anniversary of the United Nations, where President Harry Truman and others had signed the original charter in 1945. My classmate Jon Jacobs and I talked his father into driving us downtown and dropping us off near City Hall. From there we were on our own for the entire day to explore the city and the observance without parental supervision (and also without admission tickets to the event).

With the opening ceremonies beginning soon, Jon and I schemed on how we might sneak inside. We circled the outer perimeter of the Opera House and the adjoining Veterans Building looking for a chink in the security armor, but every door was either guarded or locked, and our pleas to the doorkeepers at the main entrances proved ineffective.

While we stood on Van Ness Avenue in front of the ornate gate that separates the two buildings, I noticed a few men exit the Opera House through a side door and cross over to a waiting black stretch limousine parked alongside the Veterans Building. Meanwhile, an old man staggering down the street stopped and slurred, "What's going on here, boys?" The smell of liquor on his breath almost overpowered me. As I began explaining the day's significance, he turned toward the courtyard and studied the slow-moving limousine now coming toward us.

"Wel-l-l-l-l," he called out as the car neared, "Hello-o-o-o-o, Ronnie!" I looked over and saw Governor Reagan riding alone in the rear seat. As his car rounded the turn in front of us, Jon and I waved and called to him hoping that he might stop for us. He saw us, smiled broadly, returned our wave, and then his car finished circling the courtyard and exited through the west gate onto Franklin Street.

"Good old Ronnie!" our new companion belched as he patted his pockets. "Hey, boys, anyone got an extra smoke? You don't smoke? Well, okay, see you later." With that, he toddled away.

A half century later, I still remember the impression left from my first sighting of the future president. On television and in photographs Reagan always looked tanned and ruggedly handsome, and that was true when I saw him. What surprised me was how heavily lined his face appeared and how the television camera never captured the deepness of those wrinkles. This was not my observation alone. As Reagan's car passed, the wino remarked, "Je-e-e-e-sus, he looks like a wrinkled old p-r-r-r-rune!" Wrinkles notwithstanding, it thrilled me to see Ronald Reagan in person, and I owed it all to a passing drunk.

A couple of weeks later I wrote to Reagan and recounted our Opera House sighting. I expressed my sorrow that we were unable to flag him down to shake his hand and get an autograph. Soon I received a letter from Reagan's secretary saying that the governor read my letter and wanted me to know that he was sorry that we didn't meet, but that he hoped another opportunity would present itself. He enclosed two autographed photographs as a placeholder until then, and he asked me to pass along one of them to Jon.

That delivery task proved easier said than done. Between seeing

Reagan and receiving the photographs, my family had moved away and I lost track of Jon. We didn't reconnect until 30 years later, but when we did I turned over the photograph as the governor had requested decades earlier. As they say, better late than never, but I confess that surrendering that autographed treasure to my old friend and fifth grade classmate proved a tad painful—

Jon was a lifelong Democrat.

To Jim
With Very Best Wishes
Ronald Reagan

Governor Ronald Reagan's surprise gift to me after our San Francisco Opera House encounter, 1970. (Author's collection)

• • •

I first met Ronald Reagan on May 13, 1972, when the California Republican Party held its annual convention at the St. Francis Hotel in San Francisco (see the background on this conference in my previous chapter, *Mr. Conservative*).

After arriving at the hotel for the event that Saturday morning, I walked across the street to Union Square to investigate the thousands of protesters gathered to rally against President Nixon's Vietnam policies and the Republican Party generally. While I was in the middle of the square, the protest turned into a rampage when radicals attacked police with rocks and bottles. Officers in full riot gear waded into the mob to restore order. I turned on my amateur home movie camera to shoot footage of the fracas, but before I could begin filming a rock thrown from the crowd bounced off my lens and knocked the camera out of my hands. My boldness at age 14 matched my stupidity—as I picked up my camera to try again, a policeman grabbed my arm and hustled me into the safety of the St. Francis.

I made my way into the Grand Ballroom and took a seat at the press table in time to see Governor Reagan arrive for his opening address. The delegates jumped to their feet and cheered madly for him. I positioned myself alongside the stage where I witnessed Reagan's trick that his longtime press secretary (and later my friend) Lyn Nofziger[1] explained to me many decades later:

> Reagan wore contact lenses. Just before he entered a ballroom for a speech, he'd pop out one of his contacts and leave in the other. He usually spoke from 4x6 index cards that he carried in his suit jacket pocket. When the emcee introduced him, he walked boldly to the stage and waved with both hands. He wanted everyone to see that he carried no speech. When he got behind the lectern, he slid one hand into his outer coat pocket and retrieved the cards. Here was the trick: when he gave his speech, he looked at his notes with the one eye wearing the lens, and he looked at the audience with the other eye. It gave the illusion that he spoke extemporaneously and maintained complete eye contact with everyone. I've never known any other person who could do that.

After urging his fellow California Republicans to work hard for President Nixon's reelection, he accused the 1972 Democrat presidential candidate (and eventual nominee) George McGovern of being "quite explicit in his plans for regimenting all of us into the ranks of a social order where individuality will have no place.... The domination of our lives is presented to us as liberalism." He pulled

---

1   Franklin "Lyn" Nofziger (1924-2006) was a California reporter who served as a longtime senior Reagan aide from his first run for governor, his presidential campaigns, and during the White House years.

out a copy of another political party's manifesto and said that the Democrat platform reads almost identically to what he held in his hands. He rattled off several key planks, such as nationalizing businesses and focusing less on the individual and more on the collective good. "What I have just read to you," he declared, "was the platform of Germany's Nazi Party." Then, referring to the thousands of rioters across the street, he added that their activities were "nothing more than a revival of Hitler's Storm Troopers."

When he concluded his speech, a thicket of security agents moved in to escort him out of the hotel quickly. I had hoped to meet him, but given his heavy guard and the crush of so many fans, that looked unlikely. I moved to the other side of the room to avoid the people surging toward him.

As he made for the opposite exit, he reversed course and now came directly toward me. I don't recall if I stepped forward or was shoved, but I found myself wedged inside his security bubble and walking alongside him. He shook my hand and greeted me. I asked him to sign a Nixon campaign brochure that I held in my hand. "Sure," he said. "Why don't you walk with me while I sign it?" As we strolled together, a phalanx of press photographers kept their cameras trained on us. Although I never saw a picture of us taken together from that day, in newspaper morgue files somewhere are images depicting my first meeting with a man who went on to change the destiny of the world.

I walked with him to his waiting motorcade where he handed back the autograph, shook my hand again, wished me luck in school, and then he climbed into his limousine. Throughout the rest of the day, convention delegates kept asking me in awe, "Aren't you the boy that I saw walking with the governor this morning?"

• • •

During Ronald Reagan's last year as governor, the Republican battle to succeed him was in high gear. Shortly before the California primary election, the United San Francisco Republican Finance Committee hosted a $250 per person "Governor's Dinner," both to salute him and to urge the two leading GOP gubernatorial candidates to put away their knives for an early show of unity.

On March 20, 1974, my classmates Dan Swanson, Roger Mahan, and I arrived early at the Sheraton Palace Hotel in San Francisco looking for a way to slip into the event. While in the lobby, I saw Reagan and a few aides enter the hotel from a side door and board a waiting elevator. Nobody appeared to notice him as he moved through the lobby. I recognized him only because his uncharacteristic getup caught my attention. Instead of wearing his customary tailored business suit, he wore an open-collared shirt underneath a hideous maroon belt-in-the-back polyester "leisure suit," an ensemble that enjoyed mercifully brief popularity in the fashion-bereft 1970s.

With his official entourage now taking temporary residence in the hotel, I took a page from my earlier playbook. Picking up the hotel courtesy phone, I convinced the operator to put me through to the governor's suite. I spoke with his assistant press secretary, Rudy Garcia, whom I convinced to issue us press passes and dinner tickets (I know—it's hard to believe how many times I pulled off this trick as a boy).

After changing into a proper suit, Reagan reemerged in the lobby. His entourage moved him quickly into a room marked, "Convention Sales and Catering," where he remained for ten minutes in a private meeting with the two candidates battling to succeed him, Lieutenant Governor Ed Reinecke and State Controller Houston Flournoy. Throughout their primary battle, Reagan maintained neutrality between these GOP contenders.

When the doors reopened, Reagan walked over to where we waited and greeted us. When he learned that his press aide gave us our tickets, he invited us to join him as he entered the ballroom. He led us backstage to where he and the other dignitaries lined up for their formal introductions. Talk about three kids making a grand entrance into a political event! We followed Reagan into the ballroom when the emcee introduced him. As the crowd cheered his arrival, we took our seats at a press table as waiters served dinner.

The program opened later with remarks by David Packard, the chairman of Hewlett-Packard. After brief speeches from both gubernatorial candidates, the evening belonged to Reagan, who attacked the tax-and-spend Democrats seeking to succeed him while defending the accomplishments of his outgoing administration.

In his speech, he dismissed the media expectation that the ongoing Watergate scandal forecasted doom for Republican candidates in the upcoming November midterm elections. With state and national Democrats rushing headlong to spend America into bankruptcy, he warned that, "The last hope for human liberty rests with us."

When the dinner adjourned, Reagan autographed a few items for me, including an original Turf Cigarette trading card from the 1940s depicting him in a football uniform and listing him as a Warner Brothers movie star. He put on his reading glasses to study the card more closely, and then he smiled and penned his name to it. "You've got quite a collection here," he chuckled.

Yes, I did. And each time I got the chance, I let Ronald Reagan add to it.

• • •

Ronald Reagan once gave to me the most meaningful item of political memorabilia in my collection. It not only traveled far and then returned, but it changed my life—and maybe a bit of history, as you will see.

On June 13, 1973, Governor Reagan headlined a luncheon in the Plaza Ballroom of the Boundary Oak clubhouse in Walnut Creek, California. Hosted by the Contra Costa Taxpayers Association, the invitation promised that Reagan would "present his bold initiative proposal entitled 'A Reasonable Program for Revenue

Control and Tax Reduction' [which calls for] an effective lid on state government spending."

Unbelievable by today's standards, attending this private reception with Ronald Reagan, enjoying a country club sit-down lunch with him, and hearing him unveil a major administration initiative cost "$6 per lunch including tax and tip" (per the invitation). Back then, six bucks was a lot of money to a young teenager and I didn't have it. If you have read this far in my book, you know by now that such deficiencies never discouraged me. By the way, to the hostess who left the Boundary Oak's entrance door unattended momentarily that day, I send my deepest thanks across the years.

Reagan arrived at noon and admirers besieged him. While others ate, he enjoyed little of the lunch served him. Instead, he spent most of his time shaking hands, posing for photographs, and signing autographs for admirers.

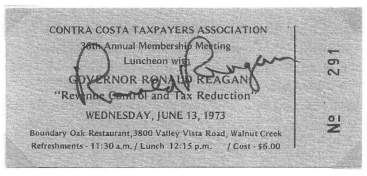

Original ticket to Governor Reagan's reception and speech, Boundary Oak clubhouse, Walnut Creek, June 13, 1973. Note the $6 admission price! This ticket rested on the table in front of Governor Reagan. At my request, he autographed it and gave it to me. (Author's collection)

Shortly before the program began, Reagan sat at the head table reviewing his stack of four-by-six cards bearing his handwritten speech notes. I decided to wait around after the luncheon and ask him if I could have them for my political collection.

Governor Ronald Reagan reviews his speech note cards before his remarks at the Boundary Oak clubhouse, Walnut Creek, California, June 13, 1973. (Photograph by the author)

After Reagan finished his speech, his security detail whisked him to the nearby La Velada room for a radio broadcast, and then for a hastily arranged meeting with Republican state legislators bussed down from Sacramento so that Reagan could brief them on his new initiative. Scores of luncheon guests lingered outside the room waiting for him to exit, but as the hours passed only three people remained: a ten year-old boy holding a vintage Brownie camera, his mother, and me.[2]

---

2   Almost 50 years after meeting Governor Reagan at the Boundary Oak, I researched his official gubernatorial schedule for June 13, 1973. Reagan was slated for only a 25 minute meeting in the La Velada Room. His meeting with state legislators ended up lasting nearly three hours, which canceled the down time his staff had scheduled for him that afternoon. https://www.reaganlibrary.gov/sites/default/files/digitallibrary/gubernatorial/pressunit/p26/40-840-7408626-p26-009-2017.pdf (accessed September 7, 2020).

Three hours later, a Reagan aide told us that the governor was about to leave, but not from the entrance where we waited. His security detail had brought his car around to the rear. The aide suggested that we wait by his car if we wanted to see him when he departed. The boy and his mother were in front of me as we made for the exit, but they moved too slowly. As we stepped through the door, Reagan had just settled into the rear of his limousine. His motorcade started pulling away.

For some reason, Reagan glanced back over his shoulder. He saw the boy holding the old camera dropping his head in disappointment. Reagan leaned forward and said something to his driver. The limousine stopped, and then it backed up to where we stood. Rolling down his window, Reagan called to the boy, "Hi, son! Were you waiting to take a picture of me?" The speechless boy nodded his head. With no reporters (or anyone else) around to witness his kindness, Reagan climbed out of the car, greeted the boy and his mother, and posed for a picture with them. He then turned to me and smiled.

Here was my chance. I praised his luncheon speech and then I said to him, "Governor, while you were reviewing your notes, I saw that they were all handwritten. Did you write them out yourself?"

"Why, yes, I did," he replied. When I asked if I could see them, he pulled them from his coat pocket and handed them to me. As I leafed through the cards, he told me he had written them the night before in his hotel room. He explained that with this speech he had formally kicked off his statewide ballot initiative campaign to reduce state taxes and curb spending. Calling this the "signature initiative of my administration," he told me he had spent three hours last night working on it because of its significance.[3]

It was now or never: "Governor, may I have them for my political memorabilia collection?"

---

3   Reagan's "Proposition 1" lost at the polls, but it was the precursor for California's Proposition 13, the 1978 Jarvis-Gann Initiative, which passed overwhelmingly and also set off a national copycat anti-tax revolt.

He grimaced. "Uh, well," he said, "you see, I'll need to give this speech more than once and I don't have another copy of it. My staff will kill me if I don't come back with it."

Sensing my opportunity slipping away, and remembering how the sad-faced boy with the Brownie camera had touched Reagan's sympathy nerve, I tried the same ploy. I dropped my chin to my chest and wiped away a nonexistent tear. "I understand, governor. It took you three hours to write it. Three hours—that's how long I've been waiting for you."

He sighed. "Okay, you win. You may not be able to make heads or tails out of my writing, but you can have them."

Brazenly, I handed back the last note card to him: "They're no good if you don't autograph them," I said. Smiling and shaking his head, he penned his name on the last card and returned it to me. Reagan then took back the cards to show me that on each one his

Two speeches for the price of one: Governor Ronald Reagan's speech notes from the Boundary Oak clubhouse, Walnut Creek, June 13, 1973 (Reagan's signed the last page for me). The recording of Reagan's Boundary Oak speech he gave from these notecards is accessible through the National Archives at this link: https://catalog.archives.gov/id/169488953.

handwritten notes were on one side for today's speech, and on the other side were speech notes typed in large black font. He explained that the typed side was his reading copy of a speech he had delivered earlier to a California Highway Patrol audience. Not one to waste paper, he said he used the back of the CHP speech to handwrite his speech notes for today's event. "So you see," he said, "you're really getting two speeches for the price of one."

• • •

The rest of the story:

Eight years later, when voters installed Ronald Reagan in the White House, I was a student at UCLA Law School. A financial crisis hit and I needed $1,500 to pay for my tuition or else the school would drop me. Knowing of my dire straits, a collector offered me the needed money for Reagan's speech notes. I refused. The new president gave them to me and I could never part with them.

As time ran out, and faced with the choice of being kicked out of school or selling the notes, I had no choice but to let them go. I kept page one of Reagan's notes in my collection, and I sold pages two through eight. The money paid my tuition. I finished law school, passed the bar exam, and my career took its course.

After I served as a House Manager in the U.S. Senate impeachment trial of President Clinton, I had lunch with Clinton's White House counsel, my friend Lanny Davis. He told me that during the House Judiciary Committee's impeachment hearings, Clinton and the White House senior staff called me, "The Domino." I asked why. He explained that they had identified several GOP Judiciary Committee members wanting to vote against impeachment but they needed cover. These congressmen said that if I voted against it, then they could use the excuse that an ex-prosecutor and an ex-judge looked at the evidence and found it lacking. "We knew if we could flip you our way, these others would follow," Lanny told me. "We could have killed impeachment in the committee." I suspected that his assessment overestimated my influence, but he insisted that they had the votes to defeat impeachment if their linchpin (me) voted no.

Not long after this lunch, I spent a rare afternoon relaxing at home and sifting through my memorabilia collection. When I came upon page one of Reagan's old speech notes, I looked at it for a long time while thinking about what Lanny had told me. If Ronald Reagan hadn't given me those notes almost 30 years earlier, I wouldn't have finished law school, which meant that I never would have become a prosecutor, a judge, a state legislator, a congressman, a member of the House Judiciary Committee, or a House Manager in the Clinton impeachment trial. Would that changed circumstance have mattered to the ultimate vote? Who knows?

As I reflected on Lanny's chain reaction theory, it caused renewed pining over the forced sale of pages two through eight, I hoped that Ronald Reagan might forgive me if he knew that I had sold them to finish my education and embark on a life of public service. Somehow, I felt he would.

A few weeks later, I was flipping through an auction catalog of political memorabilia for sale. I gasped when I saw Auction Lot #73: it was pages two through eight of my old Reagan speech note cards. The original purchaser had died and his heirs were selling his collection. I bid on the notes and then monitored the competition by telephone on the night of the auction. When the sun rose the next morning, Ronald Reagan's 1973 Boundary Oak speech notes returned home.

Some years later, I showed the notes to Martin Anderson, a former Reagan senior adviser who wrote two Reagan books sourced from the president's holographic archives. He told me that his comprehensive research throughout Reagan's body of work showed that my Boundary Oak note cards are the *only known complete set* of Reagan's famous four-by-six-inch handwritten speech notes outside the possession of the Reagan Library. More importantly, they are the *only* autographed complete set known to exist anywhere. Apparently, nobody ever thought to ask Reagan to sign his speech cards before I came along, and nobody bothered to ask after.

Because Ronald Reagan wouldn't turn down a glib fan in a parking lot half a century ago, a unique historic treasure now rests in the archives of Michigan's Hillsdale College (where I donated them in 2018). Lining the pathway to Hillsdale's repository of my donation are life-sized bronze statues of George Washington, Thomas Jefferson, Abraham Lincoln, Margaret Thatcher, and Ronald Reagan.

Thanks again for giving me those speech notes, Governor Reagan. They made an unexpected but profound impact on my life. One day, when we reunite in Glory, I'll tell you the story.

Ronald Reagan and me at the Boundary Oak clubhouse, Walnut Creek, California, June 13, 1973. (Author's collection)

8

Valhalla

National nominating conventions are to political junkies and campaign memorabilia collectors what Valhalla is to a dead Viking, so my boyhood dream was to attend one. In 1972 my chance came when I received a letter from Tom Bell, chairman of the Young Voters for the President (YVP) delegation to the 1972 Republican National Convention in Miami. Bell wanted to organize thousands of young volunteers to help staff the convention. For only $280, the YVPs offered round-trip airfare from California to Florida, hotel rooms and meals for a week, and admission to the convention to see the renominations of President Richard Nixon and Vice President Spiro Agnew. However, there was a hitch: the YVPs limited eligibility to registered Republican voters ages 18 to 30. I was a 14 year-old boy who thought of himself as a Democrat back then, but so what? The Democrats didn't invite me to their convention—the Republicans did.[1]

There was a second hitch: I needed to convince my mother to let me fly cross-country alone and spend a week 3,000 miles away with no adult supervision. Knowing the likely response if I asked permission, I bypassed the consent route and went for the fait

---

1   Because I wrote to each of the presidential campaigns and asked that they send me campaign memorabilia for my collection, my name must have ended up on the Nixon campaign's list of potential YVP volunteers.

accompli. I filled out the YVP application (*Jim Rogan, Registered Republican, Age 26*) and mailed it back to Mr. Bell with a $280 money order that I purchased with savings from my part-time job at an Oakland toy store.

"Oh, Mom, I almost forgot to tell you," I mentioned casually after dinner that night, "this August I'll be flying to Miami for the Republican National Convention. I'll only be gone about a week. I'll call you while I'm there."

She laughed. "Are you kidding? You're 14 years old. You can't just fly across the country and be gone for a week by yourself. That's ridiculous."

"Mom, I'll be with 20,000 Republicans—how much trouble can I get in? Besides, I already paid for it—$280. It's nonrefundable."

She scowled at me before extinguishing her cigarette in the ashtray. "In that case," she told me, "have a good time. And stay out of trouble." My single mother's permissive standards sometimes came in very handy.

A week later I received from the YVPs my notice of acceptance, along with a confirmed reservation aboard the *Miami Special* flight departing Los Angeles International Airport at midnight on August 18, 1972.

• • •

I was unprepared for the anarchy aboard our charter flight to Florida. From the moment our plane went "wheels up," the college-aged passengers leapt from their seats and the in-flight party began. Someone pried open the liquor galley and passed out now-complimentary bottles to all takers. Rock music blasted through the cabin and people danced in the aisles or on the seats. Recognizing the futility of trying to preserve order, our stewardess crew kicked off their shoes, tossed aside their pillbox hats, and joined in the revelry.

Growing up in liberal San Francisco, I had always heard that you could tell a Republican by his or her hair color: gray for men and blue for women. My traveling companions smashed that stuffy stereotype. They were young, hip, fun, loud, and (for many soon after takeoff) inebriated. As I surveyed this wild scene, I remembered what I had said to convince my mother to let me go on this unsupervised weeklong escapade. Now I asked myself the same question I had put to her, but the emphasis changed: How much trouble *could* I get into with these Republicans?!

My late-twenties seatmate (I'll call her Bambi—not her real name) offered a potential answer to that question. At first, she presented a severe contrast to the other partying passengers. Her old-fashioned blouse buttoned all the way up her neck-high collar. She wore glasses, a long skirt, clunky shoes, and her hair piled high in a bun. We struck up a friendly but reserved conversation.

As the plane reached its cruising altitude, she drank a glass of wine—and another, and then another. In time, the upper buttons on her librarian blouse loosened up as much as her previously reserved persona. The bobby pins came out of her bun and piles of chestnut locks dropped past her shoulders. She kicked off her klogs and stretched her legs under the seat in front of her.

Somewhere over Kansas, a deeply relaxed Bambi turned toward the window and caught me looking at her. Embarrassed, I apologized. She reached over, took my hand, and studied me over the top of her glass frames with sleepy, half-closed green eyes. Her slow transformation from frumpy seatmate into an attractive—even sexy—woman mesmerized me.

"You know," she said in a low voice, "you really seem like a nice guy. You're easy to talk to. May I tell you something?"

"Sure," I said innocently.

"I have a bit of a problem. It's a secret." After assuring her that she could trust me with her confidence, she let it fly: "I'm a nymphomaniac."

Even at 14, I knew what that meant.

Bambi leaned in closer. "Say," she asked through those sleepy eye slits, "how old did you say you are?"

We looked at each other in silence for a few beats before I answered: "I'll tell you the truth. I lied on my application. I wrote back to the national committee and said that I was 26 because I really wanted to come to the convention. But it's not true. My real age would have disqualified me."

"So how old are you?"

I cleared my throat: "Bambi—I'm 32."

As a young boy growing up in a pro-union and Democrat San Francisco household, I couldn't understand why anyone would want to be

My security credentials to the 1972 Republican National Convention, which depicts me at age 14—I mean 26—I mean 32— (Author's collection)

a Republican. Now, as our airborne jubilee continued winging throughout the night, I recognized for the first time that America did indeed have a vigorous two-party system, and that perhaps I shouldn't be so hasty in deciding which one suited me better.

• • •

Our charter plane arrived in Miami the next morning. Once we landed, organizers packed our time with campaign and convention-related events. Since President Nixon faced no serious opposition, the thousands of enthusiastic Republicans descending on Florida gathered for a coronation, not combat.

That afternoon I attended a poolside reception for Vice President Agnew at the Americana Hotel. At the conclusion of the event, and always looking for a chance to add to my collection, I shimmied up a pole mounted near the platform and yanked the convention seal off a speaker's lectern. If I met any dignitaries, I thought this might be a unique item on which to collect autographs. As it turned out, I was not disappointed.

• • •

Nautilus Middle School in Miami has a significant bit of unknown historical trivia that might surprise their current faculty and students: Over one 24-hour period in 1972, three future presidents of the United States visited their small campus. I know because I was there.

August 21 was the first full day of the convention. I boarded an early morning shuttle to Nautilus (vacant for the summer recess), which became our YVP holding area during our week in Miami. There we encamped under a large outdoor tent on the athletic field. During convention down times, we assembled under the tent painting rally signs, making new friends from 50 states, drinking complimentary Pepsi Cola from a nearby concession stand, eating boxed lunches catered by the Marriott hotels, and meeting a parade of Party dignitaries dropping by to thank us for our help.

At noon, a station wagon pulled onto the field. Out stepped a middle-aged man with thinning brown hair and wearing gray slacks and a yellow open-neck shirt—Congressman Gerald R. Ford (R-MI), the minority leader of the House of Representatives. Recovering from recent knee surgery to correct an old football injury, he hobbled on a cane over to our tent. An organizer summoned the volunteers together and introduced him to us.

Many of the YVPs were indifferent to hearing or meeting the rather obscure congressman. While Ford spoke, most volunteers remained in the back of the tent painting signs, blowing up balloons, or napping on the grass. For those of us listening, he kept his remarks brief. He welcomed the YVPs to Miami and thanked everyone for their efforts on behalf of the Nixon–Agnew ticket. He then urged us to return home at the end of the convention and work very hard to deliver a Republican congressional majority in November. This,

Congressman Gerald Ford chatting with the YVPs, Nautilus Middle School, Miami, August 21, 1972. (Photograph by the author)

he added, would bring him his greatest personal ambition—becoming speaker of the House.

Ford mingled with the YVPs, signed a few autographs, and answered questions, but his prolonged standing appeared to aggravate his knee pain. When he signaled to his driver his readiness to go, the aide had to assist him back to the car. Ford slid his cane underneath the seat and waved goodbye as the station wagon pulled away.

• • •

The next day, Miami's brutally hot and muggy weather (combined with no air-conditioning under our tent) left the cluster of YVPs increasingly lethargic. Even the free cups of Pepsi failed to bring relief. The ice melted immediately in the oppressive heat.

This sluggish spirit evaporated when a sedan pulled up to the tent and someone shouted excitedly, "It's Governor Reagan!" Unlike the reception accorded Congressman Ford, volunteers ran from all corners of the school and crammed underneath the tent to cheer Reagan as he stepped from his automobile. Where other guest speakers generated only mild interest, his surprise appearance merited a rock star-worthy reception.

During convention week, the other guest speakers visiting us wilted quickly in the heat. Neckties came off, shirt collar buttons loosened unceremoniously, and dress shirts drenched in perspiration. Reagan proved the exception. He looked crisp and fresh throughout his time with us as he discussed the Nixon campaign, the important convention efforts of the YVPs, and his own vision for an America free of bureaucratic intrusion into people's lives.

When his impromptu remarks concluded, an aide told him it was time to go. Reagan brushed

Governor Ronald Reagan, Nautilus Middle School, Miami, August 22, 1972. (Photograph by the author)

him off and told the crowd of young activists there was no place he would rather be right now than with them, and he took questions for another 15 minutes.

When a youth asked if he would run for president in 1976, the prolonged ovation almost drowned out his answer. Cocking his head and smiling, he demurred. "Well," he replied coyly, "1976 is a long way off."

The crowd mobbed Reagan when he finished. He signed autographs and shook hands as he made his way back to the car. Once inside, he rolled down his window and shook more hands until his driver pulled away.

• • •

A few hours later, another car arrived with an unrecognized dignitary: the United States Ambassador to the United Nations, former

Texas Congressman George Bush (who had lost a U.S. Senate race two years earlier). Wearing slacks, an open-neck shirt, and a security pass hanging from a chain around his neck that resembled the ones that we wore, he walked around the field introducing himself and thanking the volunteers. Bush gave a brief pep talk to the troops that drew the same lukewarm interest shown in Gerald Ford's visit. It was less a reflection of their flat oratorical skills as it was the afternoon's draining heat and humidity. Besides, let's face it, Ronald Reagan was a tough act for anyone to follow.[2]

United Nations Ambassador George Bush, Nautilus Middle School, Miami, August 22, 1972. (Photograph by the author)

• • •

I turned 15 on the opening day of the 1972 Republican National Convention, but the birthday blessing proved mixed. Getting inside the hall to witness history was more difficult than expected. Thousands of protesters descended on Miami to disrupt the proceedings. For our protection, the National Guard provided a fleet of buses with steel-barred and mesh windows to transport us through the downtown area. As our caravan barreled down Collins Avenue, I watched as troopers lining the route fought against demonstrators trying to break through the lines. Rocks and bottles crashed against our bus along the route.

---

2   George Bush returned to Nautilus the next day to play in a celebrity tennis match set up on a makeshift court.

At one checkpoint, a trooper in full riot gear and carrying an automatic rifle boarded our bus and gave us these ominous instructions: "There's a lot of tension out there on the streets and some of these people are very violent. If your bus is attacked, do not try to leave the bus. Stay on board. Your life may depend on it. If any of them break through and attack your bus, everybody needs to lean toward the rioters so they will have a harder time turning the bus over and killing you."

Lean toward the rioters if they try turning over the bus? The trooper offered no Plan B.

The scene outside the Miami Beach Convention Center looked just as grim. Police clashed with a huge mob of screaming rioters. Only a chain-link security fence separated us from the anarchy. The view unnerved me, but I hadn't come all this way to be deterred. I planned to get inside that hall no matter what.

Gratefully, our bus made it by the melee and dropped us safely at the entrance. Because security inside the arena was very tight, the line to enter the hall moved agonizingly slow. The Secret Service required each person to pass through two metal detectors and then have all personal items hand-searched. After half an hour, the line had barely moved. As the time approached for the opening gavel, I felt sure that I would miss it.

An impatient reporter at the rear of the crowd held aloft his press credentials and pushed his way through to the front of the line calling out, "CBS News—let me pass, please. CBS News...." The mass of people moved aside for him without ever looking over their shoulders. If it worked once, it might work again: I held my YVP credentials over my head. "Excuse me," I shouted. "NBC News—let me pass, please. Excuse me, please, NBC News...." Once more, the Red Sea parted and I walked directly to the security screening table inside the arena.

Any lingering bus ride anxiety dissolved when I entered the hall. The sight thrilled me. Neat rows of tri-folded red, white, and silver state delegation banners perched atop poles rested amid the thousands of seats. At the front of the arena stood a two-story eggshell-colored podium bearing the seals of all 50 states. Huge American flags and Nixon banners hung from the rafters. In the skyboxes, network news anchormen Walter Cronkite of CBS, John Chancellor and David Brinkley of NBC, and Harry Reasoner and Howard K. Smith of ABC all looked down from their glass-encased perches. Behind the podium, two large Jumbotron screens flashed a repeated admonition: "Delegates and Alternates: Please be seated."

From my seat in the gallery I watched as U.S. Senator Bob Dole banged the ceremonial gavel and called the 1972 Republican National Convention to order. Little did I dream that a quarter-century later, Dole—the 1996 GOP presidential nominee—would campaign for me in my three congressional races.

One of the first convention speeches that night was the briefest. Former Kansas Governor Alf Landon, the 1936 Republican nominee against Franklin D. Roosevelt, stood before the microphones and received a standing ovation. The 84-year old wore a huge sunflower (his 1936 campaign symbol) on his coat lapel. Landon accepted a commemorative plaque, and then he delivered a two-sentence speech: "We meet tonight in this convention in unity and enthusiasm for the winner of the next election, a great president, a great world leader, Richard Nixon. One good term deserves another."

Seeing Landon in person delighted me. A few years earlier as a young boy I had wanted him to send me an autographed picture. When I read somewhere that the Topeka telephone directory listed his home number, I decided to call him and ask for the picture personally. I waited for my mother to leave and run errands, and then I dialed *Prescott 2–2460*. Sure enough, the former governor answered the telephone himself, but the results proved frustrating. No matter how loudly I spoke, Landon kept saying we had a bad connection, he couldn't hear me clearly, and he told me to hang up and try again. I did—14 times. The next month, when my mother received the whopping $50 long-distance bill (the equivalent of

$400 in 2020) for 14 peak-time calls to Topeka, I got a slap to go with the signed picture that Landon sent me. When Landon died 20 years later, I wrote a condolence letter to his daughter, U.S. Senator Nancy Landon Kassebaum, and I shared that story. She wrote back: "I appreciate your story about Dad. It always amazes me to hear how many people have talked with him and remember him fondly. He of course loved the attention, and I am sure he enjoyed your calls as much as you did—and he didn't get spanked for it!"

Landon wasn't the only nostalgic speaker that night. Senator Barry Goldwater, the 1964 Republican presidential nominee, compared Democrat presidential nominee George McGovern to the coyotes roaming around his native Arizona: "My coyotes just bay and moan and cry over everything that exists, but they never suggest anything new, anything better, or anything constructive to replace them." He hit McGovern as an appeaser to the communist government in North Vietnam, saying, "For the first time, a candidate of one of our major parties has already surrendered to the enemy before the election has been held…. I say to the communist bosses in Hanoi that the McGoverns do not speak for America, nor will they ever get the chance."

Governor Ronald Reagan, the temporary convention chairman, used McGovern and the Democrats as fodder for his comedic talents, with each joke about them provoking uproarious laughter throughout the hall. Turning serious, he accused McGovern of pursuing utopian and extravagant policies amounting to a deliberate deception on the voters. "If we confiscated all the earnings of all the corporations in America at 100 per cent, we would have less than a third of the price of [McGovern's] promises."

The evening also proved memorable for an unexpected reason. During a filmed tribute to Mrs. Nixon (who made a brief appearance on stage following its conclusion), I stepped out of the hall for some fresh air. When I tried returning through the same gate, a guard said my pass didn't authorize readmission there and he didn't know where to direct me. I walked the outer perimeter of the auditorium trying other gate entrances, but security rebuffed me at each one.

Meanwhile, another violent confrontation erupted between police and rioters on the other side of the nearby chain-link fence. Teargas burned my eyes and throat as it wafted my way, while members of the mob directed profane jeers and gestures at the only visible conventioneer—me. Someone threw a rock that missed my head. Trapped outside the hall between a convention fortress on one side of me and a riot on the other, I didn't know what to do. Fortunately, a Secret Service agent saw my plight. He ran over, checked my credential quickly, and then he escorted me back inside the hall just as more rocks crashed where I had stood moments earlier.

Later that night, on the armored bus ride back to our hotel, I looked out my barred coach windows. Shrieking rioters again tried to break through the police lines to attack us. For the $280 I paid to be in Miami, I was getting far more of a convention experience than I ever anticipated. Still, it was an unforgettable way to spend my 15th birthday.

• • •

The next morning, the YVPs boarded buses for President Nixon's arrival ceremony. Thousands of supporters waving flags and campaign signs packed the temporary bleachers on the tarmac at Miami International Airport's Eastern Airlines hangar on 36th Street. The lineup of celebrity speakers warming up the crowd for Nixon included singer Ethel Merman and movie stars James Stewart, Mickey Rooney, and John Wayne.

Cheers arose when the gleaming Air Force One came into view on final approach. Chants of "Four More Years! Four More Years!" rang out as the plane landed and taxied to a stop. The clamor grew earsplitting when the cabin door swung open and a solitary man in a blue suit stepped onto the mobile stairs and waved.

President Richard Nixon deplaned and walked to the bank of microphones on the tarmac. Joined by First Lady Pat Nixon and their family, he thanked the YVPs for their welcome and promised to reward our efforts with a November victory. "I have not yet attended the convention," he told us. "The custom is that candidates who have not been nominated do not attend. I should not be here now, but I think I'm going to be nominated tonight, and so is Vice President Agnew!" With the 1972 election the first where 18 year-olds could vote for president, he added, "Based on what I've seen here today, those predictions that the other side is going to win young voters are wrong. We are going to win them."

When he finished speaking, he and Mrs. Nixon walked along the fence shaking hands. As he passed in front of me, I reached for his hand across the people in front of me, but he moved too quickly. I missed my chance.

The Nixon family boarded Marine One, the presidential helicopter. It circled the crowd twice before disappearing.

I didn't meet the president of the United States, but I saw him arrive on Air Force One and give a speech, and he came within a few feet of me. Not a bad way for a young political history buff to spend a morning.

• • •

Inside the convention hall that night, New York Governor Nelson Rockefeller placed Nixon's name in nomination. During the roll call of the states, organizers corralled our YVP groups into an auditorium and handed out noisemakers, flags, and floppy Nixon hats. As the balloting neared its conclusion, they escorted us to the delegate entrances on the convention floor.

Over the loudspeaker came the voice of the chairman of the Missouri delegation casting all of its 30 votes for Nixon, which gave him the needed majority. From my spot, I saw Congressman Gerald Ford, the chairman of the convention, pound the gavel and declare Nixon the 1972 Republican presidential nominee. The band struck up patriotic music, ushers threw open the gates, and the YVPs waving flags and tooting noisemakers swarmed onto the convention floor as a quarter million balloons dropped from ceiling nets.

I wandered the arena taking pictures and gathering campaign buttons worn by generous delegates. Standing near the podium, I looked up and saw convention chairman Gerald Ford off to the side of the stage speaking privately with vice chairman Bob Dole. The irony of that image returned to me four years later. Through the twists of history, these two obscure 1972 convention officials stood before the next national convention as the 1976 Republican nominees for president and vice president.

• • •

On the final night of the convention, I sat in the gallery for the acceptance speeches. In his address, Vice President Agnew pledged, "I shall do everything in my power to help reelect this great president and, after his reelection, to assist him in every way 1 can in the difficult task that lies ahead. That task is to make this nation the best possible home for all Americans.... Do we turn our country over to the piecemeal, inconsistent and illusory policies of George McGovern? Or do we entrust the future of this nation to the sound, tested leadership of Richard Nixon? There can be only one answer to that question. And in November it will be answered resoundingly with the reelection of the president."

Agnew concluded his remarks by introducing Nixon, who emerged from behind the stage to the strains of *Hail to the Chief* and a wall-shaking ovation. State banners and Nixon signs bounced up and down as the chant again rolled through the arena: "Four More Years! Four More Years!"

Once the applause died down, Nixon claimed his prize: "Four years ago, standing in this very place, I proudly accepted your nomination for president of the United States. With your help, and with the votes of millions of Americans, we won a great victory in 1968. Tonight, I again proudly accept your nomination for president of the United States, and let us pledge ourselves to win an even greater victory this November in 1972."

• • •

When the acceptance speeches ended, Nixon and Agnew wrapped their arms around each other and waved to the delegates as balloons dropped, the music blared, and conventioneers cheered themselves hoarse. Before adjourning the proceedings sine die, Gerald Ford announced that the Nixons and Agnews wanted to meet as many people as possible before leaving.

I rushed through the delegate floor entrance, which was next to the vice presidential receiving line. While waiting my turn to meet the Agnews, legendary singer Frank Sinatra and Governor Nelson Rockefeller strolled by me as they left the nearby VIP box. As a longtime Sinatra fan, I would like to have met him, but I didn't want to lose my place in line.

Agnew gave each of us moving through his line a ball point pen bearing his facsimile signature and the vice presidential seal. I thanked him and his wife, and then I hurried over to the Nixon line. While waiting, I added more autographs to my convention seal, including Governor Rockefeller, Bob Dole, future Secretary of State Henry Kissinger, and many other notables.

The Nixons greeted people in their receiving line for over an hour. As my turn neared, a security guard shut down the line. For the second time this week, I has missed my chance to meet President Nixon. (As it turned out, 20 more years would pass before we met.)

Nixon picked up a microphone and announced it was time to go: "I was just reminded that we have a rather light day tomorrow," he explained. "Let me give you an idea of what a 'light day' is for a president: I fly to Chicago and speak at the American Legion Convention. Then I fly to Detroit to dedicate the Eisenhower High School. Then I fly to San Diego and speak at a rally, and then we fly by helicopter to San Clemente and speak there."

• • •

After the Nixons left, the convention hall emptied quickly. Workers swarmed onto the floor and began disassembling the arena in preparation for an upcoming sports event. Souvenir hunters grabbed state banners off the poles, tore them into thirds, and divided the pieces. Before Miami, I had always envied the political convention cleanup crews because I assumed that they would find treasure troves of discarded campaign memorabilia when it ended. Now I combed the empty aisles looking for abandoned mementos. I found the only thing a cleaning crew inherited at the end of a national convention was a messy hall.

• • •

After joining fellow YVPs for a postconvention party at the Americana Hotel (complete with a fully hosted bar and buffet), I dragged myself back to my hotel room around 4:00 a.m. Shortly after dozing off, shouts in the hallway awakened me. I dressed quickly and opened my door. A man down the hall yelled, "Get that woman out of my room!" As a small crowd gathered around him, he explained that he had come back from the Americana party, took a shower, and then he discovered a nude woman in his bed demanding sex. I thought he might be drunk until I heard a female inside his room shouting slurred obscenities and pleading for him to return and, well, take care of business.

I peeked through his open door. A naked and crying woman stood against the far wall using the window drapes as partial covering.

Bambi! It was my seatmate from our charter flight to Miami a week earlier.

As hotel security led her from his room, I patted on the shoulder the guy she had surprised and told him, "She's a nice girl once you get to know her."

• • •

I carried home to California a suitcase filled with political memorabilia, as well as countless memories of that historic trip. Those three future presidents I had met at Nautilus Middle School had each signed the convention seal I swiped from the podium my first night in Miami. Later I added President Nixon's and Vice President Agnew's signatures to it. Today it hangs framed in my office.

Back then I never imagined that in later decades I would come to know many of the people whose autographs I collected at the convention, including those three future presidents. The Reagan family invited me to his private graveside interment ceremony when he died in 2004. Former Presidents Ford and Bush became friends; both campaigned for me and held fundraisers for my congressional races. Those experiences remained many years in the future, and they were unimaginable to a starry-eyed 14 year-old boy who stepped off a plane in Miami on a humid August morning in 1972.

By the way, that purloined convention seal returns "home" occasionally: I have loaned it to the Richard Nixon Presidential Library to display whenever the archivists request it. I do so without any concerns over legal repercussions—

—The statute of limitations on my podium seal heist expired long ago.

Podium seal from the 1972 Republican National Convention autographed for me by four presidents (Nixon, Ford, Reagan, and Bush); two vice presidents (Agnew and Rockefeller), and multiple GOP dignitaries, Miami, August 1972. (Author's collection)

9

You Didn't Wait for Me

By October 1972, polls showed that Democrat presidential nominee George McGovern's campaign appeared headed for an overwhelming defeat at the hands of President Nixon in the general election four weeks away. Anticipating the White House loss, Democrat Party leaders turned their attention to protecting their congressional majorities. Their national campaign committee scheduled all-star fundraising dinners around the country, and the San Francisco installment (at $500 per couple) came to the Fairmont Hotel on October 5.

My 12 year-old brother Pat and I slipped into the Grand Ballroom when a security guard left the entrance unattended temporarily. After entering, we had lengthy and uninterrupted time to visit with both former Vice President Hubert Humphrey (defeated recently by McGovern for the 1972 presidential nomination) and Senator Thomas F. Eagleton, McGovern's original vice presidential running mate dropped from the ticket in late July (I'll have more to say about Senator Eagleton in the next chapter). Only a few months earlier, while active candidates, both had traveled the country with an army of Secret Service agents, reporters, photographers, and cheering fans greeting them at every stop. At this event, the donor-guests paid scant notice to either of them, preferring instead to cultivate and flatter the other political leaders in attendance not branded recently by defeat. It taught me at an early age that political adulation for winners is fleeting; for losers, it's nonexistent.

I had hoped to meet one of those leaders attracting great attention that night: House Majority Leader Hale Boggs (D-LA). First elected to Congress in 1941, he had served on the Warren Commission that investigated and reported the government's official version of President Kennedy's assassination. With House Speaker Carl Albert's pending retirement, Boggs was the heavy favorite to succeed him as the next speaker of the House. Who better than to ask questions about my future congressional aspirations? Throughout the evening, each time I tried to approach him, the crowd surrounding Mr. Leader appeared impenetrable.

At the end of the formal program that evening, and as the room emptied, I saw Boggs talking privately in a corner of the room with local Congressman Phillip Burton (D-CA) and his brother, California State Assemblyman John Burton.[1] Pat and I hung back and waited for their animated conversation to end so that I could meet and talk to the future speaker.

While we lingered, a diminutive woman tapped me on the shoulder and asked if I was waiting to meet Boggs. I told her yes, but I didn't want to interrupt his discussion with the Burtons. Insisting the majority leader wouldn't mind, she took my arm and pulled me toward the object of my interest. I balked and said that I didn't want to intrude—I was content to wait.

"Oh, he won't mind at all," she said with a smile as she continued tugging. "I'm Lindy Boggs—Hale's wife."

Mrs. Boggs (with Pat and me in tow) broke into the political powwow with the Burtons and introduced us to everyone. Then she took my camera and directed our group to pose together for a photograph. Boggs signed an autograph for me after his wife snapped the picture. When she told him of my interest in politics

---

1   A month later, John Burton won election to the House of Representatives, making the Burtons the first brothers to serve simultaneously in the House in almost 200 years.

and government, he urged me to stick with it. "Maybe I'll see you back in Washington someday," he said.

• • •

Eleven days later, Majority Leader Boggs went to Alaska to campaign for Congressman Nick Begich's reelection. In Anchorage, they took off in a small twin-engine Cessna bound for Juneau. The plane disappeared somewhere in the Alaskan wilderness. Despite the lengthiest search in U.S. history, authorities to this day never have located the plane or the victims' bodies.

On January 3, 1973, the House passed a resolution declaring Boggs's seat vacant due to his death. His widow Lindy ran successfully in the special election to fill her late husband's seat. After she took office, I sent her a copy of the photograph she had taken

In the rebellious 1970s, teenage boys like me often wore their hair long. I suspect that the depiction of me in this photograph ended the fad single-handedly. From left: me, Assemblyman (later Congressman) John Burton, House Majority Leader Hale Boggs, Pat Rogan, Congressman Phil Burton, San Francisco, October 5, 1972. Twenty-five years later, when John Burton and I served together in the California State Assembly, he displayed this photo prominently in the legislative chamber to tease me mercilessly. (Photograph by Lindy Boggs, but disseminated heavily by John Burton.) (Author's collection)

that night at the Fairmont (which turned out to be one of the last pictures taken of her husband). In her gracious reply letter, she recalled our conversation regarding my goal of one day serving in Congress. She noted that in ten years I would be 25, which is the constitutional age for congressional eligibility.

"I'll wait for you," she wrote.

A quarter century later, after I won a seat in Congress, I tracked down former Congresswoman Boggs' address (she had retired after serving almost 20 years in the House) and sent her a copy of the photo she had taken and the letter she had written me long ago. On my new congressional letterhead, I penned this message: "I am so disappointed—you didn't wait for me!" Soon thereafter, she visited me in Washington for a lovely reunion lunch. After she became U.S. Ambassador to the Holy See during the Clinton Administration, we had dinner together at the American embassy during my trip to Rome.

Reunited with my photographer from 1972—former Congresswoman Lindy Boggs and me in my congressional office, 1997. (Author's collection)

• • •

A couple of years later, while in the middle of President Clinton's impeachment drama, I appeared on the ABC News Sunday show *This Week*. I broadcast my segment from the Los Angeles affiliate station via satellite. Before airtime, I heard through my earpiece ABC

News analyst and program host Cokie Roberts (in the Washington studio) thanking me for coming on her program.

While we waited to go live, I mentioned my story about her parents, Hale and Lindy Boggs. Suddenly my earpiece went dead. A few minutes later, we went on the air and she interviewed me without missing a beat.

A few weeks later, Cokie and I had lunch. I mentioned to her the curious "dead earpiece" incident from our interview. She said that my audio feed went silent because she had become emotional when I mentioned meeting her father in San Francisco, and she needed to compose herself before airtime. That event where I met her parents was the last time that she ever saw him. She added that she already knew the story of my meeting her parents because her mother had shared it with her previously, but until I had raised it, she hadn't made the connection that I was the congressman of whom her mother spoke.

Here is yet another example that this is, indeed, a small world. Maybe there's something to that "Six Degrees of Separation" theory after all.

• • •

Former Congresswoman Lindy Boggs died at age 97 of natural causes on July 27, 2013.

Reporter Cokie Roberts died at age 75 of cancer on September 17, 2019.

10

The Eagleton Question

Once George McGovern locked up the 1972 Democrat presidential nomination, speculation arose over his choice for vice president. Back when nominees gave potential running mates only a cursory vetting during the convention, McGovern chose a Senate colleague he had only met twice: first-term Senator Thomas F. Eagleton of Missouri. Before tendering the offer, McGovern's campaign manager asked Eagleton if he "had any skeletons in his closet." Eagleton said no, McGovern announced the selection on July 13, and the delegates ratified the choice later that night.

A few days after the convention ended, news reports surfaced that Eagleton had suffered previously from emotional and psychological problems. On July 25, he admitted to previous hospitalizations for nervous exhaustion and depression, and that he had undergone electric shock therapy. The revelations exploded across the headlines, and many Party leaders demanded that Eagleton resign from the ticket or that McGovern drop him. On July 26, McGovern waved off these calls and announced, "I'm behind Tom Eagleton 1,000 percent." With this renewed blessing, Eagleton hit the campaign trail trying to salvage his nomination, his name, and the wounded McGovern-Eagleton ticket.

My brother Pat and I took the bus to San Francisco hoping to see Eagleton during his July 28 campaign visit to the city's new high rise, 1 California Street, where he had scheduled his first press conference to deal with the controversy dogging his candidacy.

When his motorcade arrived, he stepped from the car quickly as he waved to supporters and ignored hecklers. Mayor Joseph Alioto took his arm and rushed him inside. With a huge crowd of reporters, campaign officials, and security guards surging at once into the building, we slipped unnoticed inside with the crowd.

We made it as far as the entrance to the press conference before a Secret Service agent stopped us. He put his hand on my shoulder and said sternly, "Come with me." Luckily, the agent recognized Pat

and me from our previous trips to see political leaders. Instead of ejecting us, he led us to a side door and slipped us inside to witness what Eagleton called the largest press conference of his career.

I squeezed my way to the front of the pack and came within a few feet from where he stood facing hostile questioning centering on his personal life and political survivability. He perspired heavily under the hot lights and intense interrogation, and he mopped his forehead frequently with a handkerchief.

Not stepping down: 1972 Democrat vice presidential nominee Thomas Eagleton insisting at a press conference that he will not resign from the ticket, San Francisco, July 28, 1972. (Photograph by the author)

Through it all, he never lost his composure. He told one reporter that after he made the disclosures, he assumed that the story would run its course in a day or so. "Obviously," he added with a grin as he surveyed the room of aggressive and shouting reporters, "I was wrong."

Through it all, he remained resolute: "I'm on the ticket to stay," he insisted, "and I won't step down. I can hack this job. George McGovern and I will win in November, and I'm going to be a good vice president." He said that he had spoken with McGovern the day before and that his running mate "repeated that he is behind me 100 percent."

"That's down 900 per cent from two days ago," a reporter shouted. Even Eagleton laughed at that observation.

After the press conference, as reporters dashed from the room to the hallway telephones to call in their stories, Eagleton stood alone, at least temporarily, and scanned the room as if seeking a friendly face. Remembering the opening quip from his recent acceptance speech, I introduced myself. "Senator," I told him as I extended my hand, "I want to hand it to you— you sure gave Roger Mudd one heck of a beating." Two weeks earlier, during the vice presidential roll call vote, one delegate cast his ballot for CBS newsman Roger Mudd. Later that night, when Eagleton accepted the nomination, he opened by saying, "Well, I sure gave Roger Mudd one heck of a beating!"

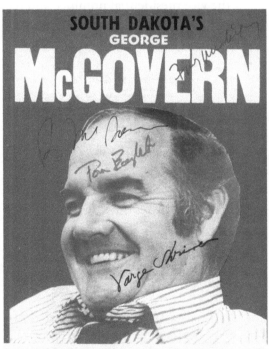

SOUTH DAKOTA'S
GEORGE
McGOVERN

"A Prairie Statesman for President in '72"

Senator Eagleton signed this McGovern campaign poster for me two days before he ended his brief vice presidential candidacy, July 28, 1972. Senator McGovern had signed it previously; Eagleton's replacement on the ticket, Sargent Shriver, added his signature later that year. (Author's collection)

At my Mudd reference, Eagleton threw back his head and laughed. "Well, I sure did!" he said as he pumped my hand. I congratulated him on both his nomination and on how well he handled himself during this brutal grilling. He draped his arm around my shoulder, thanked me for the encouragement, and then he signed for Pat and me a couple of McGovern campaign items already autographed by his running mate.

I liked Tom Eagleton. He was kind, friendly, and down-to-earth. In politics, however, such positive traits often count for little. Two days after I met him in San Francisco, McGovern dumped him as the vice presidential nominee and replaced him with former Ambassador R. Sargent Shriver.

"For my friend Jim: We know all is not well—we know that. But it is not because we have lost our way. All we have lost is the leadership to show us the way." Tom Eagleton's addition to my collection, October 5, 1972.

• • •

I met Eagleton once more. A few months after stepping down from the 1972 ticket, he attended a fundraiser for Democrat congressional candidates at the San Francisco Fairmont Hotel (see my previous chapter, *You Didn't Wait for Me*). Because many of the paying guests at that dinner treated him as yesterday's news and ignored him, he rewarded my interest by inviting Pat and me to join him at his table and visit in an unhurried atmosphere.

He showed no bitterness toward McGovern's decision to drop him a few months earlier. "I think that if I had remained on the ticket that I could have been an asset," he reflected. "At some point the story would have run its course and died out. But McGovern felt it might remain a distraction and keep the discussion on me instead of on issues like the Vietnam War." He said that he intended to campaign hard for the McGovern-Shriver ticket between now and Election Day. He encouraged me to keep up my interest in government and to get a good education as a precursor to politics. Before the formal program began, he wrote out and signed a quotation from his vice presidential acceptance speech for my collection.

• • •

Decades later, when I served in Congress and Eagleton had long since retired, I dropped him a note thanking him for his kindness when I was a young boy fascinated by the political process and tugging at his coattail for an autograph. Against my better judgment, I sent him a copy of the photograph taken of us at the Fairmont Hotel in 1972, which showed me with the very regrettable long hair I sported as a teen in surrender to the fashion of the era. I thought he would find the picture amusing, especially since I had now made a name for myself in conservative Republican circles.

He sent me this charming reply:

Dear Jim:

BURN THAT PICTURE! It will cost you votes!

Let me tell you a VP/San Francisco story. I was staying at the Mark Hopkins Hotel. On my way out of the hotel one morning, a very nice kid came up to me and asked if I would autograph two cards—one for him and one for his brother. I signed the two cards. Later that same day, I went back to the hotel, and the same kid came up to me and asked me to sign two cards for his sisters. I said, "Young man, how many brothers and sisters do you have?"

He paused and then said, "Senator Eagleton, would you be mad at me if I told the truth?"

I said, "I won't be mad; tell me the truth."

He said, "Senator Eagleton, I don't have any brothers or sisters. If I have four of your signatures, I can keep one and trade the three others for a Willie Mays." I signed the cards.

Many politicians, at one time or another, get carried away with their own importance. I think I was one of those. It is very healthy to have someone—like the kid in San Francisco— bring one down to earth.

Senator Thomas F. Eagleton and me, San Francisco, October 5, 1972. (Author's collection)

• • •

After I lost my seat in Congress because of my role in the Clinton impeachment trial, thousands of nasty letters cascaded into my office telling me, in various degrees of incivility, good riddance. A rare complimentary letter found its way to me as I packed my congressional office for the move back home to California:

November 20, 2000

Dear Jim:

I know you were Target # 1. I read somewhere about the millions of dollars being spent on both sides in your district. Although I personally did not favor impeaching Clinton, I thought that you and [Congressman and fellow prosecutor Asa] Hutchinson were the "class acts" on the Republican side. . . .

I left the Senate in '86. It was beginning to get mean. Since then, it has gotten dreadfully mean. I had some great friends on the Republican side, e.g., Mark Hatfield, Mac Mathias, Ted Stevens (his first wife and my wife were best friends), Paul Laxalt, and others. We went to dinner together. We came to each other's house. We kidded about politics. I am told that most of that camaraderie is gone. It's war! It's one side against the other! It's "shoot to kill." SAD! SAD! SAD!

You are a man of character and ability. I wish you the very best in the years ahead. I am most sincere when I say, best wishes,

Tom Eagleton

• • •

In the five decades since Tom Eagleton stood before the cheering delegates for his brief moment in the worldwide spotlight, his name has become synonymous with the notion of full disclosure. In 1985, just before tendering a job offer to me as a deputy district attorney for Los Angeles County, assistant DA Curt Livesay conducted my final hiring interview. Livesay instructed me to reveal any factor about my life that might embarrass the office if he hired me.

"That's the last question I ask in every hiring interview," he said. "I call it *The Eagleton Question*."

• • •

After retiring from the Senate, Thomas Eagleton returned home to Missouri to practice law and teach. He died at age 77 of heart and respiratory complications on March 4, 2007. In a farewell letter he wrote to friends and family, he said his dying wish was for people to "Go forth in love and peace, vote Democrat, and be kind to dogs."

To the end, Tom Eagleton was a class act.

11

Speaking of Dog Lovers . . .

As mentioned earlier, I spent countless hours as a boy looking up the addresses of long-retired national leaders to write for autographs and advice on political life. Many proved receptive to corresponding with a young person born years (and sometimes decades) after their influence and fame had waned. When I learned that one such figure lived nearby, I set out to meet him.

By 1973, few remembered that the obscure publisher of the *Oakland Tribune*, William F. Knowland, had been a political powerhouse in his day. A former state legislator, California Governor Earl Warren had appointed him to the United States Senate in 1945. Twice elected in his own right, at age 44 he became the youngest Senate majority leader in history (his minority leader counterpart was future president Lyndon Johnson). With his eye now on the White House, Knowland decided the governorship was a better launching pad for his ambitions, so he challenged incumbent Governor Goodwin Knight (a fellow Republican) for the 1958 GOP nomination. After winning the internecine battle, Knowland convinced Knight to run for his vacating Senate slot, but the clumsy switch cost both men their seats in a Democrat sweep that November. Knowland never again sought public office. He returned to his family's newspaper and became the *Tribune's* publisher upon his father's death in 1966.

Knowland proved an elusive quarry. I wrote him several letters when I was a boy and asked to meet him, but each went unanswered. Finally, I took a more direct approach. With classmate Roger Mahan along, we took the bus to Oakland and walked to the *Tribune* building. I called his secretary from the lobby, told her of our purpose, and requested an appointment. Without asking her boss, she put us on his calendar for 11:00 that morning.

To kill time, Roger and I rode up the Tribune Tower elevators to view the beautiful panorama across the Bay. When we came back to the lobby, a security guard grabbed us: "What are you kids doing hanging around here?" he demanded. When I told him of our appointment with Senator Knowland, he shook his head in disbelief, pulled us toward a telephone, and called to confirm our story. When he hung up the receiver, he grew very respectful and invited us to make ourselves comfortable in the lobby.

At the designated hour, we presented ourselves at the reception desk, and then we passed through several layers of locked doors before a guard escorted us to a private locked elevator that ran directly to the fourth floor. I couldn't understand all the security precautions involved in meeting a man almost two decades out of the public eye.

The elevator opened in Knowland's outer office. We waited by his secretary's desk for over ten minutes listening to her answer a frequently buzzing telephone and responding, "Yes, senator . . . Yes, senator...." Finally, after answering another loud buzz, she led us toward two large wooden doors, opened them, and invited us to step inside.

My collector's eye swept across the political and historic memorabilia crowding the office walls and shelves of the unsmiling man seated behind a large desk. He rose, offered a perfunctory handshake, and then he motioned for us to have a seat across from him. An uncomfortable silence filled the room as he stared at us and said nothing. I broke the ice and thanked him for letting us come up to meet him and get his autograph. "I'll sign it now," he replied, and then he motioned for me to join him behind his desk to collect the signature. I wanted a tour of his mementos and to ask him about his career, but he clearly had no interest in prolonging the visit. The signing chore done, he stood, thanked us for coming, and led us to the door.

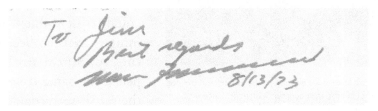

Here's your autograph—what's your hurry? Signed for me by Senator William F. Knowland, Oakland Tribune office, August 13, 1973. (Author's collection)

Desperate to stall for time, I tried asking about his memorabilia displays, but he gave a disinterested answer as he continued shooing us to the door. In a last gasp effort to avoid the boot, I pointed to a large color picture of two Saint Bernard dogs hanging on the wall next to the exit. "Are those your Saint Bernards?" I asked. "I have a Saint Bernard, too."

He removed his hand from the small of my back and stopped steering. Looking at me with great intensity, he asked, "*You* have a Saint Bernard?" I opened my wallet and showed him a photo I carried of Pumpernickel, our family pooch. He took the picture of my dog and studied it, and then his eyes grew moist as he spoke of his love for his two dogs (one had died recently, and the other was now 14).

Knowland's demeanor softened, and his eagerness to eject us evaporated. With an unexpected bond forged, he brought us back into his office and offered us coffee as he asked about our families, our school, and our interest in politics. He told us the story of his own career in publishing, politics, and his service in the Army during World War II. He was still overseas when he learned of his appointment to the

Saint Bernards are known for coming to the rescue, and my dog Pumpernickel did her job after Senator William F. Knowland saw her picture. (Author's collection)

U.S. Senate. "Guess how I found out I had been appointed?" he asked. "I read about it in the newspaper! My wife tried to call and tell me, but she couldn't get through the military censors because the appointment happened the same day that the Japanese surrendered and World War II ended."

He gave us a leisurely tour of his collection of political mementos, and he showed us all of his gavels, plaques, and other souvenirs of his role in history. Among the framed treasures I noticed were signed photographs of him with luminaries such as Senator Robert A. Taft (whom Knowland succeeded as majority leader), President Dwight D. Eisenhower, and a very young Lyndon B. Johnson (depicting both men as the majority and minority leader). He pointed out his certificates of election to the United States Senate and as majority leader (the latter bearing the faded brown signature of Vice President Richard Nixon), his commission from President Eisenhower appointing him a delegate to the United Nations, and an original oil portrait of Lincoln painted by Eisenhower and given him as a gift.

A large color photograph of Knowland swearing in Richard Nixon as vice president hung in the center of the room. "Nixon served two terms as vice president, but I swore him in three times for that job," he said. "Do you know why?" I did, but I decided not to ruin his story. He related that Inauguration Day 1957 fell on a Sunday, so Eisenhower and Nixon followed tradition and had a private oath ceremony at the White House that day for their second term. They held the public ceremony the next afternoon.

Half an hour after we arrived, his secretary tried rescuing her boss from his young fans with a reminder of another meeting. He dismissed her. She returned a few minutes later and insisted that he needed to keep to his schedule. "Okay," he sighed with an air of surrender in his voice.

He wrapped his arms around our shoulders as he led us out to the security elevator across the hall from his office. He shook our hands, thanked us for visiting, and he

After making our dog connection: a smiling Senator William F. Knowland and me, Oakland, August 13, 1973. (Author's collection)

didn't leave until the elevator doors closed on us. Having viewed us as nuisances when we arrived, he seemed sorry to see us go.

• • •

Apparently, Knowland showed us uncharacteristic warmth. In later years his biographers, Gayle B. Montgomery and James W. Johnson, wrote that even as a senator, "Knowland was uncomfortable in close contact with people.... Although he could mesmerize a room full of admirers with his speeches, a one-on-one talk with the senator was painful for both parties. His son, Joe, said once, 'The hardest thing I have to do is carry on a conversation with my father.'"[1]

---

1   Gayle B. Montgomery and James W. Johnson, *One Step from the White House: The Rise and Fall of Senator William F. Knowland* (1998), 80.

When I read that passage, my experience with him made sense. After our meeting, I came away thinking that for all his power and position, he was one of the loneliest men I had ever met.

• • •

Six months after our visit, Knowland spoke at the Oakland Tribune's 100th anniversary party. A reporter covering the event described him as tired, emotional, and having lost weight.

Two days later, on February 23, 1974, he drove alone to his vacation home in Guerneville, California. He went to the rear of his house and descended the steps leading to the edge of the Russian River. After wading waist-deep into the water, he raised a .32-caliber revolver to his right temple and pulled the trigger. Authorities recovered his body later that afternoon.

He left no suicide note, but investigators learned of his crumbling private life. After divorcing his wife of 45 years, he married a woman 25 years his junior (they separated shortly afterward). In debt and

Senator William F. Knowland posed for me in his private office, Oakland Tribune building, August 13, 1973. (Author's collection)

fearing financial ruin, he had also developed a security phobia. With the recent kidnappings of Patricia Hearst (granddaughter of publishing magnate William Randolph Hearst) and *Atlanta Constitution* editor Reginald Murphy, he feared he was next on the abduction list, which explained the protective security layers we navigated to reach his private office. With multiple stresses pressing in on him, he found his escape on the bank of the Russian River.

When I heard the jarring news of his suicide, I felt tremendous sadness for him and for his family. I also remember wishing that people who loved dogs—as he did—had spent more time with him.

12

Thanks for the Memory

When I served in Congress, Bob Hope told people I represented him even though his North Hollywood home fell just outside my district. No matter. He told me that he wanted to claim a Republican as his congressman, so I assumed the honor gladly.

During my youth, there were few people on the planet more universally recognizable than Hope. In a show business career spanning over 80 years, he achieved fame on Broadway, in vaudeville, on radio and television, and in motion pictures. Those feats, along with his entertaining our troops during four wars on overseas USO tours, endeared him to almost a century of fans.

Like most people of my generation, I grew up loving Bob Hope, so as a teen I looked forward to meeting him when he came to San Francisco in early 1975 to promote his new book, *The Last Christmas Show*, which chronicled his decades of performing overseas for the military. The San Francisco Emporium, a famous Market Street department store that operated for 99 years, proclaimed "Bob Hope Day" and featured a free showing of his films before he appeared in person to autograph copies of his book.

My brother Pat and I arrived at the Emporium two hours before his scheduled appearance and found an unhappy sight. A thousand people formed a line starting at the sixth floor auditorium; it wrapped up the stairs to the roof and encircled it. We took our place at the end.

After a three-hour wait, we made it inside the auditorium where the one line branched off into two: the "buyer" line (for book purchasers), and the "looker" line (nonbuyers wanting a glimpse of the star). Since I had purchased his book, a clerk directed me to the preferred line.

Hope sat at a table greeting his fans. Parents brought young children to meet him, while World War II, Korea, and Vietnam vets carried faded snapshots of him entertaining them during their service years or decades earlier. He studied each photograph shown him and he shared recollections of those shows with the aging warriors.

When my turn came, a store clerk opened my book to the title page and handed it to Hope, who inscribed and signed it for me. As he did with everyone in front of me, he thanked me for coming and shook my hand. He not only signed 1,000 books that day, but when he finished, he remained for another hour signing autographs for anyone who couldn't (or didn't) buy a book.

No wonder fans loved Bob Hope for so long: he loved them right back and in spades.

Bob Hope signing photographs for fans who couldn't afford to buy his book, San Francisco, February 21, 1975. (Photograph by the author)

• • •

I saw Hope a few months later in a venue where he shined: the concert hall, when he appeared live at the Concord Pavilion (now the Sleep Train Pavilion), a beautiful outdoor theater in Concord, California. The septuagenarian packed the 12,000-seat arena for the evening performance.

After the orchestra played a medley of tunes from his movies, he walked onstage to a standing ovation. Wasting no time, he launched into an hour-long rapid-fire series of songs and gags. He joked far faster than I could take notes, but I managed to memorialize a few. The first zingers came at the expense of his longtime costar in the classic *Road* movie series, singer Bing Crosby:

During World War II, Bing and I had to room together while we were entertaining the troops overseas. The man snores terribly! I finally found a way to cure him of it. One night while he was snoring, I walked over to his bed, bent down, and kissed him on the lips. Not only did that cure his snoring, but he stayed awake all night watching me sleep!

Once Bing and I were out in the jungle taking a jeep ride. We parked and took a walk. A coiled snake sprang and bit him in the crotch. I told Bing to lie down and rest while I rushed back to get medical advice about how to save him from the poisonous bite. When I found the medic, he told me to suck the venom out of the wound. I returned to where Bing was resting. He asked what the doctor said. I told him, "He says you're gonna die."

After working over Crosby, he moved on to other topics:

A young fellow walked down the streets of Belfast late at night. A hand in the shadows reached out, grabbed him, and put a knife to his throat. A sinister voice asked, "Are you a Protestant or a Catholic?" The terrified young man didn't know what to say, thinking he'd be killed if he gave the wrong answer. Finally, the young man decided to play it safe. "I'm a Jew," he responded. The voice said, "I must be the luckiest damn Arab in Ireland tonight!"

I took a plane flight to Oakland from LAX to come up here for the show. A little guy was sitting next to a big monster that was sound asleep. After we were airborne the little guy, who was terrified of flying, heaved up his Waldorf salad all over the sleeping man. When we were landing, the big guy woke up and found the mess all over him. The little guy leaned over and asked, "Are you feeling better now?"

A man was doing poorly at golf one day. Suddenly a genie appeared. The man told the genie he would do anything to hit a hole in one. The genie said the man must give up five years of his sex life. The man thought it over, agreed, and then made a hole in one. The genie said he could make a birdie if he gave up ten years of sex. The man again agreed and made a birdie. The genie asked the man's name. The man replied, "Father O'Toole."

A hunter sent his dog to retrieve a quail. The dog walked on top of the water to fetch it. The hunter's friend said, "There's something wrong with your dog." "I know," the hunter replied. "He can't swim."

A gorilla at the zoo grabbed a woman. He began to hug and caress her. "What should I do?" the woman cried. Her husband said, "Do what you always do—tell him you have a headache."

A woman told the psychiatrist that her husband keeps climbing into the bathtub and goes fishing in the toilet. The shrink asked her, "Are you sure you aren't the one who needs to see a psychiatrist?" "I don't have time," the woman said. "I'm too busy cleaning fish."

A man called his seven children together and asked which one of them pushed the outhouse in the lake. When none of the children confessed, the father said, "George Washington never told a lie when his father asked him who chopped down the cherry tree, and he grew up to be president." Finally, one of the kids confessed. The father slapped the hell out of him. The bewildered kid said, "I thought you said George Washington didn't lie, and he became president." "That's right," the father said, "but Washington's old man wasn't sitting in the tree when he chopped it down!"

During the show, a drunken woman in the third row heckled Hope repeatedly for his prior support of President Nixon and the Vietnam War. Theater ushers tried to silence her unsuccessfully. He ignored the disturbance and continued his routines. When she resumed her jeers, security guards arrived and scooped her from her seat. As they dragged her away, she threw a coin onto the stage and yelled, "Here's a nickel, Hope. That's all your show is worth."

Hope stopped his monologue. In silence he bent down, picked up the nickel, looked at it, and then slid it into his pants pocket. The crowd howled.

Bob Hope in concert, the Concord Pavilion, September 6, 1975. (Photograph by the author)

By the time the orchestra played Hope's exit theme song, *Thanks for the Memory*, the audience suffered from laughter exhaustion. He bowed and walked off-stage to lengthy applause. The crowd pleaded for an encore, and he reappeared to another standing ovation. After firing off a dozen more jokes, he sang his signature song, blew a final kiss, and said good night.

For those of us present for this live concert, Bob Hope was half-right: he should have said, "Great night."

• • •

During my last few weeks as a student at UCLA Law School, Hope came to my campus to tape his Thanksgiving television special for NBC, "Bob Hope Goes to College," with comedy skits filmed at various universities across the country. The network scheduled the UCLA segment for outdoor filming on the Janss Steps, but on the day of the show a steady rain fell. One hour before show time, the director ordered the production moved to the Women's Gym steps (which offered the entertainers some covering from the elements). Unfortunately, the venue provided no similar protection for the audience during a sustained downpour. Although I arrived for the taping only 20 minutes before its scheduled start time, I found a front row seat. The heavy rainfall discouraged the otherwise expected large crowd from coming.

As the engineers concluded their sound and equipment check, a man behind me patted my shoulder and said in an easily identifiable voice, "You kids sure are brave to be here in this rain. Thanks a lot for coming out." I turned and saw Hope, dressed casually in a necktie, sports jacket with patches on the elbows, and a badge on his lapel with the letters USC and a red slash through them.

He walked onto the makeshift stage as the couple hundred assembled students cheered for him. "You know, you kids are just marvelous," he said as he looked out at everyone huddled under ponchos and umbrellas. "I didn't think anyone would show up today because of the rain, but this is going to be great."

His show lasted two hours. He read his monologue and gags off huge cue cards held aloft behind me. When he flubbed a line, he simply reshot the scene with this request: "When you hear the punch line again, do me a favor—laugh as if it was the first time."

During a break in the taping, he complained about roof water dripping on his head. A student in the audience ran onstage and offered his blue UCLA baseball cap. Hope liked the gesture so much that he returned the cap to the student and asked him to repeat the gesture for the cameras. He donned the hat and wore it for the rest of the show.

Bob Hope's cue-card man enjoying his job during the comedian's monologue, UCLA taping, November 11, 1983. (Photograph by the author)

I contributed a spontaneous moment to the performance. As he set up a joke about the networks cancelling television programs, he asked, "How do you know anymore when your show's been canceled?" Before he could deliver the punch line, the rain caused an electrical short and the lights and power went out momentarily.

"That's how you can tell, Bob!" I yelled from my seat. Hope and the audience laughed.

After shooting wrapped up, he again thanked the students for turning out in the rain and asked if he could do something for us. I ask him to sing his theme song, *Thanks for the Memory.*

"I'll do the best I can," he said, "but in the last 50 years I've sung

Bob Hope taping his TV show at UCLA, November 11, 1983. (Photograph by the author)

so many parodied versions of that song that I've forgotten the real lyrics!" He then warbled several verses of the tune before receiving a standing ovation.

With the taping over, the UCLA homecoming king and queen presented him with gifts, including a certificate from the chancellor naming him an Honorary Freshman. At the bottom of the document was this added sentiment: "We hope you never graduate."

• • •

A few years later, when I was a young lawyer, I came to know Hope's longtime publicist, Ward Grant. I once mentioned to Ward that I had seen Hope in person a couple of times over the years, but lamented that I never had the chance to chat with him. Ward gave me Hope's private mailing address and told me to write him a note and reference our discussion. He said that the comedian would be pleased to set up a meeting. I sent the note, and a couple of weeks later I received this reply:

October 6, 1986

Dear Jim:

I would be happy to see you. The only problem is when. If you're ever around my way, drop by and see if I'm home. Either that, or come to NBC Studios on December 6 or 7 when I'm taping. You can tell the usher you have an appointment with me (either that or yell out at me from the audience). And if you get arrested I'll try and fix it. Anyway, there must be a way. Maybe I'll come by your house.

Regards,

Bob Hope

Despite his kind invitation (and notwithstanding the brashness I showed as a kid), I didn't want to barge over to Bob Hope's house and bang on the gate, so I opted for the second suggestion. His secretary sent along four tickets for his 1986 annual Christmas show taping at NBC Studios in Burbank.

Along with my former college roommate Bob Wyatt and our dates, I arrived at NBC for the 6:00 p.m. taping and took our places in the long line for his show wrapping around the complex. About an hour before the doors opened, I saw Hope exit a studio back door. He was dressed casually in slacks and a silver auto racing-style jacket bearing American flag patches on the sleeves. Only a few people in line recognized the comedian as he and a couple of friends climbed into a car and pulled out of the driveway.

"We're going for some quick dinner," he called out to a surprised fan. "We'll be back!"

At 6:00 p.m. the audience began filing inside the studio. Since we had special tickets, an usher brought our group to the front of the line. My letter from Hope also granted me special dispensation to bring a camera inside the building, which is otherwise forbidden during a taping. We took seats on the steep audience bleachers inside the soundstage.

At 7:30 p.m., Hope walked out and received a standing ovation. Dressed in a black tuxedo, he bantered with the audience and crew while the technicians set up the first shot. When the show started, he again read his monologue from large cue cards held underneath the main camera. The audience laughed appreciatively, even when his jokes were old, corny, and predictable. After all, the legendary Bob Hope was telling it, which made them funnier.

When he left the stage for a costume change, the director played on a large monitor the segment they shot a day earlier to gauge audience reaction. Hope reappeared a few minutes later wearing Australian bush clothes and carrying a large rubber alligator. He then filmed a comedy segment spun off from the recent hit film *Crocodile Dundee*. It was almost 10 p.m. when the skit ended. The producer called an end to shooting for the night and invited the audience back for the final taping the next morning. Hope thanked everyone for coming, said goodnight, took a final bow, and left to another standing ovation.

An NBC page asked our group to remain in the bleachers until the rest of the audience had departed. He then escorted us across the soundstage to Hope's private dressing room. Still in his *Crocodile Dundee* costume and heavy television makeup, he waved us inside with a hearty welcome. After he saw our two dates huddled outside the door (too shy to enter), he went out and got them: "Hiya, dolls. Come on in and join us."

Throughout our visit, he teased and joked with everyone. He grew serious only when he asked detailed questions about the various skits and gags he had just performed during the taping. "Since you're keeping an old man up past his bedtime, the least you can do is give me your critique, from an audience's perspective, which jokes worked and which were flops." It was a wasted question to four Bob Hope fans. We loved all of them.

He asked us to come back tomorrow to see the rest of the taping. Sorry, I told him, I had a court appearance in the morning and couldn't make it. "Can't make it, eh? Then give me back the picture we took!" With that he snarled and lunged for my camera jokingly.

On the way home that evening, my date told me how impressed she was over my ability to get us into Hope's dressing room for a private meeting. "Oh, that was nothing," I said as I feigned indifference. "He asked to come over to my house but I turned him down. If he wants to see me, he has to entertain!"

"To Jimmy Rogan—Glad I'm Dressed Formal." Comedian Bob Hope (still in his Crocodile Dundee costume) and me, NBC Studios, Burbank, December 7, 1986. (Author's collection)

• • •

In 1993, America prepared to celebrate Hope's 90th birthday on May 29. Pre-birthday celebrations began early. Burbank renamed the main street near NBC Studio "Bob Hope Drive," and the network planned a two-hour birthday special produced by his daughter Linda.

Ward Grant offered several times over the years to set up a photo op with Hope for my family, but we never seemed to make the time to do it. With age 90 rolling up, I thought I had better take him up on it. At Ward's request, Hope's secretary called and invited my family over to his house three days before his birthday milestone.

We drove to his longtime home at 10346 Moorpark in Toluca Lake (the Hopes moved there in 1939 and remained for 63 years). The house rested on a quiet, tree-lined street with tall hedges hiding most of the property from public view. A secretary greeted us outside the black iron gates emblazoned with a large *H*. We pulled into the driveway and parked alongside the large two-story white brick building circled by manicured gardens. Next to the main house were small white cabanas, a pool in the rear, a driving range, and a massive yard where workers set up tents for the upcoming television show taping.

All of Hope's secretaries and staff came out to greet us and look at our infant twin daughters, dressed in red, white, and blue sailor dresses and white bonnets. Claire was alert, smiling and laughing at the attention. Dana (just awakened from her afternoon nap) was more circumspect and studied everyone.

An assistant said her boss was concluding an interview and would join us in a few minutes. While waiting in the bungalow, I admired the photographs adorning the walls depicting him with notables such as Cary Grant, Jackie Gleason, President Eisenhower, and General George Patton. There was a golfing print signed by the artist and President Gerald Ford, a pencil sketch of Hope with Bing Crosby, a plaque inducting him into the Golf Hall of Fame, and several sketches and paintings portraying him during various phases of his career.

Hope left the main house and walked over to the bungalow where we waited. The old spring in the comedian's step had turned into a hunched, slow shuffle as he negotiated the couple of stairs leading into the building. He had aged significantly since I last saw him a few years earlier, and the fund of energy that sustained him for almost a century appeared to be depleting. Still, he didn't let the infirmities of age dampen his spirit: he entered singing an old Bob Wills song, *San Antonio Rose*.

When he saw me holding Dana, he let out a high-pitched cackle: "Well, hello, baby! Hello, baby!" he said as he waved playfully at her. "My God, you're beautiful. What's your name?" When he saw Christine holding Claire, he laughed even louder: "Oh, God, look at them! Twins! They're beautiful!" Turning to his secretary, he told her, "Go get Dolores [Mrs. Hope] and tell her to get over here! She needs to see these twin girls!"

A few minutes later, Dolores Hope (his wife of 59 years) joined us. She fawned over the twins, and she and Hope took turns holding their hands, kissing their cheeks, and talking to them. Claire took it all with a good nature, laughing and smiling at the attention. Dana studied Hope as he wiggled his finger before her. "Be careful, Bob," I warned. "She's cutting teeth and may think that finger is lunch." Sure enough, she leaned forward and took a nip on it. Hope howled playfully and pretended she had bit it off at the knuckle.

Dolores asked if Christine had a rough delivery when the girls were born. "Actually," Christine smiled, "it was a perfect delivery!" She shared the story of our adopting the girls. Hope listened intently, and then he told us the story of how he and Dolores also adopted their children.

He talked about his ninetieth birthday, now only three days away. "Ninety years old—can you believe it!" he exclaimed, and then he looked at Dana in my arms. "I remember as if it were yesterday picking up my daughter Linda from her bassinet in that Chicago hospital after we adopted her and holding her in my arms like you're holding Dana," he said with a smile. "Now she's my producer. I'm very proud of her."

He drafted a maintenance worker into photographer service. As we lined up inside the bungalow, Dolores tried begging out of the picture ("Oh, look at me, I'm a mess") but we insisted she stay. Just as the worker prepared to take the picture, I asked him to hold up for a moment—Dana had just spit up on my tie. After a quick wipe-up, we posed again.

Dana Rogan, tickling her favorite comedian's chin (from left): Dolores Hope, Christine and Claire Rogan, Bob Hope, Dana Rogan, and me, Toluca Lake, May 26, 1993. In the photograph you can see Christine's arm draped behind her back. Look carefully and you will see she is hiding the diaper she used to mop Dana's face and my necktie after Dana threw up on it. (Author's collection)

Chris remained behind with the girls talking to Dolores while I escorted Bob back to the house. I held his arm to steady him as he climbed down the steps. Just before we said goodbye and he went inside, he looked up at the sky. "You know, the weather's too nice to stay inside. I still need to get in some golf before the day gets away from me."

Bob Hope was hunched, a bit unsteady and 90, but he still played with a 12 handicap.

• • •

On July 27, 2003, in the same Toluca Lake house where we had visited, Bob Hope died at age 100. A comedian to the end, when Dolores asked him on his deathbed where he wanted to be buried, he replied, "Surprise me."

Dolores Hope died at age 102 of natural causes on September 19, 2011. Like her husband, she passed away in their Toluca Lake home.

13

President of What?

When an unknown, one-term governor of Georgia told his mother in December 1974 he had decided to run for president, she asked, "President of what?" Jimmy Carter labored in obscurity through most of his 20-month lead-up campaign to the 1976 Democrat National Convention. Once he started winning the early primaries, however, he became a rapid favorite for the nomination.

Carter brought his campaign to San Francisco in May 1976 a few weeks before reaching the delegate count needed to secure the nomination. Since I had read much about Carter by then but had never met him, I went to the event and (eschewing my childhood habits) actually bought a $25 ticket. Back then, that was a lot of money for an 18 year-old: I had to spin pizzas at a 525-degree oven at my fast-food job for about ten hours to earn it.

When Carter arrived at the Hilton for his reception, I took pictures as he greeted supporters (many of whom wore "Damn Yankees for Carter" campaign buttons). He didn't look very presidential to me: he was short and had wide lips encasing long teeth, but he worked the room effortlessly as he treated everyone there to a handshake and famous wide smile.

My chance to meet him came during the dinner service. While everyone else ate, he skipped the food and walked around the room shaking hands. During one lull, he stood alone against the rear wall with nobody near him except a lone Secret Service agent. I went over and introduced myself. He treated me to the same friendly grin everyone else received. When I told him about my political memorabilia collection and asked if he would sign one of his campaign brochures for me, the big smile disappeared quickly. "No, I'm not signing any autographs," he snapped. "If I sign one for you, then everybody will want one."

His refusal didn't upset me. I understood that sometimes such requests are neither convenient nor welcome. What caught me off guard was his quick personality change at my polite request—he went from smiley to surly.

I told him that I understood. As I thanked him and said goodbye, I chuckled slightly to myself. That chuckle appeared to annoy him. He asked what I found so amusing about his refusal. I explained that as a boy I had snuck into countless events to meet political leaders to get autographs for my collection. Now, at the first one where I actually saved my money and bought a ticket, the candidate had turned me down.

"Bring it over to my table later and I'll sign it," he said coolly, and then he turned and walked away.

A short time afterward, when Carter had returned to his table and was unoccupied by admirers, I took up his invitation and walked over with my brochure. When he saw me approaching, he made a hand signal to the agent who earlier had stood with us when he had told me to bring it to his table. The agent stopped me and said that Carter wouldn't be signing anything. I reminded him of Carter's earlier promise. "No, he didn't tell you that," the agent replied. "He told you to mail it to his home in Plains, Georgia." Carter sat a few feet away and watched this exchange with an approving eye as the agent told me to beat it.

Weird.

After Carter's speech that evening, and just before he exited the ballroom, he climbed on a chair and raised his arms in the air as if to embrace the cheering crowd. "Good night, everybody!" he shouted. "I love you all!"

Sorry, but I felt the only thing Jimmy Carter loved about me that night was the 25 bucks he had grinned out of my wallet.

"I love you all!" Former Georgia Governor Jimmy Carter, San Francisco Hilton, May 26, 1976. (Photograph by the author)

• • •

I saw Jimmy Carter a few more times during his 1976 presidential campaign. One appearance he made late in the race leaves me with an unsettled memory, but the reason has nothing to do with him.

Three weeks before the election, on October 6, 1976, Carter debated his general election opponent, President Gerald Ford, in San Francisco. Carter's campaign scheduled a post-debate rally with Carter and local Democrat candidates at the Civic Auditorium, which was only a few minutes away from the debate location.

Carter partisans at the rally site watched the debate on Jumbotron screens. Shortly after it ended, the auditorium's rear doors opened and the band played *Happy Days Are Here Again*. Accompanied by a large entourage that included his wife Rosalynn, California Governor Jerry

Brown, and Democrat National Committee chairman Robert Strauss, Carter walked down the center aisle shaking hands. A standing ovation greeted him when he reached the stage.

"Anybody here want to debate me?" Carter joked before delivering a brief campaign speech pledging to lead the Democrats to victory in November. After introducing his wife, he thanked everyone for attending and waved goodbye. Security whisked the Carters from the auditorium to the Fairmont Hotel for a fundraising dinner.

"What's so bizarre about that routine campaign event?" you may wonder.

One of the main organizers of this rally was Jim Jones, the founder of the San Francisco "Peoples Temple" church. The following year, Jones moved 1,200 members of his cult from the city to the tiny nation of Guyana to establish an agricultural colony. Later reports surfaced that Jones used beatings and extortion against members to enslave them. In November 1978, Congressman Leo Ryan led a congressional delegation to Guyana to investigate. During

"Anybody want to debate?" I took this photo of Governor and Mrs. Jimmy Carter acknowledging the applause during his post-debate campaign rally in San Francisco. At far right Mayor George Moscone (in a light-colored suit) is depicted smiling and clapping, while Congressman Leo Ryan whispers to him. Two years later, both men were murdered within a week of each other. (Author's collection)

the visit, Jones ordered the murder of Ryan and his party. While the executions took place at the nearby airstrip, Jones instructed his entire flock to commit suicide. His thugs murdered those who refused to drink the poisoned Kool-Aid potion concocted for his doomed parishoners. Almost 1,000 people died in Guyana that afternoon, with very few Temple members surviving the horror.

I remember seeing many of Jones' glassy-eyed followers at the Carter rally as they cheered wildly on cues from Jones, who stood on the stage with the other dignitaries. Later, when I studied the fuzzy photographs I took from my seat in the bleachers, I saw Congressman Ryan depicted with Carter. Ironically, Ryan stood next to San Francisco Mayor George Moscone. Only a week after Ryan's assassination, San Francisco Supervisor Dan White murdered both Moscone and fellow Supervisor Harvey Milk in their city hall offices.

• • •

Over the next 40 years, I met Carter many times and under various circumstances. Candidly, I found him to be prickly most of the time (I will share a few of those encounters later in the book). I never really liked him until decades later, when organizers of his 90th birthday party dinner invited me to Plains as the guest "roast" speaker at a dinner tribute for him. We had a fun, sweet, bantering encounter that weekend, and as far as I am concerned, it canceled out his San Francisco snit from 1976 when I shelled out 25 bucks to meet him.

Alas, that 90th birthday party story awaits a future sequel to this book. For now, we move on from politicians to paladins.

14

A Night of Heroes

Every two years, the living recipients of the Congressional Medal of Honor reunite for a weekend of reminiscences, drinks, laughs, and tears shed for fallen comrades. The 1977 biennial celebration, held in San Jose, was a two-day jubilee featuring receptions and a parade before the banquet finale. The 167 decorated veterans who journeyed west for the event covered every twentieth century military conflict to date: Vietnam, Korea, World Wars I and II, and even the 1900 Chinese Boxer Rebellion. Their theaters of battle differed, but they shared in common a blue ribbon around their necks acknowledging America's tribute to their valor.

My college radio station press credentials helped me obtain two tickets to the Congressional Medal of Honor Society reception and dinner at the Civic Auditorium, so I brought along my longtime friend Bob Wyatt. We arrived that evening and picked up our passes in the media center.

At the private cocktail reception for the banquet speakers and honorees, I spotted legendary movie star James Stewart chatting with guests and signing autographs. His accomplishments went beyond the silver screen. At the outbreak of World War II, he enlisted as a private in the Army Air Corps, flew 20 bombing missions over Germany, earned the Distinguished Flying Cross, and retired from the reserves as a general.

Bob and I met Stewart, whom I found both cordial and humble.

He said that he felt very honored to receive the Society's "Patriot Award" tonight. As he shared some memories of his Hollywood career, I told him how much I enjoyed his classic films *The Philadelphia Story*, *Harvey*, and *It's a Wonderful Life*. "Boy, we sure made good pictures in those days," he replied, and then he shook his head in dismay. "But they sure don't make them like we did anymore." After mentioning that I saw another of my favorite films recently, *Mr. Smith Goes to Washington*, I asked if they filmed the congressional scenes inside the U.S. Senate chamber. "No," he explained, "they wouldn't let us shoot in there. Frank Capra [the director] did everything he could to talk them into it, but the answer was no. So the studio spent over $1,000,000 to build an exact re-creation of the Senate." He chuckled as he said, "After they spent that million, do you know what they did with that set when we finished the picture? They chopped the whole thing into firewood!"

Actor James Stewart and me, San Jose, November 12, 1977. (Author's collection)

During the reception, Bob and I noticed an elderly woman standing alone and shifting in and out of her shoes as if her feet hurt. He brought her a chair. She thanked him for the courtesy and introduced herself as Josephine ("Call me Joe."). While we chatted, she said she was so glad to meet two young men with manners and that she wanted us to meet her husband. "He's around here someplace," she said as she scanned the room. Spotting a short, bald, elderly man across the room, she called to him, "Oh, Jimmy! Jimmy—come join us!"

Like many of the tuxedoed men at the banquet, "Jimmy" wore the Medal of Honor hanging from a blue ribbon around his neck. Joe made the introductions, and Bob and I were stunned when we realized "Jimmy" was General James H. Doolittle, one of America's great military heroes from World War II.

Doolittle had gained fame originally in the 1920s as a test and stunt pilot, winning many national races and flying cross-country when aviation was still in its infancy. He had pioneered the concept of "flying blind," where the pilot relies on instruments only for takeoffs and landings. But it was after the outbreak of World War II that he had earned his lasting fame. Commanding a squadron of planes taking off from the USS Hornet, he led the daring bombing raid over Tokyo and other Japanese cities. Every plane in the mission was shot down or forced to crash-land, with Japanese soldiers capturing and executing some of his crew. For his gallantry, President Roosevelt awarded him the Medal of Honor.

Doolittle showed great interest in my current studies at the University of California in Berkeley because it was his alma mater. He said that he had enrolled there in 1916 to study mining engineering, but he had dropped out the following year to enlist in the military. After World War I, he returned to obtain his degree in 1922. Mrs. Doolittle, also an alumna, shook my hand and said, "We *Cal* folks need to stick together!"

He showed us his medal, which bore on the reverse an engraved

General James Doolittle wearing the Congressional Medal of Honor, November 12, 1977. (Photograph by the author)

General and Mrs. James Doolittle and me, San Jose, November 12, 1977. (Author's collection)

account of his exploits for which he received the commendation. She reached into her purse, retrieved her wallet, and produced a faded snapshot of Franklin Roosevelt presenting him the award. "I remember that night so well," she said. "I got a call late at night from [General Henry] 'Hap' Arnold, who said to come to the White House right away. He didn't give me any other information, and I had no idea what the visit was all about. When I got there, I saw Jimmy for the first time in many months. He looked thin, pale, and near-dead. We went into the Oval Office and met the president, who gave Jimmy the medal. Nobody told me anything ahead of time!"

• • •

When the Society presented Stewart its award, he choked up as he called the honor "the proudest moment of my life." Noticing tears in his wife Gloria's eyes as well, he pointed to her and said, "My wife seems to be crying!"

"Oh, shut up!" she called out from the audience amid laughter.

• • •

Midway through the program, Mrs. Doolittle spied Bob and me at the rear of the ballroom. She insisted we join her table. As she escorted us forward, she told us about her husband's current activities: "These days he serves on the board of directors for Mutual of Omaha," she said. "It's the only real business venture he's ever been involved in." She said at 81 he still keeps active: "We're flying home tomorrow, and then he leaves on a pheasant hunting trip."

Throughout the evening, whenever I asked the medal winners that I met what they did to earn their decoration, most replied with humility. Typical responses included, "I was in the wrong place at the wrong time," or, "I acted before I thought about it." That initial storytelling relaxed as the evening progressed and the liquor flowed. General Doolittle was no exception. When we joined him at his table, he was discussing the Tokyo raid with another medal winner. After Bob and I showed obvious interest in his firsthand account, he pushed all the plates and flatware aside, took out his pen, and sketched out for us on the tablecloth the details of his famous mission. (I returned later to salvage the tablecloth for posterity, but a waiter had already consigned the relic to the laundry chute.)

During this incredible first-hand history lesson, he interrupted his narrative and introduced us to the man with whom he was so engrossed in conversation when we joined them: retired Marine Colonel Gregory "Pappy" Boyington. As legendary as his tablecloth-defacing companion, Boyington led World War II's famous "Black Sheep" squadron. He shot down 28 Japanese planes, and he won both the Navy Cross and the Medal of Honor. His exploits later became the basis for a 1970s network television show, *Baa Baa Black Sheep*.

Not exactly a lounge singer: Here I am with the incomparable Pappy Boyington, November 12, 1977. (Author's collection)

Boyington didn't look like the rest of the decorated warriors. He eschewed a formal black tuxedo and showed up in a blue suede blazer and pale blue ruffled shirt. His wardrobe, coupled with his bangs combed down on his forehead, made him look more like a Vegas lounge singer than a roughneck Marine combat hero.

Boyington introduced us to his other tablemates, Thomas A. Pope and Phillip C. Katz. When I asked Pope how he had earned his medal, he replied modestly, "I got it in 1918 while fighting in France," and he left it at that. I learned later that he had charged a German machine gun nest to keep enemy soldiers from firing on his platoon. After hand-to-hand combat with the enemy, he and his platoon captured more than 100 prisoners. He became one of World War I's 95 Medal of Honor winners.

Another World War I recipient was Phil Katz, then age 90. When I asked him the same question, he grinned and said, "Oh, it was just something I did." Doolittle filled in the rest of the story for me: Katz had climbed out of a trench near Eclise Fountaine, France and ran through German machine-gun fire to rescue a wounded friend, Phil Page. When Page begged Katz to leave him there and save himself, Katz replied, "Go to hell." Dragging Page to safety through more machine-gun fire, he earned both a medal and a life-long friend. Years later, Page managed Katz's successful campaign for the San Francisco Board of Supervisors.

• • •

In 1990, journalist Joseph L. Galloway wrote that the Congressional Medal of Honor itself is a modest bronze star suspended from a pale blue ribbon, but since its inception during the American Civil War it has come to represent the highest honor a grateful nation could bestow on its warriors. He noted that most who serve in the military do so to retirement without ever meeting even one of the men entitled to wear it. "When they do, they rise automatically to show respect for the man, the medal, the deed."[1]

As Galloway noted, most people never meet a Congressional Medal of Honor recipient. When I was a young college student, I spent a privileged evening with more than 100 of them. I came away from the experience with the understanding that the medal, by itself, means little. But when worn around the neck of its recipient, it means liberty, sacrifice, freedom.

It means everything.

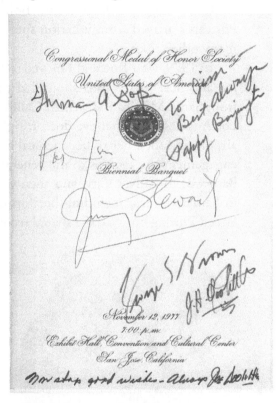

My program from the Congressional Medal of Honor Society banquet, November 12, 1977, autographed for me that night by General and Mrs. James Doolittle, James Stewart, Colonel Gregory "Pappy" Boyington, General George S. Brown (Chairman of the Joint Chiefs of Staff), and Thomas A. Pope. (Author's collection)

1   Joseph L. Galloway, *Medal of Honor: Profiles in Courage*, U.S. News & World Report, September 10, 1990.

• • •

The Doolittles and I corresponded frequently over the next few years. Age didn't slow down either of them. The letters Joe and the general sent me came postmarked from adventures such as elk hunting in Idaho, fishing in Washington, antelope hunting in Wyoming, cattle ranching in Oregon, and Bohemian Grove encampments. Postcards arrived from vacation spots in London, Honolulu, and many other cities.

In 1979, after Bob and I moved to Los Angeles to attend UCLA, Joe and her "master" (as she called the general playfully) moved from Santa Monica to Carmel, California. When she flew back to Los Angeles to see her eye doctor, Bob and I picked her up at the airport and took her to her medical appointments. After one such engagement she took us to the general's favorite restaurant, Stern's Barbecue in Culver City, and then we toured her favorite haunts in Santa Monica, including her former home at 233 Marguerita Street. During our visit she shared recollections of their old military friends: General "Georgie" Patton ("A great historian and egotist who only wanted to lead a battle."); General "Doug" MacArthur ("Jimmy says he was as good a general as he thought about himself, but my, how he desperately wanted to be president."); "Ike and Mamie" Eisenhower ("During the war, Mamie liked to play mahjong with me, but she grew disappointed when I tired of the game

General Doolittle's bomber jacket sleeve patch from his Eighth Army Air Force Command, 1943. Given to me by General and Mrs. Doolittle. (Author's collection)

and stopped playing with her."); and General Mark Clark ("He calls Jimmy 'Junior' since Jimmy's three months younger.").

Once I wrote to her and asked if the general had any of his World War II military patches left. She wrote back an apologetic note stating that all such memorabilia had been donated years ago to the Smithsonian. However, a few weeks later, I received another note from her. She said that while cleaning out an attic trunk she found his old Eighth Army Air Force Command flight jacket (from 1943). She removed its embroidered sleeve patch and sent it to me, writing that the general wanted me to have it.

More than forty years after receiving it, the patch remains a prized treasure in my memorabilia collection.

• • •

Academy Award–winning actor James Stewart died of a heart attack at age 89 on July 2, 1997. His wife, Gloria, had died of cancer three years earlier on February 17, 1994.

General James Doolittle died peacefully at his home in Carmel at age 96 on September 27, 1993. His wife Joe had died five years earlier, on Christmas Eve 1988—their 71st wedding anniversary.

Colonel Gregory "Pappy" Boyington died of cancer at age 75 on January 11, 1988.

Thomas A. Pope became the last surviving World War I Congressional Medal of Honor recipient. He died at age 94 on June 14, 1989.

Phil Katz was America's oldest surviving Medal of Honor winner when he died one month before his 100th birthday on October 29, 1987. A few years earlier, the California State Legislature awarded Katz and the state's 35 other Medal of Honor recipients a special "Congressional Medal of Honor" license plate. As the oldest of the medal winners, they issued to Katz plate number one.

15

Memphis

Midway through Jimmy Carter's presidency, the Democrat National Committee (DNC) convened a three-day national "mid-term" party convention in Memphis. Carter hoped to use the forum to solidify his base and quell liberal dissidents hoping to convince Senator Edward Kennedy to challenge Carter's 1980 renomination bid. Although Kennedy stated he "expected" to support Carter, he criticized the administration's social policies frequently. These potshots fueled the Carter campaign's concern over both Kennedy's steady lead in the polls and the feverish media preoccupation with the senator's intentions. From the White House's perspective, Ted Kennedy was an irritant, not a soul mate.

The Carter loyalists in control of the convention couldn't silence Kennedy, but they could sequester him. They scheduled Carter for the primetime keynote address on the opening night (with his speech preceded by a pro-Carter documentary film). The DNC relegated Kennedy to a 15-minute afternoon speech at an off-site health care workshop where he would share the forum with ten other panelists.

At age 21, I attended the Memphis conference as an elected delegate from Alameda County, California. As my diary notes show from our first delegation meeting upon arriving, my growing dissatisfaction with the Party of my youth was apparent even then:

Memphis, December 7, 1978

Today I attended the caucus of the California delegation in our hotel. Mary Warren, chair of our delegation, issued our convention credentials and presided over the election of a vice chair. A representative from every conceivable group nominated one of their own for the position, urging us to vote for their favored candidate based solely on "qualifications" such as race, gender, union membership, sexual preferences, and similar factors. Not one nomination speech urged the selection of a vice chair based on ability, merit, or party service. It was a quota free-for-all, with each group trying to "out-victim" the other. The spectacle distressed me. I walked out without casting a vote.

• • •

When I entered the Cook Convention Center for the first session, it became clear that the White House dominated the agenda. Jimmy Carter's face adorned the convention program, the official convention schedule, and even the DNC magazine tucked in every participant's "Welcome to Memphis" bag. As delegates entered the hall, people checking their credentials issued them a green-and-white campaign button reading, "Carter Mondale 1980."

I wandered the arena taking pictures while awaiting the opening gavel. At the Arkansas delegation, news photographers trained their lenses on the president's son, Chip Carter, as he chatted with a shaggy-haired 31 year-old state politician wearing a tweed coat with wide lapels and shank buttons on the pockets. This young Southerner's moment in the convention sun would come the following afternoon when he served as moderator for the much-anticipated panel discussion featuring Senator Kennedy. But on the convention floor, attention focused on the presidential offspring and not on his conversation mate.

In what presaged the next three days, the convention began half

Here I am as a delegate to the 1978 Democrat National Midterm Convention, Memphis, December 7, 1978. (Author's collection)

an hour behind schedule. Once it convened, an orchestrated series of increasingly disruptive motions from various state delegations delayed the program further. To make up lost time, organizers scratched many of the scheduled speakers, including Democrat National Committee Chairman John C. White and Speaker of the U.S. House of Representatives Thomas P. "Tip" O'Neill, Jr. By the time the lights dimmed for the Carter propaganda film, the convention ran two hours behind schedule.

At the film's conclusion, White introduced President Carter. The Memphis State Marching Band played "Hail to the Chief" as Jimmy and Rosalynn Carter appeared from behind the curtains and greeted Vice President and Mrs. Walter Mondale at the lectern. Carter and Mondale joined arms and waved to the delegates while acknowledging surprisingly brief applause.

Carter began his remarks by joking that the film preceding his speech was "the best network news program I've seen since I became president!" That proved the best line of a lackluster speech outlining his administration achievements to date.

When he finished, Mrs. Carter and the Mondales joined him onstage. The audience applauded politely, but the uninspiring speech struck no emotional chord with the delegates. A reporter later described Carter's missed opportunity:

> [The midterm conference] seemed like the perfect setting for Jimmy Carter. . . . [Yet] when he pronounced his grand theme, no one clapped. One delegate from New York munched a ham sandwich; one woman from Texas fixed her makeup. When the band played "Happy Days Are Here Again," it looked as though nobody believed it. "It showed both his problems and his potential," said a delegate from Illinois. "How do you bring a crowd to its feet by talking about inflation?" Even many of Carter's supporters seemed lukewarm. "He creates no great enthusiasm and he creates no great hostility," sighed Rep. Paul Simon of Illinois. "There's simply no verve of any kind."[1]

If Carter came to Memphis to do oratorical battle with Ted Kennedy, then his mission had failed even before Kennedy had shown up and uttered a word.

The "exclusive" invitation I had received to a private reception honoring the Carters and the Mondales following the president's address from

President and Mrs. Jimmy Carter, Democrat Mid-Term Convention, Memphis, December 7, 1978. (Photograph by the author)

North Carolina Governor Jim Hunt was anything but that. When I learned that the guest list included *every* delegate and alternate to the convention, I decided to skip it. During the benediction, I

---

1   *Newsweek*, December 18, 1978.

slipped out of the hall and headed in the opposite direction of the presidential soirée hoping to avoid the maddening crush of delegates flocking to Carter's event.

As I made my way through the near-empty lobby of the convention center, I stopped to put away my camera. Someone from behind tapped me on the back. I turned and faced a ramrod-straight military officer with close-cropped hair and a large presidential emblem on his chest. "Excuse me," the officer said, "but the president would like to greet you." As he spoke, he placed both hands on my shoulders and spun me gently 90 degrees until I looked directly into the blue eyes of Jimmy Carter. I was so taken off guard by the encounter that it took a moment before I recognized him.

Carter shook my hand: "It's nice to meet you," he said. "How did you like my speech?"

Mercifully, I didn't have time to answer. Someone nearby shouted excitedly, "Hey, there's the president!" From nowhere a sudden horde of people converged on the scene. "Thank you," Carter said as he gave my hand a quick pump and then he push-pulled me toward Mrs. Carter, Vice President and Mrs. Mondale, and Governor Hunt (whose "pump-and-go" handshake marked the end of the reception).

• • •

The next day, the convention held 24 domestic and international policy workshops for delegates, with administration officials plugging Carter's programs at each one. Two competing workshops promised to attract the most attention: one with President Carter and the other with Senator Kennedy.

At Carter's workshop, delegate attendance inside Conference Room N proved sparse enough for me to find a center seat in the front row. The panelists filed in and took their places: U.S. Senator John Culver (D-IA), two Carter administration officials (National Security Adviser David Aaron and Under Secretary of Defense

William Perry), and the moderator, South Carolina Governor-elect Richard Riley. One seat remained empty at the table.

Riley introduced Aaron and Perry, each of whom promoted the Carter administration's goals of increased defense spending while seeking arms reductions with the Soviet Union. Liberals in the audience cheered Culver, who urged cutbacks in the military to help fund more social programs. Someone passed a note to Riley, who read it and then interrupted: "Senator Culver," he said, "I apologize, but it is time for me to introduce our mystery guest. Ladies and gentlemen, the president of the United States." Surrounded by Secret Service agents, Carter entered from the rear of the room and shook hands with delegates as he made his way to the table.

President Jimmy Carter after arriving for a defense policy workshop, Memphis, December 9, 1978. (Photograph by the author)

During the workshop, Carter defended his military spending goals to the dismay of the heavily liberal audience. When Culver challenged the administration's military priorities, Carter delivered a stern rebuke: "As long as I am in the White House, I will keep a strong defense."

• • •

A few hours later, I squeezed into Dixon-Meyer Hall for the health care workshop, which drew national media attention because of Kennedy's attendance. Earlier that morning, only a few hundred people had shown up for Carter's symposium. More than 2,500 people—standing room only—had packed the hall to hear Kennedy. The young Southern politician I had seen talking to Chip Carter the previous night served as the forum moderator.

When Kennedy arrived and joined the other ten panelists, the audience went wild. His brief speech calling for implementing guaranteed national health insurance and a greater commitment to domestic spending programs drew repeated and enthusiastic standing ovations. In a direct slap to Carter's earlier remarks at the defense workshop, Kennedy thundered: "We cannot accept policies that cut spending to the bone in areas like jobs and health, but allows billions of dollars in wasteful spending for defense. The party that tore itself apart over Vietnam in the 1960s cannot afford to tear itself apart today over budget cuts in basic social programs." As the crowd cheered and chanted his name, Kennedy vowed to continue speaking out "as long as I have a voice in the U.S. Senate."

Finishing his speech, Kennedy left immediately, and almost every spectator in the hall filed out with him. Only a handful remained to hear the other panelists.

Two hours after Kennedy's departure, the other speakers still hadn't finished their opening statements, which were now delivered to an empty auditorium. The smiling young moderator apologized for the program falling behind schedule. Two more hours went by, and it was well past the dinner hour when he adjourned the session after allowing for only two audience questions.

Nobody besides me paid attention to the moderator as he collected his papers and prepared to leave. I had recognized him the night before when he spoke with Chip Carter, but only because I had read a previous news story about his rapid statewide political rise. Two years earlier, at age 30 (and only a few years out of law school), voters back home had elected him state attorney general.

I introduced myself to the moderator and said that I hoped to follow his lead into law school and, later, politics. We chatted for maybe 15 minutes about the political and professional opportunities that a law degree opens. He encouraged me to study law, continue my interest in government, and he told me to keep him posted on my progress. I told him how much I appreciate his taking so much time with one who wasn't an Arkansas constituent.

Although the young moderator circulated in Memphis anonymously that week, in later years he played on a profoundly larger stage.

His name was Bill Clinton.

• • •

During his Memphis speech, President Carter chided Democrats who complained that the price tag for the midterm conference paid out of Party coffers was a waste of money. Although Carter later proclaimed the conference a success, I suspect he came to regret the expense. The midterm convention gave anti-Carter forces a national platform from which to showcase their organized hostility. The seeds of belligerence planted in Memphis in 1978 grew into a divisive and bitter struggle between Carter and Kennedy for the 1980 Democrat presidential nomination. When the warfare ended, Carter won a Pyrrhic victory over Kennedy. A few months later, Ronald Reagan's juggernaut swamped Carter and his Party in the general election.

The Democrat National Committee never held another midterm convention.

• • •

As for the young moderator at Senator Kennedy's health care conference, it was 20 years after our pleasant meeting in Memphis—not only to the day, but almost to the very hour—that I sat as a member of the House Judiciary Committee and cast my vote to impeach President Bill Clinton. When the committee's clerk called the roll on that tense and rancorous evening, a river of thoughts ran through my mind as I voted on the historic question.

But mostly, I thought about Memphis.

16

Something to Tell
Your Grandkids

As the 1980 presidential campaign neared its conclusion, every poll suggested the race between President Jimmy Carter and former California Governor Ronald Reagan was too close to call.

On Election Day, November 4, 1980, I took the night off from my Hollywood-Sunset Strip bartending job to watch the returns. In preparation for an anticipated late-night vigil, I had a clipboard, charts, and pens spread out on the coffee table to help me track races and trends. Since the networks began broadcasting live election coverage on the West Coast too early for any meaningful developments, I laced up my running shoes for a quick afternoon jog before anything significant happened. When I returned less than an hour later, it was over. NBC's map had America colored almost solidly red for Reagan. News anchorman John Chancellor appeared stunned that modern polls could have been so wrong. Returns now showed a Reagan landslide. Just as surprising, Carter delivered his concession speech almost three hours before polls closed on the West Coast (many incumbent Democrats later blamed their loss on Carter's premature surrender).

Although still a registered Democrat, I voted for Reagan in 1980 because I supported his platform of economic growth through lower taxes, peace through strength, and eliminating bureaucratic strangulation. Reagan's common-sense petition to individual responsibility appealed to me greatly. Still, I felt like a sneak thief entering the voting booth that morning. After glancing over my shoulder to see if anybody watched, I marked my ballot for the straight Republican ticket. As it turned out, millions of Democrats around the country did the very same thing—and for the very same reason.

When my boyhood friend Frank Ambrose dropped by, we watched the live news coverage of Reagan leaving his Pacific Palisades home in the late afternoon to dine with friends before proceeding to his 19th floor suite at the Century Plaza Hotel to await the final results. Frank agreed to my impulsive suggestion that we drive to the Century Plaza and try to see Reagan's victory speech in person later that evening.

• • •

As dusk settled, reporters, camera crews, satellite dishes, and delirious crowds packed the inside and outside of Reagan's hotel. Frank and I tried to enter the Grand Ballroom for Reagan's appearance, but the Secret Service had by then blocked all entrances and exits onto the lower floor ballroom location.

Suddenly, from the main lobby, we heard the walls shake. A thundering ovation greeted Reagan and his family as he stepped onstage to claim victory. The deafening chant of "We Want Reagan! We Want Reagan!" could be heard in every part of the huge building.

Undaunted by the lockout, I looked for an unsecured means of entry. I grabbed Frank's arm and told him, "Hey, follow me." I opened an unattended service door and we wended our way through a maze of hallways, corridors, and pantries looking for a ballroom entrance.

I saw a door ajar and opened it quietly. By accident we had stumbled into the Secret Service observation booth above the ballroom! The agents stood with their backs toward us as they watched Reagan and the ballroom crowd below through binoculars and communicated with other agents through radios. I exhaled only when I realized they didn't notice our entry.

Frank panicked: "Holy shit!" he whispered. "Let's get the hell out of here!" He didn't wait for my reply. He turned and dashed back down the hallway trying to retrace his steps. Since I expected the Secret Service to arrest me anyway, I remained by the doorway to watch Reagan through the observation booth as he introduced his family, and then he promised to unify the nation: "I consider the trust you have placed in me sacred, and I give you my oath that I will do my utmost to justify your faith."

After Reagan finished his momentous appearance, I slipped out of the room and closed the door behind me. The Secret Service agents posted in the room never knew of my intrusion.

When I returned to the mezzanine, I found a very agitated Frank pacing back and forth. He wasted no time in giving me an earful: "You stupid bastard!" he shouted. "Are you crazy? You and your stupid, *Hey, follow me.* We could've been shot! Besides, I've got an arrest warrant out for me—and I've got weed in my pocket! Don't you *ever* do that to me again!"

"Frank," I reminded him gently, "you'll be able to tell your grandkids someday that you saw Ronald Reagan on the night he was elected president of the United States. Isn't it worth going to jail for something like that?" Frank glowered at me, and then he stopped yelling.

• • •

Later, a select VIP group of Reagan's earliest supporters and closest friends exited from one of the small ballrooms after a private meeting with the new president-elect. All wore orange buttons reading, "November 4, 1980—President-Elect Ronald Reagan," distributed to them exclusively inside this historic private reception with the new president.

Frank disappeared as I bartered with attendees trying to get one for my political memorabilia collection (I succeeded eventually).

One guest leaving the reception not wearing the coveted badge was Lyn Nofziger, Reagan's campaign press secretary. Nofziger may well have been the only person in the entire hotel not dressed for the event. His hair stood on end, his Mickey Mouse tie was askew, and his suit looked as if he had slept in it for a week. Given the frantic pace of the campaign's closing days, he probably had.

I located Frank posed in an unlikely tableau. My uncouth and unemployed pal sat atop a marble table in a busy corridor. Seated alongside and engaged deeply in conversation with him was the legendary comic from radio, television, and movie fame, Red Skelton. Frank and Skelton laughed and joked as if they were long-lost brothers while puffing on expensive cigars from Skelton's private stock. The star didn't seem to mind Frank's

Rare election night badge from the private reception held with Ronald Reagan and his longtime friends on the night he won the presidency, Century Plaza Hotel, Los Angeles, November 4, 1980. (Author's collection)

earthy expression of appreciation for his talent: "Red! You're a funny fuckin' dude! Hey, thanks for the stogie, babe! Yeah, Red, you're a funny fuckin' dude."

Frank saw me approach: "Hey, Jimbo, come over here. Hey, Red, here's my friend, Jim. Give him a cigar too, Red."

I shook hands and accepted a cigar from Skelton, but I was still too dumb-founded by the weird scene to make sense of it. Skelton whispered something to Frank. They shared another hearty laugh, Skelton patted him on the back, said goodbye to me, and then he left.

"What the hell was that all about?" I asked.

Frank smiled and shrugged: "What can I say? I'm a man of the people."

A few minutes later, a sudden commotion erupted in the hallway. Skelton ran by shouting, "Somebody took my briefcase! Where's my briefcase? Call hotel security!" I looked at Frank (known to have more than a bit of larceny in his veins).

"I swear to you!" Frank whispered as he raised his hand in oath-like fashion.

"Relax, Frank," I said. "You might swipe a case of beer from a delivery truck, but I know you'd have no use for Red Skelton's briefcase. Grab your cigar and let's go."

With the Reagans having departed, security guards reopened the Grand Ballroom where the jubilee remained in full swing. The band played while happy celebrants danced, sang, and toasted their victory from one of several open bars in the festively decorated room. Reporters and camera crews interviewed local and state Republican Party leaders. The celebrants dashed my hope of finding campaign memorabilia for my collection. Nobody parted with or left behind mementos of a very historic night where, only minutes earlier, the Reagan Revolution began.

• • •

Frank never did explain how he ended up seated on that table smoking cigars with Red Skelton, nor did he offer any explanation about the missing briefcase. The last time I asked him he told me, "There are some things that you just don't need to know—and some things that ain't going in one of your books."

• • •

Comedian Red Skelton died of pneumonia at age 84 on September 17, 1997.

17

What Case Is He On?

The American Film Institute added Cary Grant's name to its list of the "Greatest Male Stars of All Time." With the rich legacy of motion picture roles he left behind, few question the ranking. Twice nominated for the Academy Award for Best Actor, Grant starred in such classic movies as *The Awful Truth*, *Bringing Up Baby*, *Gunga Din*, *The Philadelphia Story*, *His Girl Friday*, *Arsenic and Old Lace*, *The Bishop's Wife*, *An Affair to Remember*, and *North by Northwest*.

In 1986, when I was a young prosecutor in the Los Angeles County district attorney's office, I had an acquaintance who once worked with the legendary actor. Knowing I'm an old film buff, he gave me Grant's private post office box address and suggested that I drop him a note. "Tell him who you are, that you know me, and that you'd like to meet him," he said. "He might say yes, and then you can spend time with him talking about his career. What have you got to lose?" I took the advice, wrote a note to Grant, and then I forgot about it almost as quickly as I mailed it.

A few weeks went by. On November 21, after a long morning in court, the judge recessed our trial for lunch. I was leaving the DA's office with my boss, Walt Lewis, when the receptionist paged me to the phone. I picked up an extension line and heard a woman with a British accent say, "Good afternoon, Mr. Rogan. This is Mr. Grant's secretary. Please hold for Mr. Grant."

Assuming that some lawyer named Grant wanted to talk about a matter I was prosecuting, I asked her, "What case is he on?"

"I beg your pardon?"

"Do you know what case this is about so I can get the file before I talk with him?"

She cleared her throat. "Please hold for Mr. Cary Grant."

Oh.

Within moments an unmistakable voice—imitated by thousands of impersonators over the decades—boomed over the receiver: "Hello, Mr. Rogan. This is Cary Grant." I stood speechless as he continued:

"I received your note, and I want you to know how very flattered I was to get it. I was touched by the kind words you expressed in it. I would very much like to meet with you, but I can't set up anything for a couple of months. I'm traveling extensively doing shows right now, and I am leaving for a trip to Iowa. I don't get a lot of rest for a man my age—I'm 82 years old. But when I get back, I'll give you a call and we'll set up something."

As I listened to Grant speak, Walt started tugging on my elbow. "Come on," he griped, "I'm hungry; let's go. Who is it, anyway?"

I put my hand over the mouthpiece. "It's Cary Grant," I whispered.

Walt laughed. "Oh, sure—tell Cary hello for me! No, really—who is it?"

"It's really Cary Grant."

I told Grant I was shocked, but honored, to get his call. "Oh, don't mention it," he replied. "I always prefer to dispose of my business over the telephone. It's much easier that way for me." I said I looked forward to meeting him when his schedule settled down, and asked if he might send me an autographed picture as a memento of our conversation.

"Well, I wish I could," he said, "but I retired from motion pictures over 20 years ago, and I haven't had a picture taken since then.

I'd hate to send one of me looking like an old goat!" He balked when I offered to get one and send it to him: "The problem with you mailing one to me is that my staff routinely returns or ignores those things when collectors send them in, and I'm afraid your picture will get lost in the shuffle. When we get together, I'll be happy to sign it."

I thanked Grant for the call and said that nobody would believe me when I told them about it—including my boss who was at my elbow and didn't believe me right now.

"You're a district attorney," Grant laughed. "Don't you have any credibility?"

"Mr. Grant, now you sound like an ex-girlfriend!" He laughed louder and said he would get in touch with me when he returned. I wished him a successful trip and thanked him again.

When I hung up the receiver, Walt asked, "Okay, who was that, really?" When I told him again, he said, "Bullshit. Let's go eat. You can buy lunch for keeping me waiting."

When it came to assessing my credibility, I guess Cary Grant was right.

• • •

On November 29, a week after calling me, Cary Grant arrived in Davenport to do his one-man show, *A Conversation with Cary Grant*. While getting ready to leave his suite at the Blackhawk Hotel for the theater, he suffered a stroke and died that night.

To this day, Walt Lewis still doesn't believe that Cary Grant delayed our lunch.

18

Pretend I Am Dead

Spiro T. Agnew's political career rose like a rocket. A local Maryland attorney, he ran successfully for Baltimore county executive in 1962. In 1966 he won the governorship, and in 1968 Republican presidential nominee Richard Nixon picked him as his running mate. The Nixon–Agnew ticket defeated the Democrat nominees narrowly that year, but four years later they won reelection in a landslide. In 1973, as Nixon's presidency dissolved with each Watergate revelation, federal prosecutors indicted Agnew for allegedly accepting bribes of more than $100,000. On October 10, 1973, he resigned the vice presidency and pleaded no contest to a single charge of failing to report income.

Unlike many former political leaders, Agnew craved anonymity. Eschewing almost all requests for interviews and public appearances after leaving Washington, he lived quietly in the Palm Springs area pursuing his private business interests. Of course, as a student of history, I wanted to meet him and discuss his years in Washington. Knowing he refused interviews, I wrote him anyway and made my request. In my letter I mentioned that I had witnessed his acceptance speech when I was a member of the Young Voters for the President delegation to the 1972 Republican National Convention.

Once again, brazenness paid off. On January 5, 1987, I returned home from work to a voice message on my answering machine. "Mr. Rogan," the nasal voice intoned, "this is Mr. Agnew. Please call me back." When I dialed the number left for me, he answered the phone himself and suggested that we meet at Los Angeles International Airport a few days later. "I am flying to Korea on Wednesday," he said. "Meet me in the VIP lounge of the Korean Air Lines terminal about 10:45 in the morning. You can ask your questions then."

I thanked him for the opportunity and for his call.

Two days later, Agnew called me at work to delay our meeting by a day. The district attorney's receptionist answered the telephone. "Is Mr. Rogan there?" the former vice president asked.

"I'm sorry," she responded. "He's in court. May I take a message?"

"This is Mr. Agnew."

"Who?" the receptionist asked, not knowing with whom she spoke.

"Mr. Agnew," he said again. "A-G-N-E-W."

She repeated back the spelling, and then she asked, "Agnew—is that spelled just like Agnew the crook?"

Later, when I returned his call, I made no mention of the receptionist's horrible social blunder. Gratefully, neither did he.

• • •

After making an early court appearance, I drove to LAX and checked in with the clerk at the Korean Air Lines lounge. She escorted me inside a private waiting area where a couple dozen businessmen sipped tea and read newspapers while awaiting their flights. Agnew sat alone at the far end of the room working quietly on the *New York Times* crossword puzzle. The other travelers took no notice of him. When I introduced myself, he put down his newspaper, stood, and welcomed me. Neither the years nor his prior travails appeared to have impacted him physically: he looked tanned and fit.

He invited me to join him for tea. "I'm in no hurry," he assured me. "I have almost an hour to kill before my plane arrives."

He asked how long I had been a prosecutor with the Los Angeles County District Attorney's Office, and then he mentioned that he kept following news reports on the lengthy McMartin preschool child molestation trial that dominated the local news in the 1980s. "Your boss, Ira Reiner, is doing a good job," he noted, "although I don't care much for prosecutors after what a bunch of them did to me. Nothing personal, but I felt the prosecutors looking into my case were dishonest."

Not wanting him to dwell on his distaste for my profession, I changed the subject and handed him a few items to autograph for my collection, including his memoir, *Go Quietly . . . or Else.*

"Have you read the book?" he asked.

When I told him I had just obtained it for our meeting and hadn't read it yet, he leaned forward and locked his eyes on mine: "When

you read it, you will see what I mean," he said. "It shows how the prosecutors in my case relied on perjured testimony and unreliable statements from known criminals to pursue their case. They gave them immunity for their lies and made me an open target. I was given nothing before entering my plea. I obtained my discovery documents later

The card that helped start it all: 1962 Agnew for Baltimore County Executive palm card, which he signed for me at Los Angeles International Airport. (Author's collection)

under the Freedom of Information Act. Had I known how terrible their case was against me, I never would have been blackmailed into pleading no contest."

Agnew inscribed the book, and then he signed for me a small campaign card from his first race in 1962 for Baltimore County Executive. "Where did you get this?" he asked as he studied the card. "This was from my first political campaign. I never really wanted to go into politics and didn't intend to run for office. I got started accidentally when I joined the local Kiwanis Club. Once I got started, they would not let me out."

I asked Agnew if he ever missed politics. "No," he said forcefully,

I didn't like politics and I don't miss it. The press hated me and still hates me. They were not satisfied to beat me politically. They wanted to destroy me personally. Long after I left office, they kept trying to look into my private business deals. After going broke from having to defend myself against every crank lawsuit filed, I tried to get a consulting business going. Eventually I set up a lucrative deal with the government of Indonesia that would help my family and me get back on our feet. The New York Times learned about it and began calling every government leader in Indonesia to interrogate them. The Indonesian government did not need or want all of the publicity, so they pulled out of the deal.

As far as the press and the world are concerned, I want them all to forget me and pretend I am dead. I try to be as anonymous as possible wherever I go. I travel alone. I take no associates with me. Whenever a reporter calls to interview me, I hang up. I don't give interviews. Ted Koppel of ABC News keeps calling and trying to get me on his show. I tell him no way.

Pausing only to take an occasional sip of tea, he continued calmly: "The thing that really gets to me after all these years is this: I can never really be anonymous. No matter where in the world I travel, people still recognize me and think, 'There goes Agnew the crook.' Last year I was picking up my luggage at the airport in Korea and I noticed a few Americans standing across the baggage carousel. They were pointing at me and whispering. I knew what they were saying: 'There's Agnew the crook.' The stares really get to you."

Remembering my receptionist's faux pas, I tried again to direct the conversation to more neutral topics: "Mr. Vice President," I asked, "what was it like for you to stand on the steps of the Capitol and raise your hand to be sworn in as vice president? What thoughts went through your mind as you took the oath of office?" I expected him to offer some nostalgic or patriotic memories, but his answer was devoid of such sentiments.

"It was no big deal," he replied. "I was used to such ceremonies. I went through the same thing when I was sworn in as governor of Maryland. The one big advantage to being vice president was the logistical support one gets when traveling. The Secret Service coordinated all my travel. I never drove a car in over six years while I was running for and serving as vice president."

When I asked if he ever spoke with former President Nixon, the man who had picked the obscure Maryland governor as his running mate in 1968, he shook his head: "I haven't seen him or spoken with him since the day I resigned," he replied, "and I have no desire to see him or speak with him. I was very bitter over the way he treated me. He tried to use my legal troubles as a way to avoid the bad publicity he was receiving because of the breaking Watergate scandal. He treated me terribly. I have heard from friends who remain in touch with Nixon that he is now sorry for the way he treated me during those years, but he only expresses such sorrow through intermediaries. He has never expressed it to me. The only person who treated me worse than Nixon was his chief of staff, Alexander Haig, who is a terrible man."

For all the apparent hard feelings, I found him unemotional and very matter-of-fact when discussing such unpleasantries. His forthright answers proved surprising, especially since he shared them with a stranger.

Agnew's tone softened noticeably when he discussed his current activities. He said that his business travels take him to Korea at least six times a year. "Mrs. Agnew travels with me once or twice a year," he said, "I've made 56 trips to Korea since resigning the vice presidency. It's a 13-hour flight each way, so when I go, I stay for two or three weeks to get in as much business as possible. I've piled up my frequent-flier miles. They owe me five free flights!"

Former Vice President Spiro T. Agnew and me, Los Angeles International Airport, January 9, 1987. (Author's collection)

As we posed for a picture shaking hands, the photographer asked if he ever felt like a beauty queen when posing for photos. "Oh, I've done this a lot of times over the years," he replied. "I remember one day when I posed with 435 members of Congress for individual photographs. Even the Democrats were excited about having a picture taken with me. But that was a long time ago." His sad voice trailed off.

The time came for Agnew to board his plane. I thanked him for the invitation and for taking the time to visit. As we finished our tea, I asked him one last question: Given everything he had achieved and then endured, was his time in political life worth it?

He paused for a moment and then he grinned. "If I had to do it all over," he said, "I still would have joined the Kiwanis Club—but nothing else!"

• • •

On September 17, 1996, Agnew fell ill suddenly. Tests run at a local Maryland hospital revealed undiagnosed advanced-stage leukemia. He died at age 77 only a few hours after receiving the diagnosis.

19

In the Shadows

Under other circumstances, history might remember Mack Robinson as one of America's great athletes. An Olympic medalist, he set records in NCAA, AAU, and Pacific Coast Conference track meets. He is enshrined in the Oregon Sports Hall of Fame and the University of Oregon Hall of Fame. Yet few remember him today because he lived under two mighty shadows.

As one of America's first black Olympic track stars, he represented the United States at the 1936 Berlin games presided over by Adolf Hitler. In the historic 200–meter race, Mack (who had no running coach) wore the same beat-up track shoes he had used in college competitions. By the time he got to Berlin, those shoes were disintegrating on his feet as he ran a close second in that race, and Jesse Owens went on to sports immortality instead by nosing out Mack for the gold medal by 0.4 seconds. Then, a decade later, America's fixation on the accomplishment of his younger brother Jackie, who smashed through the segregation line of Major League Baseball, again overshadowed Mack's athletic legacy.

Unpleasant circumstances brought about my encounter with Mack Robinson. In 1987, I was a Los Angeles County Deputy District Attorney prosecuting the double murder case of *People v. Hamilton*. The defendant's girlfriend at the time of the killings was Mack Robinson's daughter Kathy, and she proved a very reluctant witness for the prosecution. My co-counsel, Bill Holliman, and I wanted to make sure she hadn't given police less-than-complete information about her boyfriend's whereabouts on the night of the killings, so we set up an interview with her parents to measure the credibility of her statements.

Along with Los Angeles Sheriff's Department homicide detective Janet Stewart, we arrived at the Robinson family home at 550 MacDonald Avenue in Pasadena. Del Robinson (Mack's wife) greeted us at the door and escorted us inside. When I apologized for our early morning appointment, she waved off my concern. "I've been up since five this morning giving Mack his insulin shots," she explained. "He's a diabetic."

Once inside, Mack Robinson leaned heavily on his cane as he rose to welcome us. Now in his seventies, the man bore no resemblance to the lean young runner depicted in an old photograph displayed nearby. His gray hair sat atop thick mutton-chop sideburns and a mustache. His portly stomach hid under a too-snug T-shirt. On the walls hung framed sports mementos related mostly to his younger brother. Photographs depicted him at various celebrations for Jackie: Mack alongside a Jackie Robinson statue, Mack christening Jackie Robinson Park, Mack holding the official Jackie Robinson postage stamp. The only relic I saw from his career was a certificate captioned "XL Olympiade Berlin 1936" hanging on a wall near the kitchen.

Our questioning of the Robinsons produced only the vaguest recollections and provided little information. The only revealing comment Mack made was when he shared his grief knowing that his daughter might have dated a man involved in a double murder. "I don't know," he said glumly. "Kids don't listen. They never do. That boyfriend of hers never even worked. Kathy worked. I don't know." His eyes filled with tears.

Hoping to change the mood, I pivoted from investigation-related questions and asked him to tell us about his 1936 Berlin experience. That didn't have the desired result. His demeanor went from glum to resentful:

Hitler was in the stands when I ran in that race with Jesse Owens, but I wasn't watching Hitler. I was too busy running. Besides, those Nazis in Germany didn't treat us any worse than America did after the Olympic Games. Ten out of the 11 blacks on our Olympic team won medals in Berlin, but our own country ignored us when we came home. I used to sweep streets here in Pasadena wearing my Olympic jacket. The City of Pasadena has yet to honor me. They have never had a 'Mack Robinson Day' and they never will. Nobody remembers me and nobody cares. I'm ignored and forgotten. Jesse Owens won the race by an eyelash and he is the one now in the history books. People remember Jesse Owens and Jackie Robinson, but they don't give a damn about Mack Robinson.

Photograph of 1936 Olympian Mack Robinson autographed for me on December 30, 1987. (Author's collection)

Del looked down at her shoes saying nothing. I suspected that she had heard this before.

I told him that he was wrong if he thought nobody remembered him. "Listen," I told him, "here we are 50 years after you ran in Berlin, and I don't want to leave without getting your autograph." Bill and Jan chided me for asking, but when Del dug through a box and found a few old pictures of him running in the 1936 Olympics, they almost trampled over me to get one.

His demeanor softened at the appreciation we showed for his career. He smiled, put on his glasses, and signed a photograph for each for us.

When it was time to go, the Robinsons walked us to our car. Mack appeared oblivious to the cold late-December weather as he stood in a T-shirt at the small gate in front of his driveway and talked about his daughter. "I used to wait here for Kathy to come home at night," he said. "We tried to raise her right. That boyfriend never worked." Shaking his head, he said goodbye. I watched as he turned slowly and walked back inside.

Dedication plaque at the United States Matthew "Mack" Robinson Post Office Building located at 600 Lincoln Avenue, Pasadena, California. Created by Act of Congress, 106th Congress, H.R. 4157, authored by Congressman James Rogan.

• • •

Many years later, I was Mack and Del Robinson's congressman when he died of complications from diabetes, kidney failure, and pneumonia in Pasadena at the age of 85 on March 12, 2000. Had he lived a few months longer, he would have seen Congress pass and President Clinton sign into law congressional legislation I authored naming the U.S. Post Office in Pasadena after him. By the way, that building is down the street from what is now the Jackie and Mack Robinson Memorial Park.

Both the Post Office building and the park's large sculpted bust of Mack are on the same streets that he once swept while wearing his Olympic jacket.

20

Bob Fink on Nixon
(and a Few Others)

Robert H. Finch owned a historic footnote not widely known but confirmed by Richard Nixon in his presidential memoir. When Nixon won the 1968 Republican nomination, he asked Finch to be his running mate. Because of Finch's one-word answer to that question, when I met him in 1988, he was a solo-practicing lawyer in a small Pasadena office. Had Finch given a different answer, today there likely would be a Robert H. Finch Presidential Library, and Gerald Ford would be the name of an obscure former Michigan congressman. (By the way, in later years Finch hosted a fundraising lunch for me when I ran for the state legislature. After he introduced me, I told this story, and then made this observation: "If Bob had said yes instead of no, today he would be the former president of the United States—and I could have charged all of you a hell of a lot more than the lousy 50 bucks you paid to get in here!")

Finch's Republican roots dated back to Wendell Willkie's 1940 presidential campaign. A few years later he befriended a young World War II returning veteran, Richard Nixon, who won election to Congress in 1946. After Nixon became Eisenhower's vice president in 1953, Finch joined Nixon's Washington staff; in 1960, he managed Nixon's national presidential campaign that year against

John F. Kennedy. In 1966, Finch won election as California's lieutenant governor, and he outpolled the winner of the governorship—Ronald Reagan. In 1969 he resigned his statewide office to join President Nixon's first cabinet.

My relationship with Finch began that same year. I was 11 and in the seventh grade when I wrote him and asked for an autographed picture for my fledgling political memorabilia collection. A month later he responded with a gracious letter and enclosed signed pictures of both Nixon and him.

Two decades later I worked as a prosecutor at the Pasadena courthouse in the Los Angeles County DA's office. While reading the morning newspaper, I spotted a "Where Are They Now?" article about Finch. Although his own political career ended in 1976 with a failed U.S. Senate race, he remained a powerful behind-the-scenes presence in California Republican politics. I grew particularly interested when I read that his law office was just a few blocks down the street on Colorado Boulevard. I sent him a copy of his 1969 letter and invited him to lunch. He called, and that started a friendship that lasted until his death.

During one conversation over lunch, I jotted down some of his recollections of his years with Nixon, of whom he spoke more as an older brother than as a boss:

My association with Richard Nixon dates back to 1946, when Nixon first ran for Congress against incumbent Jerry Voorhis. Nobody thought Nixon had a chance to win, but he upset Voorhis on Election Day. Because we became close friends, I went from being a local Republican county chairman to a member of his inner circle.

When Nixon became vice president in 1953 under Dwight Eisenhower, he asked me to run his office. In 1960, when he ran against John F. Kennedy, Nixon appointed me chairman of his national campaign committee. One of the worst mistakes Nixon made that year was picking Ambassador Henry Cabot Lodge as his vice presidential running mate. The idea of picking Cabot Lodge for VP was pushed by Ike, who, for some reason, really liked Lodge. But Lodge proved to be a disaster as a candidate. He was lazy and would only do one or two speeches a day. He needed to take frequent naps throughout the day. His candidacy embarrassed us and hurt Nixon, who needed a fighter on his team. Lodge was a joke.

It's true that when Nixon won the 1968 Republican presidential nomination, he asked me if I would be his running mate. After discussing the option with my friends and family, I turned him down. You can read about it in Teddy White's book, The Making of the President 1968. I felt being a lieutenant governor did not give me sufficient national exposure to bring strength to his ticket. After I refused, he turned to Spiro Agnew, who of course accepted and went on to become vice president. After Nixon won, he gave me my choice of whether I wanted to be Attorney General, Secretary of Commerce, or Secretary of Health, Education and Welfare. I chose HEW because that was the department where I was most interested.

At the mention of Agnew's name, Bob grimaced and showed little regard for the man who later resigned the vice presidency:

I never had a good relationship with Agnew. He resented me because I was Nixon's first choice for the vice presidency. Agnew was Nixon's fourth or fifth choice. That ate at him.

Agnew was never in the president's inner circle. He was a whiner who always complained to me that he didn't have enough access to Nixon or enough things to do. I explained to him that this was the role of a vice president. Nixon went through it with Eisenhower, so now it was his turn in the barrel. Nixon also grew tired of Agnew's whining to the point that Nixon once sent me over to the Old Executive Office Building to meet with Agnew to tell him how good he had it. Nixon wanted Agnew to know that Eisenhower treated Nixon pretty badly when Nixon was vice president. Agnew was living like a king compared to the way Nixon was treated. When Nixon was vice president, Eisenhower didn't even give him an office in the White House.

As to two other future presidents with whom he worked, Bob shared these thoughts:

In 1966, I ran for lieutenant governor the same year Ronald Reagan ran for governor. Although both Reagan and I won in 1966, I received more votes than he did. In fact, I was the top vote-getter across the nation in those elections. This made Nancy Reagan mad that I had outdistanced her husband. Two years later, when Reagan ran against Nixon for the 1968 Republican presidential nomination, I deepened Nancy's resentment when I endorsed Nixon. Truthfully, Reagan was not "running" for president—his staff ran him. Reagan knew Nixon and I were close, and when I told Reagan I would support Nixon, Reagan said it was okay and he understood. He never held it against me. But my support for Nixon sent a chill between our respective staffs, and Nancy never forgave me for it.

George Bush and I became pretty good friends. He was a middle-level official in the Nixon Administration who was competent and bright, but nobody ever thought of him as presidential mate-rial. Maybe as a future Secretary of State, because he had a good résumé, but never president.

Following Nixon's resignation, Bob returned to California to run for the U.S. Senate in 1976. His voice grew tense as he explained how Nixon's Watergate scandal and later resignation doomed his own return to elective office:

> I always wanted to be a senator, and I felt that is where I could have served with the most effectiveness. In 1976 I expected to win that Senate race. All the polls showed I was ahead and winning until the last couple of weeks. But my association with Nixon was made an issue suddenly, and the Watergate scandal tainted everyone around Nixon, even those of us who had nothing to do with it. My relationship to Nixon was well-known, and it hurt, and my Republican opponents capitalized on it.

• • •

As the years went by, Bob Finch became more than a friend. He became a mentor (despite the fact that I was a Reagan conservative and Bob had helped lead the more moderate wing of the GOP), a valued consultant, and an immeasurable political resource. He held my hand through my change in political parties, administered my oath of office when I became a judge, and hosted one of my first fundraisers when I ran for the State Assembly.

In 1995, as I contemplated a run for Congress the next year, Bob was the first person I called for advice, and he was the first person who urged me to do it. Around this time, he told me that he had decided to start work on a political memoir that would pay special attention to his long relationship with Nixon. When he showed me his outline for the book over lunch, I told him, "Only you can tell many of these inside stories from the Nixon years. Make sure you don't take them with you to the grave."

A week later, I was in full congressional campaign mode when Bob celebrated his seventieth birthday on October 9, 1995. A scheduled speech precluded me from joining his staff for a surprise party at his office. That afternoon I took a break to call Bob and wish him a happy birthday. I caught him just as he was leaving the office, and he turned the conversation immediately to my congressional race and matters of strategy and tactics. "I guess I won't be able to call you Jim anymore after you win this race next year," he chuckled. "You'll be 'congressman' then."

Our conversation that day grew so engrossed in campaign details that after I hung up I realized that I had forgotten to wish him a happy birthday. I started to call him back, and then remembered him telling me that he was walking out the door. "I'll call him back tomorrow and give him belated greetings," I thought, and then I rushed off to my next event.

That night, Bob Finch died of a heart attack.

A few days later, at his funeral, California Governor Pete Wilson and Herbert Klein (Nixon's former communications director dating back to RN's first congressional race) delivered the main eulogies. Wilson described his friendship with Finch starting when Wilson was fresh out of law school and worked as an advance man in Nixon's 1962 gubernatorial campaign:

> Bob was a man who could have succeeded Ronald Reagan as governor had he chosen to remain in California. He could have been elected to the United States Senate in 1970 if he had been willing to push aside his old friend George Murphy. He declined the vice presidential nomination from Nixon in 1968 to protect his friend against the charge of cronyism. After Nixon was elected, Bob chose the less glamorous position of HEW secretary because it was where he could make a difference in people's lives. He was a thoughtful and unselfish patriot who fought for the betterment of his country. California and the nation lost a man who wanted the best for all of us.

Klein recalled first meeting Finch in 1952:

I was traveling on a bus with then-Senator Richard Nixon, who had just been named as Eisenhower's running mate. Nixon's campaign bus was traveling to Redondo Beach. He told me that when we arrived at our destination he wanted me to meet a fellow named Bob Finch. "Bob is running for Congress against an incumbent," Nixon said, "and he is probably going to lose. But he will go on from the loss to do great things for California and the nation." And Nixon was right.

With my wife Christine and Bob Fink (aka Robert H. Finch) at a Rogan for State Assembly fundraiser, Burbank, California, October 1994. (Author's collection)

I well remember Nixon's 1968 presidential campaign against Vice President Hubert Humphrey. When President Lyndon Johnson decided to halt the bombing of Hanoi just before Election Day, we felt it would hurt our effort and we decided to attack LBJ's decision as sheer opportunism. None of us wanted to take on Johnson ourselves, so we asked Bob to do it. Bob dutifully came through, and at a press conference he really laid into LBJ. He must have done a great job, because a short time later Johnson personally called Nixon about Bob's attack.

"Dick," Johnson demanded, "you need to get rid of that guy 'Fink' on your staff, or we'll have some real problems." Nixon looked at us and winked as Johnson complained about "That guy Fink" and groused that "I don't want to hear from that Fink no more!"

From that day, Bob had a new nickname among his colleagues— *Bob Fink.*

• • •

When I think about Bob Finch (and a few others like him in this book), I recall how he took the time to write an 11 year-old interested in politics. To me, that embodies the man that I knew: he made time for strangers, and he inspired them along the way. If someone can say that about me after I'm gone, it will mean that my time in public life was worth it. It will mean that I made a difference.

It will mean that I was a little bit like Bob Finch.

21

Curses—Foiled Again

In 1988, former California Lieutenant Governor Bob Finch (see previous chapter) invited me to join his family and attend former President Richard Nixon's speech to the Orange County World Affairs Council. I looked forward to seeing Nixon with great anticipation. The last time was 16 years earlier at the 1972 Republican Convention in Miami, when I missed narrowly the chance to go through his receiving line and meet him. Knowing of my long-ago unfulfilled opportunity, Finch planned to introduce me at this event to his former boss and longtime friend.

At the last minute, business commitments forced Finch to skip the luncheon, so I went with his wife, Carol, and my pals Priscilla (Bob's daughter) and Chris Gooch (his secretary) for the drive to the Disneyland Hotel. During the trip, Priscilla shared stories of growing up with a father in the center of White House power. She told me her favorite Nixon story:

> I was at a party in New York a couple of years ago and was surprised to find Nixon there. I introduced myself to him and he was very charming, asking how my mom and dad were doing. His ease surprised me because he always struck me as a man who was uncomfortable meeting people. I knew he was a family man, so to make conversation I mentioned to him that my sister had recently had a baby, and that her friend Julie Nixon Eisenhower [Nixon's eldest daughter] sent the baby a stuffed bunny.

When I told him that, Nixon howled with laughter unexpectedly: "She would send a bunny!" He then explained why that amused him. When he ran for the U.S. Senate in 1950, he and his family did a live television campaign commercial. When Nixon finished his speech, he was supposed to step back and his two young girls were to sing their father's campaign theme song. Throughout the commercial Julie Nixon was clutching her favorite stuffed animal, a bunny, and refused to put it down.

So here I was at this party, surrounded by famous people and standing with President Nixon, when Nixon himself began singing the words to their 1950 campaign song that his daughters performed that night: Here we go on to Washington, to Washington, to Washington; Here we go on to Washington—vote for Nixon. He said that as the girls were about to sing the last line, Julie held up the doll and instead of singing Vote for Nixon, she sang, Vote for Bunny! as the camera faded out.

For the first time in all the times I met Nixon, he looked relaxed—and human."

• • •

Our group arrived at the Disneyland Hotel, where more than 1,000 people jammed inside the ballroom for the luncheon. My tablemate was Maurice Stans, Nixon's former Secretary of Commerce who also worked as his chief fundraiser during the 1968 and 1972 presidential campaigns. A Watergate grand jury had indicted him, but he won an acquittal. When he learned I was a deputy district attorney, the courtly Stans smiled: "You won't have any trouble from me!" he said.

I spoke with him about his career while we waited for the program to begin. A farm boy from Minnesota, he became an accountant in the 1920s and worked as a CPA until Washington beckoned:

I joined the Eisenhower administration in the 1950s as an assistant postmaster general, and then later became director of the
Bureau of the Budget. I took that job on one condition: I told
Eisenhower I would need to meet with him for an hour or so
to go over his budgetary priorities. Eisenhower agreed and we
met privately. I told him I could give him a balanced budget his
last year in office if he would give me the necessary support to
back up the tough decisions I would need to make. Eisenhower
agreed, and I went to work. Eisenhower called a meeting of his
Cabinet and senior staff and said I was acting with his authority.
Later I made the necessary cuts and Eisenhower backed me to
the hilt. We presented the American people a balanced budget in
1960—it was the last time America had one. Ike was a wonder-
fully charming man who was very bright and very quick-minded.

As to his future boss, Stans told me:

I didn't know Richard Nixon that well back in the old days. I
got to know him during the Eisenhower years when he was vice
president and I was working on the budget. When Nixon ran
for president in 1968, he asked me to be his national campaign
treasurer and I agreed. I essentially did all the fundraising for
that campaign.

After Nixon won, John Mitchell [Nixon's first Attorney General]
called and said Nixon wanted me to be his postmaster general.
I said I didn't want the job. Congress runs the Post Office
Department, and I had a taste of it under Eisenhower. Mitchell
ran down some other options to me, but I had no interest in
becoming Secretary of Agriculture or Secretary of Housing
and Urban Development. I told Mitchell I could handle either
Treasury or Commerce. Two weeks later, Mitchell called and
said, "It's Commerce."

Stans said he stepped down from the cabinet at Nixon's request to become his 1972 reelection finance chairman. Once again, he found himself as Nixon's chief fundraiser: "During the '72 campaign I read a story in the *Wall Street Journal*. A wealthy businessman was quoted as saying if George McGovern won the election over Richard Nixon, the businessman would commit suicide. I called him on the telephone and told him I was planning to save his life. We met a short time later on his yacht, and I told him we needed a check to the Nixon campaign for $250,000. He wrote it on the spot."

Stans' government service came to an abrupt halt with the Watergate scandal. "It ruined everything and everyone it touched," he lamented. "Federal prosecutors went after everyone connected to Nixon. They never understood that we kept finance and politics separate. I went on trial in New York with John Mitchell. I was charged with ten felony counts. The jury found me not guilty on nine counts, and the judge dismissed one count. I felt like another former Cabinet member who said after going through the same experience, 'Where do I go now to get back my good name?'" He said these days he spent his time raising money for the Nixon Library, and he took pride that it would be the only presidential library built without taxpayer assistance.

A sudden burst of applause and cheers interrupted my conversation with Stans: former President Nixon had entered the room and walked to his place at the head table. After giving a stiff-arm wave to the cheering crowd, he took his seat and the waiters served lunch.

During the meal service, I watched Nixon as he greeted and signed autographs for people at the head table. Because of the setup, the only way to reach Nixon would be to get atop the stage and walk its length to where he sat in the middle of the head table (the table sat too high on the stage to approach from the audience level). Having waited almost 20 years to meet him, I didn't want to let this opportunity go by without trying.

I noticed that a small stairway at the far left side of the stage led up to the head table, and no security guard monitored it. (Nixon was the only former president to give up his Secret Service protection.)

"What the hell?" I thought.

With a copy of Nixon's recent book in hand to have him sign, I approached the stairs, climbed them, crossed the stage, and walked to where Nixon sat. When I reached my target, I knelt beside him and waited while he finished signing an autograph for his seatmate. Just as he started turning in his chair to acknowledge me, a very agitated man in a three-piece suit with a radio earpiece squeezed my arm and demanded I leave the stage—now. I stood and followed him back down the stairs with my tail between my legs.

"Just who the hell do you think you are?" he growled as we walked away. "You have a lot of nerve walking up to Nixon like that!" As he continued upbraiding me, I noticed he wore pinned to his vest under his coat an oval plastic Disneyland employee name tag—the same kind worn at the Magic Kingdom by all the churro cart vendors and the guy who runs the Dumbo ride.

"Hey, you're not part of Nixon's security detail," I challenged him. "You're a Disneyland employee!"

"Nixon doesn't have security," the man said as his face reddened, "so I'm guarding him today."

"*You're* guarding him? Are you kidding me?"

After almost two decades of waiting, I missed my chance to meet Nixon—again. I shook off the glorified ticket-taker and was about to resume my mission when the program began. Reluctantly, I abandoned the effort and returned to my seat while fuming over my lost opportunity.

The emcee introduced the numerous former presidents of the Council, and then he welcomed Nixon home and reminded the audience that Orange County is the place from where Nixon hailed and began his political career.

Nixon received a sustained standing ovation when he rose to speak. "Mr. President," Nixon began, and then pointed to the assemblage of ex-club leaders, adding, "and my fellow former presidents." The audience laughed and applauded.

Nixon stood at the microphone and folded his hands in front of him. He moved them rarely from that position during his 45-minute speech. Speaking without notes on world affairs, he traversed the globe mentally while discussing policy challenges that would confront the next president.

He directed the primary focus of his remarks on the Soviet Union and its leader, Mikhail Gorbachev.

Gorbachev is a charming man, but to be a good prime minister, as Gladstone noted, one must be a good butcher. Gorbachev is unlike any other Soviet leader I have known. He is cool. Khrushchev was more like Lyndon Johnson—he liked to grab people by the lapel and arm. I remember Brezhnev standing next to Khrushchev during our 'Kitchen Debate,' and then he later deposed Khrushchev. Gorbachev will not allow that to happen. What we will need in the next president is a man who can deal with Gorbachev."

Former President Richard Nixon addressing the Orange County World Affairs Council, Disneyland Hotel, Anaheim, California, May 4, 1988. (Photograph by the author)

Nixon finished his speech and then answered written audience questions read to him. Here he shined: during his formal speech, he appeared rigid and with an intense focus. During the Q&A, he smiled, joked, and looked relaxed as he handled each question deftly.

Although some queries touched on foreign policy, most focused on the upcoming presidential election. He felt the two presumptive nominees (Republican George Bush and Democrat Michael Dukakis) would run a close race, with Bush winning by a whisker. He refused to suggest who might be the strongest running mate for Bush, and named a list of the most oft-mentioned possibilities. Then, with a smile, he pointed to the battery of television cameras in the rear of the ballroom: "To my friends in the media," he quipped, "if I forgot to mention someone, please list their names in your newspaper columns for me!" Even the reporters joined in the laughter.

"Dukakis," Nixon added, "may be too cerebral for the Democrats. He's tough and a good debater, but not very warm. Democrat candidates need to be like Hubert Humphrey and love the people and really mean it." As he spoke these words, he reached out his arms and wrapped them in an imaginary embrace. "I don't see this quality in Dukakis."

At the end of the questions, Nixon received another standing ovation. Guests began filing on the stage to greet Nixon and get his autograph. Another chance! I started to get in line to meet him, but Mrs. Finch (my ride home) foiled that plan: she had an appointment to keep in Pasadena.

Once again, meeting Richard Nixon must await another day.

• • •

Maurice Stans died of a heart attack at age 90 on April 14, 1998.

22

Plains

When I was 12, I joined the American Political Items Collectors (APIC), a national organization of campaign memorabilia aficionados. During the summer of 1988, a subset of APIC held their first "CPIC" (Carter Political Items Collectors) meeting in Plains, Georgia, the hometown of former President Jimmy Carter. During the weekend meet, Carter and his wife planned to join the festivities. It sounded like my kind of event.

My friend Bob Wyatt and I flew to Atlanta, and then we drove a rental car down Highway 280 to Plains. After walking around our destination for a few minutes, I found it difficult to grasp that in this modern era a peanut grower from this small, remote town could reach the White House. In Plains (population 700), things like movie theaters, fast-food establishments, and department stores didn't exist; the nearest ones were ten miles away in Americus. One could drive past Plains in the blink of an eye without taking notice—if a former president of the United States didn't live there.

• • •

Main Street consisted of a water tower and about eight small, side-by-side, brick-and-wood buildings. These structures bore historical significance in Carter's early life. At one time they housed the Carter family's peanut office, farm business, and his early county and legislative campaign offices. When I first visited in 1988, most of these buildings stood vacant. The only ones still in operation were the "Carter Worm Farm," and the antique store run by Hugh Carter (the former president's first cousin), who stocked his store with antiques and (mostly) Jimmy Carter souvenirs. Cousin Hugh sold bargain priced hand-signed, cloth-bound copies of Jimmy's early memoir, *Why Not the Best* for the original price of the book alone—$7.99. One of the locals told me later that Jimmy hated signing cartons of these books for Hugh's store, but he felt obliged to help his cousin remain in business.

A sign taped to Hugh's store window read, "President Jimmy Carter will teach the Sunday school lesson this Sunday at Maranatha Baptist Church. You are invited. 10:00 a.m." This would be an added bonus to our Plains trip.

A couple of blocks away stood Jimmy Carter's home on Woodland Drive. Trees, shrubs, and a large wrought-iron fence surrounded the single-story house. A television camera, security kiosk, and automatic guardrail blocked access. A sign directed passing tourists: *Keep Moving.*

• • •

The next morning, two dozen Carter collectors gathered under the wooden awning on Main Street and set up their "bourse" (displays of Carter campaign memorabilia for sale and trade). Unlike the bustle of the Plains I remembered from television when Carter ran for and held the White House, today no reporters, television camera crews, satellite trucks, or armies of staffers awaited his arrival. When a Ford Range Rover with tinted windows pulled up, most people didn't notice when Carter, his wife Rosalynn, and three Secret Service agents climbed out.

Carter greeted CPIC president Bobby Linzey, who in turn introduced me: "Jimmy, this is Jim Rogan. He's come the farthest—he's from California." Carter and I shook hands, and I showed him an item from my own collection: a letter I had sent him when I was 16 asking whether he would make what was then considered a very long-shot run for the presidency (the top corner of my letter bore Carter's handwritten reply to my questions).

"Mr. President," I said with a smile, "this shows I was prescient." He looked at the letter, smiled, handed it back, and then turned and walked away without saying a word.

Oh.

He ambled down the street viewing the Carter campaign memorabilia displays. Several CPIC collectors requested an autograph: "Sorry," he told each one while nodding toward the lemonade cup he held. "I've got my hands full." He made an exception to the "full hands" excuse if people asked him to sign a prepaid copy of one of his books. When a wide-eyed young boy approached nervously and asked him to sign a card, Carter refused and used the lemonade pretext.

Remembering how Carter had stiffed my own youthful request years ago, and feeling sorry for the dejected boy, I stepped forward: "I'll hold your drink for you, Mr. President," I volunteered. "Now you can sign the kid's autograph."

Carter shot me a cold stare. He handed me the cup silently, scrawled his signature for the lad, and then he took back his cup and walked off.

"Jimmy doesn't like to sign autographs," Bobby Linzey whispered to me. "He thinks people are trying to make a buck off him. He's really funny that way. He resents people asking for his autograph. He's afraid they will turn around and sell them."

"Then he should have stayed a peanut farmer," I replied. Curiously, as time went by with the collector group, Carter's signing mood swung from cold to charming and back again. One minute he refused all autograph requests icily, and the next he was smiling and signing for anyone who asked. I didn't understand what triggered the fluctuations.

During this visit, a pale, thin man dressed in blue jeans and suspenders followed closely behind Carter. His face looked worn and tired; his graying hair hung limp. I paid little attention to him at first, but as the Carters prepared to leave, I noticed someone asking the gaunt man for his autograph. The man took the pen and signed, "Billy Carter." My heart sank. I had heard earlier that the president's infamous brother (whose outlandish redneck antics during Carter's presidency presented unending press fodder) now suffered from terminal cancer. The cherubic face and beer belly I remembered from the 1970s were gone. Hollow eyes now betrayed the ravages of illness. A Secret Service agent gently helped Billy enter the van.

Mrs. Carter, an incredibly charming lady, welcomed me to Plains before she departed with her family. "I hope to see y'all in church tomorrow," she said to me.

Former President Jimmy Carter (holding his autograph-precluding lemonade cup) reviewing a display of memorabilia; brother Billy Carter is at left in striped shirt and suspenders; CPIC President Bobby Linzey stands between them, Plains, July 9, 1988. (Photograph by the author)

After the Carters departed, I returned to the bourse. Bobby introduced me to an elderly woman dressed in sweatpants and a blouse. "I want you to meet Miss Allie," he said. "This is Rosalynn's mama." Miss Allie Smith, mother of the former first lady, also welcomed me to Plains and chatted about life in their small town. "I used to be the postmaster here," she said, pointing to the small post office building down the street.

• • •

Later that morning, the assembled collectors buzzed about a local Plains resident (now running Billy Carter's former gas station) with a fistful of rare campaign buttons from Carter's unsuccessful 1966 race for Georgia governor. Throughout the morning CPIC members went to the gas station and tried to buy or trade for one of those badges, but the owner wouldn't budge. By mid-afternoon I decided to take a look. Amid glass cases stocked with Carter souvenirs for sale were several examples of the desirable Carter buttons. A sign next to them read, "For display only. Not for sale."

"Hey, how y'all doing?" called out the chuckling man behind the counter. "You here with those Carter collectors?" I introduced myself to the owner, Bobby Salter, a jovial fellow serving a joke and a story with almost every breath he took. Within minutes we became fast friends.

"Bobby," I warned as I pointed to the glass case, "I've come for one of those Carter for Governor buttons. I need one for my collection and I'm not leaving here without one."

Bobby laughed and slapped his knee. "Nobody yet has talked me out of one! They've been coming in all day, beggin' and pleadin' and offering me lots of money and great trade stuff. But those buttons are stayin' here!"

"You might as well know right now that I sold vacuum cleaners door-to-door as a boy and I never left a house without a sale, so I'm not leaving here without a badge!"

Still laughing, Bobby rocked back in his folding chair, and then he called his two clerks to come join him. "Boys," he cackled, "grab yourselves a bottle of pop and come watch this Yankee boy try to talk old Bobby out of one of those Carter badges." The two men sweeping the store pulled up stools, popped the caps off their Coke bottles, and joined Bobby.

It took over an hour, but I left with one of the badges—and made a new friendship that has lasted decades after my Plains trip ended.

In between my pleading, arguing, and cajoling, Bobby shared a few anecdotes about growing up in Plains with the Carters:

I was much closer to Billy growing up than I was to Jimmy, since Billy and I were in the same class. Truthfully, everyone in town always liked Billy much better. Billy will give you the shirt off his back. Jimmy's so tight that he'll squeeze a nickel until the buffalo jumps off! We all know Jimmy's holding the first dollar he ever earned.

Funny thing about Jimmy: we're all mighty proud one of our own became president, but Jimmy Carter has never carried his own precinct in any election he has ever run in—not for school board, not for the state legislature, not for governor of Georgia, and not for president of the United States.

The coveted 1966 Carter for Governor badge that I brought home from Plains. Don't bother asking what I traded Bobby Salter to get it. (Author's collection)

I asked Bobby how he had voted when Carter ran for president. Bobby leaned forward, cupped his hand to my ear, and whispered so his clerks couldn't hear:

"Confidentially, I'm a Reagan man."

• • •

The next day, CPIC members attended the Sunday school class Carter taught at Maranatha Baptist Church, a small brick building nestled in a charming wooded setting. We settled in a classroom to await the beginning of Carter's class. When two large buses carrying Japanese tourists arrived unexpectedly, Hugh Carter moved the class into the main sanctuary. Although small, there were enough seats for everyone in the pale green chapel, where a wooden lectern without a microphone or sound system stood in the front.

At 10:00 a.m., Jimmy and Rosalynn Carter entered from the side door near the choir loft. He walked to the lectern while Mrs. Carter sat behind me. A lone Secret Service agent sat nearby.

Former President and Mrs. Jimmy Carter outside Maranatha Baptist Church, Plains, Georgia, July 10, 1988. (Photograph by the author)

"When I entered the regular Sunday school room it was empty," Carter said, "so I thought nobody was coming to my class today!" He noted the presence of many visitors, and then he went around the room asking from where everyone came.

He put on his glasses and announced the lesson this morning would be titled "Maintaining Confidence in God" from Exodus 13:17–14:31. "Does anyone here ever worry?" he began. "Sometimes we do more than worry; sometimes we panic. That happened to me once on a duck-hunting trip when I was lost in a swamp. It took me a while to remember to ask God for guidance. The point is that we have someone who will sustain us if we only ask Him to do so. Just as the Israelites doubted the presence of God when the Egyptians chased them, we often doubt His presence when we are in need. But God is with us just as He was with the Israelites. Thus, there is no need for despair if we are working to achieve Christ's purpose in our lives."

Carter read from Exodus, joking that during his presidency, "I got to know the map of the Sinai as well as I did the map of Sumter County, Georgia." He then began quizzing the class on their knowledge of the selected reading, saying, "I hope you all did your homework." He asked if anyone knew what the Israelites carried with them during their trek. Only Mrs. Carter had the correct answer (the bones of Joseph).

Continuing with his lesson, he said, "People are afraid to be like Jesus. They fear they might be called a 'bleeding heart.' Back in the 1950s, the worst epithet one could be called around these parts was a 'nigger lover.' People avoided the epithet then, and they avoid epithets now. We shouldn't avoid being like Jesus. We can't be afraid to reach out and love people. But we are held back because we lack faith in God to protect and shield us. In Bible times, death or slavery was certain for those who trusted in the God of Israel. So trust in God has always involved a risk. Even the Israelites turned against Moses because they did not want to put their faith in God."

Carter again called out a question to the audience. When nobody volunteered an answer, I broke the awkward silence and raised my hand. He called on me. Unfortunately, I misunderstood his question. I thought he asked, "Who *are* we more like: Moses or the Israelites?" instead of what he actually asked: "Who *should* we be more like: Moses or the Israelites?"

I answered, "The Israelites."

"No," he admonished me. "We should be more like Moses." People in the audience (none of whom had braved raising their hands) nodded their vigorous agreement with him. Some looked over and frowned at me while Carter highlighted my biblical ignorance. To make things worse, I had referred accidentally to the Israelites as the "Israelis," which made them nod their heads more furiously as he pointed out that error, too. My buddy Bob patted my shoulder as he leaned over and whispered, "You'd better shut your mouth before you embarrass us more."

When Carter paused to inhale from his ongoing correction, I raised my hand. I saw eye rolls from the audience when he called on me again. I took another swing at the pitch: "When I said we are more like the Israelites, I meant that we constantly lack faith in God, despite many manifestations of His presence and love, whenever we are faced with a crisis. I agree we should be like Moses, but in our flesh we respond more like the Israelites. This is our great challenge as Christians."

Carter smiled and said he agreed with my assessment. Nearby faces chiseled in chagrin moments earlier now relaxed their cheek muscles as they looked at me and nodded approvingly. Apparently, I had leave to cancel my appointment with the Baptist Dunce Cap fitter.

At the conclusion of the class, he summarized his lesson: "How should we deal with our problems? We should ask what portion of our life we devote to serving God's will, even when such service is not in our own personal interest. Remember God's promise: He will not forsake us. His mighty hand may be seen in a strong east wind or in some other transformed miracle. No situation is too difficult for Him, and His command for us is to go forward."

After leading the class in a closing prayer, he said, "Generally, when church service is over, Rosalynn and I will pose for pictures outside if there is time. But please do not ask for autographs, because I never sign at church." He collected his notes and Bible, and then he joined Rosalynn in the pew directly behind me.

The pastor opened the regular service by leading the congregation in the hymn *Holy, Holy, Holy*. Both Carters had loud singing voices; Mrs. Carter's soprano was pleasant, but Carter's wavering baritone was simply awful—about like mine.

The service lasted an hour. At the conclusion, I followed behind the Carters as we exited church. Secret Service agents protecting Carter kept their distance. Once outside, the Carters posed for pictures with each attendee. During the photo op, Carter gave stage directions to each person when their turn came. He positioned

Former President and Mrs. Jimmy Carter with me, Maranatha Baptist Church, Plains, Georgia, July 10, 1988. (Author's collection)

me to his left for our shot. I noticed the Bible that he held had "Governor Jimmy Carter" stamped in gold on the cover.

Carter thanked me for participating during his class. I told him, "I'm sorry I needed to clarify my earlier comments, but I didn't want you to think I was sleeping through your lesson!"

"You did fine," said Mrs. Carter.

Whew!

• • •

A couple of years after I traded with Bobby Salter for that old Carter campaign badge, he invited my brother Pat and me back to Plains for a visit. Our trip coincided with another CPIC meeting and "Plains Days," an annual weekend celebration commemorating the founding of the rural community.

A carnival-like atmosphere filled the small town for the festivities. I entered the Plains Days race through town. The Carters also signed up for the run, but both canceled at the last minute. Instead, they were on hand at the finish line to greet the runners.

After the race, Pat and I chatted with Rosalynn Carter. When she saw the shield insignia on my running shirt, she asked if I was a police officer. I explained it was a Los Angeles County District Attorney badge. She smiled and said, "Jimmy and I are going to California to build Habitat for Humanity housing in San Diego and Mexico soon. You're both welcome to come and help us build."

The Carters presented the race's winner with an award at the old train depot, after which he did a brief television interview. He and Mrs. Carter then strolled hand-in-hand back to their home on Woodland Drive.

Former First Lady Rosalynn Carter with my brother Pat (at right) and me after the Plains Day race, Plains, May 19, 1990. (Author's collection)

Pat and I drove over to Andersonville to tour the cemetery and Civil War prison camp. When we returned, we found Plains deserted—strange for a town in the middle of a weekend-long celebration. When I located Bobby Salter, he told me that everyone was over at the old Plains High School for a special reunion. I grabbed my camera and walked the few blocks to the school Carter had attended 50 years earlier. There I found a large crowd of townspeople sitting in folding chairs on the grass, with Jimmy and Rosalynn Carter among them.

After joining the audience in singing the school song, the Carters went on stage and shared memories of their high school teacher, Miss Julia Coleman (whom Carter saluted in his 1977 presidential inaugural address), and school principal T. Y. Sheffield. He credited both educators with helping him achieve his later successes.

• • •

The next day, we attended Carter's Sunday school class and church services at Maranatha Baptist Church. He arrived for his lesson a few minutes late and apologized for his tardiness: "I was on the telephone with the president of the Dominican Republic. I have been back there to investigate voter fraud charges in their recent election. I've spent much time watching elections on a commission for both the Dominican Republic and for Panama. My internal clock is still a bit off, because I just flew back home to be here this weekend for the Plains Days celebration."

Former President Jimmy Carter teaching his Sunday school class, Maranatha Baptist Church, Plains, Georgia, May 20, 1990. (Photograph by the author)

Carter said his lesson would be brief, and that there would be no regular church service this morning: "In honor of Plains Days," he said, "all of the local churches will come together to conduct a joint outdoor service on Main Street at 11:00 a.m. You are all invited to join us there." He then asked if any people in the small sanctuary were visiting pastors. A man raised his hand, so Carter asked him to start the service by offering the opening prayer.

Carter's lesson came from 1 John 5:1–15. He shared the story of William Carey, the first Baptist missionary, and how it took Carey seven years to win his first convert to Jesus. "This is the fortitude

God calls us to demonstrate in the long struggle to trust and believe in Him," he noted. "We should never give up."

After the lesson, the Carters greeted everyone on the patio. Pat and I later joined them for the outdoor service on Main Street, where choirs sang hymns and pastors from each neighboring church offered prayers.

Former President and Mrs. Jimmy Carter at outdoor church services, Plains, Georgia, May 20, 1990 (Photograph by the author)

• • •

At the conclusion of the joint service, Pat and I joined Bobby and Jean Salter for lunch with their family. During this lunch, I made a historical discovery.

Bobby told me that when Carter's sister Gloria learned she had terminal cancer, she told him she wanted to sell all of her assets and give the proceeds to her church. She sold him the old abandoned Carter Warehouse on Main Street (the Carter family had used the warehouse during the 1950s and early 1960s as the operations center of their peanut business).

While cleaning the attic, he found two dirty boxes buried amid the dust. The cartons contained some of Jimmy Carter's old 1950s business records from his peanut farm. Apparently, when Carter had moved his enterprise to a new building in 1962, he had abandoned these boxes. The cartons and their contents showed extensive water, insect, and rodent damage throughout, yet despite the inadequate storage conditions, material of historic interest survived. The boxes contained hundreds of scraps of paper bearing Carter's spidery scrawl on old invoices, bank checks, diagrams, and notes.

The most significant discovery was Carter's handwritten desk calendar books for the years 1954–1961 (except 1959, which was missing). These books traced Carter's daily routine after returning home to Plains from the U.S. Navy (when his father died in 1953) to assume responsibility for the family peanut farming business. For a presidential and historic memorabilia collector, this proved the find of a lifetime.

I told Bobby the material was worth more money than I could afford. When I suggested he contact an auction house to get the best price, he balked: "I don't want this stuff going to some collector who turns around and resells it immediately. I want it to go to someone who will enjoy it for history's sake. I want you to have it." He mentioned that since Gloria Carter wanted the proceeds from the sale of the property to benefit her church, he wanted to sell the boxes to give her church the money according to her wishes. He told me to make him my best offer; I did, and he shipped the boxes to my home.

I pored over Carter's personal date books, reading them alongside Hugh Carter's biography of growing up in Plains with Jimmy. For example, Hugh Carter wrote that Jimmy's first political involvement came in 1954: after returning from the Navy, Jimmy joined the Lions Club and helped raise money to build a local swimming pool. Thumbing through Jimmy's 1954 desk diary, I found entries that chronicled these Lions Club fundraising efforts—his first steps on an unimaginable ascent to the White House. Other interesting entries memorialized Carter's sightseeing trip to Washington, D.C., (January 1958), his work as an officer overseeing an upcoming local election and getting the ballots printed (July 7, 1961), and his increasing political involvement that year when he started attending local board of education meetings.

Despite Carter's social enlightenment, hints of the 1950s segregated Georgia popped up in his handwritten entries. For example,

Carter noted he had helped get the "colored school" piano fixed (January 7, 1960). On one diary page, he listed all the people he signed up for the Red Cross blood drive, while on the next page he listed those he signed up for the "colored" blood drive. On another page he noted drafting a letter advising customers there would be an increase in the price of peanuts; on his next day's entry, he indicated he had drafted a similar—but different—message for his "colored" customers.

Also of interest were documents relating to the Wise Sanitarium, the local hospital where Carter was born on October 1, 1924. After his father's death, Carter became secretary of the Wise Corporation and kept its records until it dissolved in the 1950s. The original incorporation documents, stock certificate book, and other items were there. Inside the original stock issuance book was the receipt for one share of stock purchased for the future president, "James E. Carter, Jr.," when he was only two.

As I sifted through each sheet, a picture of Jimmy Carter emerged. Here was a man who, true to his engineering background, paid meticulous attention to every detail of the family business and accounted for every penny he spent. He threw nothing away: irrelevant scraps of paper bearing Carter's mathematical calculations and doodles were bundled with more important documents. He saved notes and letters from other businesses and recycled them as scratch paper for later use. He saved insignificant receipts, whether for a $5 gasoline purchase at the local filling station, or for a bottle of Coca-Cola. Carter or his wife, Rosalynn, docketed almost every statement received by the business. Other handwritten notes from him proved he showed no timidity in challenging suppliers he suspected of overcharging him.

Perhaps the most fascinating aspect of going through these records was realizing that a peanut farmer in a sparsely populated and rural Georgia town focusing on things like finding spare parts for a shelling machine, applying for an SBA loan (with his mother as cosigner), watching a late 1950s French soft-core porn film (by standards of that era), or wondering whether Sears Roebuck would deliver in a timely manner the adding machine he had ordered, would—within the span of two decades—negotiate nuclear disarmament accords and Middle East peace agreements. These business records represent more than a silent testimony to one man following his dream.

They represent a testimony to America.

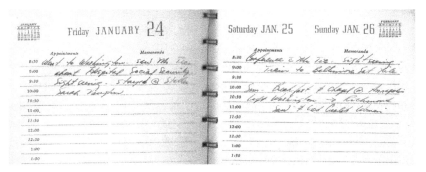

In future President Jimmy Carter's personal handwritten daybook, January 24–25, 1960, he recorded his visit to Washington, D.C. Carter noted that he stayed at the Statler Hotel; he went sightseeing for two days, saw a Sarah Vaughn concert, and then he took the train to Baltimore to attend a lunch at his alma mater, the United States Naval Academy. Later he left Washington for Richmond and saw the film, "And God Created Woman"—the French film that launched Brigitte Bardot's career as an international sex symbol. According to film historians, when distributors released the film in the United States in the late 1950s, they censored it heavily because it pushed the limits of allowable sexuality under then-American standards of decency. (Author's collection)

• • •

Two months after I met him in Plains, Billy Carter died of cancer at age 51 on September 25, 1988.

Miss Allie Smith, Rosalynn Carter's mother, died at age 94 on April 1, 2000.

23

It's Good to be Home

After Ronald Reagan left the White House, anyone wanting to meet the former president could do so on almost any Sunday by showing up for the 11:00 a.m. service at Bel Air Presbyterian Church. If in town, Reagan usually attended, and he always made time to greet people there. A friend of mine who belonged to the church invited me several times to services, and I encountered Reagan each time I went.

Bel Air Pres (as its members call it) is a lovely church nestled in the mountains above Beverly Hills. It looked like any other church on a Sunday morning with the exception of the men wearing dark glasses and discreet radio receivers in their ears congregating outside whenever "Rawhide" (the Secret Service code name for Reagan) attended.

The first time I saw Reagan at Bel Air Pres was only a month after his presidential term ended. I recognized a Secret service agent I knew from my time in the district attorney's office. He directed me to the corner of the church as a good place from which to take pictures. "The man always enters over here," he said as he walked me over to the west side of the church, where a small flight of stairs led to a pathway from the parking lot to the main entrance. "Wait here and you'll get some great photos." Two additional agents stood nearby, but they didn't keep anyone from assembling along Reagan's pathway into the sanctuary.

A black limousine pulled into the parking lot a few min-

Former President Ronald Reagan and me, Bel Air Presbyterian Church, February 26, 1989. (Author's collection)

utes before the service began. Former President and Mrs. Reagan stepped from the car without fanfare or ceremony. They walked along the path greeting everyone and signing autographs for those who asked. My agent friend introduced me to the Reagans.

When the service ended, the Reagans again greeted people outside. Mrs. Reagan moved toward the car faster than her amiable husband, who obliged each autograph collector, including the one requesting (and getting) a half dozen signatures. [Author's note: No—the collector wasn't me.] While she waited for him near the top of the stairs, we struck up a conversation. I mentioned that we once met when I was 14 at the 1972 Republican National Convention in Miami. She smiled: "That was so long ago," she said. "A lot of water has gone over the dam for us since then."

I held out my arms in mock surprise. "Mrs. Reagan, that was only 16 years ago—don't you remember me? I was wearing a blue jacket that night!"

She laughed; "Oh, sure, of course! Now I remember you!"

The Reagans approached their car and waved goodbye to the small applauding crowd. An older man called out, "Welcome home, Ronnie! It's good to have you back!"

Reagan turned to the small applauding crowd and responded: "And it's good to be home!"

• • •

Bobby Linzey, the longtime Jimmy Carter supporter who had organized our earlier memorabilia collectors' visit to Carter's hometown in Georgia (see my previous chapter, *Plains*), visited me in 1989 and wanted to meet Reagan. Reminding him of Carter's rather icy attitude when he had introduced me in Plains to the man Reagan had vanquished, I told him teasingly, "I'll take you to meet a *real* president."

When the Reagans arrived at their church that Sunday, they mingled as usual with the small group of waiting admirers. Bobby had a chance to meet them both. When he admired Reagan's cowboy tie pin, Reagan treated him to a mini fashion show. He showed Bobby his cuff links depicting a horse and said, "These cuff links and tie pin remind me of my ranch when I'm in the big city."

Thanks to my friend Bob Finch (Reagan's former lieutenant governor), Reagan knew that I was a young prosecutor whom GOP party leaders had mentioned as a future candidate for office, so he invited us to join the service.

Inside the sanctuary, Reagan chose his usual seat.[1] We sat alongside him on the opposite aisle. During the service, he closed his eyes and dozed off repeatedly. However, when the congregation sang *America the Beautiful*, the *Doxology*, and *Battle Hymn of the Republic*, nobody sang with heartier gusto than he.

At one point in the service he nodded off again. I watched with amusement when a beautiful young woman in a clinging red sweater, short dress, black nylons, and stiletto heels entered the sanctuary and walked slowly to her seat a few rows in front of Reagan and me. The scent of her wafting perfume caused him to perk up. His gaze fixed on her every move, he looked her up and down, and he even straightened his back and rose slightly in his seat to have a

---

1   Memo to Bel Air Presbyterian church historians: As one enters the sanctuary, Reagan always sat on the left side of the church, aisle seat, third row from the back.

better look when she took her place in a forward pew. Mrs. Reagan appeared unaware of her husband's sudden wakefulness.

• • •

Later that day, as Bobby recounted his experience, I asked if he had changed his mind about Reagan.

"Well," he replied, "I'm still a Carter man through and through. But I hate to admit it—he sure is a nice fellow. He even signed a few autographs for me."

Yes, he did. And, as I reminded Bobby, unlike a mildly cranky former president we met together in Plains the previous year, I didn't have to hold Ronald Reagan's lemonade cup to get him to do it.

24

He Remembered Me

After he left the White House in 1989, I had the chance to meet Ronald Reagan privately in his office a few times. The first time, in August of that year, was again thanks to my friend Bob Finch (Reagan's former lieutenant governor during the former president's first term in the Sacramento statehouse).

Bob, who set up the meeting, told Reagan about my Party switch and his belief that I might make a good GOP candidate down the road. Finch instructed me to give Reagan a copy of my recent article on why I had changed parties from Democrat to Republican. "I told Reagan he needs to read it," Finch said. "Reagan's an old ex-Democrat himself, so he'll like it a lot."

On the morning of our meeting, Christine and I had a disagreement about a gift I had for the former chief executive. With his presidential library currently under construction, I wanted to donate an item to his archives from my political memorabilia collection. I settled on a pair of Reagan slippers. Each shoe looked like a bed covered with a flag-designed comforter; poking out from under the covers and resting on a pillow was a rubber head—a smiling Reagan in a nightcap was on one slipper, and his wife Nancy on the other. I planned to hand-carry the gift in a plain brown shopping bag.

"If you carry those hideous slippers with you, especially in that awful brown bag," she warned me, "I'll wait in the car. You'll embarrass yourself." As a compromise, I promised not to present the gift unless Reagan's staff approved in advance.

Along with the slippers in the grocery bag, I also carried large pieces of cardboard to protect the two Reagan campaign posters that I wanted him to autograph. In Christine's eyes, this added insult to injury: "You want to visit President Reagan carrying a brown paper shopping bag and cardboard?" She shook her head and asked, "Are you *trying* to look homeless?"

We drove to Reagan's office in Century City and took the private elevator directly to the 34th floor for our 11:45 a.m. meeting. When the doors opened, I thought we might be at the wrong place. Nothing in the bare room suggested we had entered Ronald Reagan's suite. To the left was a door with a glass and wire mesh window and a telephone on the wall. A lone receptionist was visible on the other side of the window. The only clue to our location was the jellybean jar I spied on her desk (Reagan's love for jellybeans made their jars standard White House desktop décor during his administration).

I picked up the phone and identified myself. She buzzed us through and invited us to wait in an anteroom decorated with photographs of Reagan alongside various world leaders. She said the entire floor was a secure area housing the private offices of Ronald and Nancy Reagan, as well as the Ronald Reagan Library Foundation.

An aide escorted us through a second security door and invited us to wait outside Reagan's private office. Remembering my promise to Christine, I opened the brown bag and produced the slippers for approval. I asked if she thought it an appropriate gift. "Oh, absolutely!" she exclaimed. "He'll love them! He's seen a picture of these slippers but he doesn't have a pair and he wants them. We were trying to find them for him." I turned to Christine and smirked.

The door to Reagan's office was cracked open. From inside we overheard him talking with another man. "President Reagan's with his ghostwriter, Edmund Morris," she said. "He's dictating his memoirs right now. I'll let him know you are here." A few moments later, Morris left the office and nodded a greeting to us. He sat on a couch and flipped through a magazine as another aide approached: "President Reagan will see you now."

Ever the political collector junkie, as we entered Reagan's office I noted his memorabilia

Slippers fit for a president: my gift to The Gipper, August 1989. (Author's collection)

decorating the room. On a coffee table sat a silver tray with an engraved replica of the 1981 presidential inauguration invitation. The bookcases behind his desk housed an assortment of Remington miniature bronze saddles, along with autographed photographs from England's Queen Elizabeth and Prince Charles, British Prime Minister Margaret Thatcher, and Japanese Emperor Hirohito. Family photographs crowded his credenza; an unattractive green and brown mountain landscape painting hung over his chair (the same chair he had used in Sacramento and in the Oval Office). On his desk sat a gold eagle that once belonged to President John F. Kennedy (given to Reagan by Senator Edward Kennedy). Binders, folders, calendars, and notepads cluttered the work area. I recognized the brass plaque from his Oval Office desk that read, "There is no end to what a man can accomplish if he does not mind who gets the credit."

Wearing a green and red plaid jacket, gray slacks, and a red necktie, Reagan rose from his desk and welcomed us. He looked tall, sturdy, and much younger than his 78 years. The only concessions to advancing age I noticed were the touches of gray now streaking through his otherwise dark hair, and a miniature hearing aid concealed in his ear.

An office photographer followed behind us and suggested we take a group photograph. As she focused her lens, Reagan posed the shot: "Let's put Christine in the middle," he said. "If she is between us, it will be a prettier picture."

"If you and I get out of the picture, Mr. President," I replied, "it will be even prettier."

To Jim and Christine Reagan
With best wishes,
Ronald Reagan

President Ronald Reagan, Christine, and me, Office of President Reagan, Century City, California, August 3, 1989. (Author's collection)

After the photo op, I made the presentation Christine dreaded, telling Reagan about my memorabilia collection and desire to give him a memento for his library collection. When I removed the slippers from the shopping bag and handed them to him, he laughed as he studied them. "Well," he said, "these are wonderful. There is just one problem with them: I'm sleeping in one slipper, and Nancy is sleeping in the other. I don't think she will like the separation!"

To sign my two campaign posters, Reagan spread them across his desk. He studied the first poster, which was a color jugate from his 1984 reelection campaign depicting him alongside his running mate, George Bush. "I'll sign over my head," he said. "This way,

I'll leave room if you ever want to have this other guy sign it," he said with a wink as he pointed to Bush's picture. He inscribed the poster with slow, deliberate pen strokes. He stopped writing when he reached my last name and began fumbling through his schedule trying to remember it. I could tell he was stuck.

"Mr. President," I reminded him, "it's Rogan, R-O-G-A-N. Just like 'Reagan,' only with an 'o.'"

President Reagan and I share a laugh over the slippers, August 3, 1989. Christine is not in the picture because once I picked up the brown paper bag to give them to him, she stepped as far away from me as possible. (Author's collection)

He looked up and smiled. "You know," he said, "I once looked at research on the derivation of the Reagan name. It was pretty comprehensive. It told all about the Reagan heritage and where all the families hailed from, mainly from Ireland and Scotland. It also covered the history of all my close cousins—the 'Regans,' the 'Ragens,' and of course, the 'Rogans.' So this one is just for you, cousin!"

He said the second poster was special to him. It was the most graphically beautiful produced during his 1980 presidential campaign. Captioned *America: Reagan Country*, it showed a color photograph of him wearing a cowboy hat. Surrounding his image were sketches of Americana scenes. He started to sign the poster on the Statue of Liberty sketch and then caught himself, saying, "I have to be very careful not to mark on this lady. Nancy and I were invited to the centennial celebration of the Statue of Liberty in New York in 1985. The statue was the most beautiful sight I had ever seen, with her all lit up and fireworks exploding over her head. Later we flew over her in a helicopter, and it was an even more beautiful sight from the air. I leaned over to Nancy and told her, 'Honey, there will always be two ladies in my life.'"

"America: Reagan Country" poster that President Reagan signed for me. Lady Liberty—Reagan's other love—is on the opposite side of where he inscribed it. (Author's collection)

He told us that these days he kept busy writing his memoirs. I said I hoped that his book would answer my question: "Mr. President, you are one of the few men in history called to assume the awesome duties of the presidency. I have often wondered what goes through a man's mind when he stands on the steps of the Capitol with his hand raised and takes the oath of office for that job."

"You won't have to wait for my book to learn that answer," he said, smiling. "I will tell you right now exactly what I was thinking. I was praying for guidance and wisdom. I was just praying silently the whole time I took the oath."

"Judging from your accomplishments, I'd say God answered your prayers."

Before leaving, I gave him an envelope with a copy of my earlier article that he had requested. "As another ex-Democrat," I said, "you might appreciate this." He thanked me and put the envelope in his jacket pocket, and then he asked,

Do you know the story of how I first registered Republican? Here's how it happened. I had always been a liberal Democrat, but in the 1950s I began to feel my Party had left me. In 1960, I headed Democrats for Nixon. Although I voted for Nixon, I never changed my registration after the election.

In 1962 I was speaking for Nixon's gubernatorial campaign in some auditorium. An old lady in the audience raised her hand to ask a question. I called on her and she yelled out, "Have you changed your registration yet?" I confessed I had been too busy and hadn't changed.

"Well," she said, "I'm a voter registrar!" With that, she marched onstage with a form in her hand and she reregistered me on the spot! She returned to her seat to a standing ovation.

When it came time to resume my speech, I forgot where I had left off. I asked the audience, "Now, where was I?"

We thanked him for the visit. As Christine and I were leaving, I looked back before closing the door and saw him sitting at his desk opening the envelope I had handed him.

• • •

To my delight, Reagan read my article. More significantly, he liked it.

A couple of days after meeting him, I returned home from work and found a full-page handwritten letter awaiting me. It read in part:

August 3, 1989

Dear Jim:

I haven't the words to properly describe how impressed I am with your article. Thank you for giving such an account of what has actually happened to the political parties in our land in your article. Like you, I left the Democrat Party, and like you I don't believe we changed. We still support the same beliefs we always held, but the party leadership set off on an entirely different course. It is this that you so eloquently explained. It is the best and most complete exposition I have seen of the philosophical reversal of the Democrat Party.

Your essay should be the basis for freeing up Democrats who are discontented but still not aware of how far their party leadership has turned from what they as individuals believe. After dealing with a Democrat majority in the House of Representatives for eight years—a majority they've had for 55 of the last 59 years—I can't help but think our very safety requires that your exposition be widely distributed.

I want you to know that I'll be quoting from your essay on my own mashed-potato circuit lectures.

My very best to Christine and again my thanks to you.

Sincerely,

Ronald Reagan

RONALD REAGAN

Aug. 3 - '89

Dear Jim

I haven't the words to properly describe how impressed I am both with your letter and your article. Thank you for sharing your life with me in the letter, and for giving such an account of what has actually happened to the political parties in our land in your article.

Like you I left the Dem. party and like you I don't believe we changed. We still support the same beliefs we always held but the party leadership set off on an entirely different course. It is this that you so eloquently explained in your article. It is the best and most complete exposition I have seen of the philosophical reversal of the Dem. party.

Your essay should be the basis for freeing up Democrats who are discontented but still not aware of how far their party leadership has turned from what they as individuals believe. After dealing with a Dem. majority in the House of Representatives for 8 yrs. a majority they've had for 55 of the last 59 years I can't help but think our very safety requires that your exposition be widely distributed. I want you to know that I'll be quoting from your essay on my own mashed-potato circuit lectures.

My very best to Christine and again my thanks to you.

Sincerely Ronald Reagan

Reagan's generous comments left me humbled. Remembering how long it took for Reagan to inscribe a poster for me, I speculated on the time expended in penning this comprehensive letter. I showed it to Christine, who read it with tears in her eyes. This caused me to puff with pride.

"So," I asked her, "you like what The Gipper wrote about your husband, eh?"

"Truthfully, I wasn't paying any attention to what he wrote about you," she replied. "I'm crying because of this part here—'My very best to Christine.'

"He remembered me!"

• • •

Weeks later, I watched a cable news broadcast of Ronald Reagan giving a speech somewhere. He stunned me when I heard him using language right out of my article on the fundamental differences between Democrats and Republicans. Reagan proved true to his word: he really did quote me on his own mashed-potato circuit. The only thing I didn't hear as he finished his speech was any mention that those words came from me!

I didn't mind. Since he once gave me his speech notes at the Boundary Oak clubhouse in Walnut Creek back in 1973,[1] it was only fair that I now give him mine.

---

1   If you are reading these chapters out of order, see my story on encountering Ronald Reagan at the Boundary Oak clubhouse in the previous chapter, *My Governor*.

25

Spanky and the Boss

For five generations, audiences have laughed at the antics of those irrepressible kids from producer Hal Roach's *Our Gang* comedy films made in the 1920s–1940s (later dubbed *The Little Rascals* for television syndication). Of the many child actors who came and went during the life of the classic series, perhaps the best known and most beloved was George "Spanky" McFarland, the chubby leader of the gang. Along with pals Alfalfa, Buckwheat, Darla, Butch, and others, the Gang stumbled from one hilarious childhood circumstance to another.

After a decade of starring in these comedy short subjects, Spanky became a Hollywood has-been at age 14 in 1942. He and his family moved back to Texas, and for the next 50 years he worked in various sales jobs while making occasional guest appearances on television and at Hollywood memorabilia shows.

When executing his 1930s movie contracts with the Hal Roach Studios, Spanky's parents signed away the rights to his name and image forever. Decades later, Spanky filed strings of lawsuits against people and companies using his childhood image. It galled him that these legal efforts hit repeated brick walls. That was how we first met: I did some legal work for him as a young lawyer in the early 1980s, and we kept in touch afterward.

During the years I knew him, he called often to update me on his newest litigation battles and to complain about his most recent failure in preventing someone from using his likeness for commercial purposes. Despite the realities of his original contractual terms and the discouraging results he encountered, he kept at it. "I'm damned tired of people getting rich off me and my work after all these years," he told me in exasperation. "My name and face are *mine*." Sadly, I don't think he ever found a judge or jury that agreed with him.

In March 1991, he called and told me he was coming to Los Angeles the next day to shoot a television commercial for Quality Inn motels. "They have me climbing out of a damned suitcase," he complained, "but what the hell. The money's good." He invited me to join him for lunch. Although our friendship had by now dated back years, this would be our first face-to-face meeting.

I picked him up in front of his hotel. Now in his sixties, he looked like an older version of the still-roly-poly boy remembered by his fans.

George "Spanky" McFarland and me catching up over lunch in Hollywood, March 28, 1991. (Author's collection)

We drove to the Daily Grill in Hollywood for lunch, where most of our conversation centered on several new lawsuits that he filed against businesses that had again appropriated his name and likeness. Since the canons of ethics precluded me (as a sitting state court judge) from dispensing legal advice, I listened while he shared his frustration with lawyers and the legal system. He told me that litigation had become such a major part of his existence that he couldn't focus on writing a long-intended book about his Hollywood experiences.

After polishing off our hamburgers, and before dropping him off at a rental car agency, we drove by his former home at 1616 Queens Road in West Los Angeles. "Here is where I lived when I was a kid working on the Roach lot," he said. "A studio limousine picked me up for work every day, and I would get the driver to race down these winding streets each morning." He said that members of the pop-music group The Jackson 5 later bought the house, and that he had his picture taken with singer Michael Jackson standing on the balcony.

As we drove, he set aside his legal travails briefly to talk about his relationship with "Alfalfa" (Carl Switzer), another beloved character from the *Our Gang* series. According to him, Alfalfa was beloved only by his movie fans. "Alfalfa was a kid who was always in trouble," he explained:

He was such bad news that my mother wouldn't let me play with him. We weren't friends off the set. He could be a mean little bastard even when he was a kid. He used to go up on the catwalk above the set and piss down on the hot klieg lights and the crew.

When the Gang movies ended, I moved home to Texas. I never saw him again until 1957 at a reunion show. That was two years before he died.

When Alfalfa wasn't working, he had trouble with alcohol. He was the kind of guy who would steal a truck filled with wood, then try to sell the wood door-to-door. [In 1959 he died] when he pulled a knife on his business partner in a dispute over a $50 debt. The partner shot and killed him. He was trouble right to the end.

• • •

Movie producer Hal E. Roach created the *Our Gang–Little Rascals* film treasury. Nicknamed "The Boss" by the actors and crew who worked on Roach's "Lot of Fun," he began his film career in 1912 when he did extra work in silent films. Within a couple of years he started his own production company that became the premiere comedy factory in Hollywood. Harold Lloyd, Will Rogers, Jean Harlow, and Charley Chase were some of the actors in his stable. Aside from discovering them and creating the *Our Gang* comedies, he also paired as a team two of his minor contract players. This union gave the world perhaps the best-loved comedy duo in film history: Stan Laurel and Oliver Hardy.

Hal Roach remained the last living witness to Hollywood's transition from fruit orchards to entertainment Mecca. In 1990 I traveled to Catalina Island for a celebration of Stan Laurel's centenary. While attending a special showing of Stan and Ollie movies at the Avalon Theatre, an elderly man seated in front of me laughed heartily at the comedy antics on-screen. At the end of the showing, the house lights came up and the emcee announced, "Ladies and gentlemen, all these films will live forever because of the vision and foresight of the movie pioneering genius who created and produced these classic treasures, Hal Roach. Mr. Roach will celebrate his 100th birthday next year and we are honored to have him with us tonight. Please welcome Mr. Hal Roach." The audience rose in an ovation, and the old man seated in front of me who had laughed throughout the films stood and waved.

Later that evening, Roach attended Laurel's celebratory birthday banquet in the Carno Ballroom. Inviting me to join him at his table for coffee and cigars, he introduced me to Eddie Quillan, a character actor from the 1930s and 1940s most noted for his role in the classic film *The Grapes of Wrath*. During our visit Quillen appeared drawn and fatigued; two weeks later he suffered a fatal heart attack.

Movie producer Hal E. Roach (looking decades younger than his 99 years) and me, Catalina Island, June 15, 1990. (Author's collection)

The party remained in full swing long past dinner. When I bid Roach goodnight around midnight, he was still holding court at his table, smoking thin cigars, signing autographs for fans, and greeting well-wishers. I later learned that The Boss stayed until the celebration ended after 2:00 a.m.

• • •

In the fall of 1992, Spanky called and said he planned to visit Los Angeles to meet with his onetime boss Hal Roach (now almost 101). "I've only seen the old man once in 50 years," he told me, "and that was when I presented him his honorary Academy Award in 1984. I've never had the chance to sit and talk to him one-on-one as an adult, so this could be an interesting meeting. I want you to come with me."

As it turned out, the desired reunion with his former employer had a motivation beyond nostalgia. He wanted Roach to sign an affidavit regarding the interpretation of a 1936 contract between Roach Studios and Spanky's parents. Spanky felt the document would help in his pending lawsuit against yet another business using his name. "Some bastards in New Jersey have opened a bar called 'Spanky McFarland's,'" he griped. "They're using my name and likeness, and a statement from Roach might help me in the lawsuit." Although I doubted a contemporaneous affidavit regarding a half-century-old contract would have much legal heft, especially since Roach had disposed of his rights to the *Our Gang* films decades earlier, any excuse to visit Roach was good enough for me.

On the appointed day, I picked up Spanky and his wife Doris at the Beverly Hilton Hotel where they were staying for the weekend. As we exited, we encountered about a hundred movie fans awaiting the celebrity arrivals for the American Cinema Awards being held at the hotel that evening. Someone behind the rope line outside the entrance recognized Spanky and asked him to come over and sign autographs. He waved them off and grumbled to me that these "autograph hounds" would pester him throughout his stay.

We drove through the winding roads leading to Roach's Beverly Hills home and parked in front of the single-story ranch-style house overlooking a hilltop at 1183 Stradella Lane. Roach's nurse, Don Aho, greeted us at the front door and led us into the living room, which was decorated unpretentiously with worn furniture. Stacks of magazines and inexpensive photo albums lay in piles on tabletops. In the midst of this clutter stood Roach's special Oscar, bookended by photographs of Roach with President Reagan.

Aho escorted Roach into the living room. Leaning on his metal cane and moving slowly, Roach wore hearing aids in each ear. When he saw Spanky, his face brightened and he shuffled quickly toward his portly discovery. Embracing him warmly, he patted Spanky's girth and chuckled, "You haven't slimmed down since you were five years old!"

"The Boss" settled into his chair and told Aho to serve us drinks. A few minutes later, Aho returned with a tray of Diet Cokes. "Spike mine with some vodka," Roach instructed his nurse. Then he turned and said to me with a grin, "I'm almost 101 years old. At this age, I'll have some vodka when I want it!" Spanky asked for his the same way.

Spanky and "The Boss" holding Roach's honorary Academy Award, September 11, 1992. (Photograph by the author)

Roach said he wanted some photographs taken with his guests and produced two cameras, but one was broken and the other had no film. Fortunately, I had brought mine to record the reunion. Roach liked my suggestion that he and Spanky pose with Roach's Academy Award; I handed the heavy Oscar to Spanky and he held it aloft as my shutter clicked.

Roach pointed to actor Roddy McDowall's oversized book on the coffee table that compiled celebrity photographs coupled with tributes from other stars who knew them. Printed next to the photograph McDowall took of Roach was Spanky's testimonial. Roach handed the book to Spanky and asked him to read it aloud. As Spanky recited his homage to "the man who gave me my first job when I was five years old," his voice broke and both men wept.

Once Aho served the drinks, Roach lit a cigar and spoke generally about the old days of filmmaking. He said people had often tried to buy or borrow his film rights. He joked about taking a trip years earlier to Germany where a film producer had given him an envelope stuffed with cash while requesting the rights to exhibit his films. Roach turned to Spanky and said, "Never sign away your likeness or film rights. They are worth a fortune now." This comment served as an introduction to the business purpose of the meeting.

Spanky told Roach about his pending New Jersey lawsuit, and then he handed Roach the affidavit that he wanted signed. As Roach took the document, he smiled and said, "I'll sign it without even reading it!" Despite this comment, he reviewed the document carefully before scratching his signature on it. "I hope this will help you," he said as he handed it back.

Spanky produced several photographs of the Boss and asked Roach to sign them for family members. Roach obliged and penned his name slowly on the pictures. While he signed, he invited me to tour his trophy room and den. There I saw memorabilia and dozens of inscribed photographs framed on the wall: Bette Davis, Cary Grant, Franklin D. Roosevelt, Walt Disney, and Lucille Ball were there alongside pictures of Roach dining with Laurel and Hardy and playing polo with Will Rogers. A presidential commission signed by Harry Truman was displayed amid countless plaques and awards. In the midst of all was a framed poster depicting the *Our Gang* children.

Over in a corner, Aho showed me boxes on the floor filled with stacks of photographs of Roach. He invited me to select a couple to have The Boss sign for me. When I asked where all the pictures came from, he pointed to a separate four-foot-high stack of envelopes: "This is fan mail that's come in," he said. "The old man signs maybe two or three things a day. The rest go in this pile and are never returned. He just can't do much of this anymore."

Using his cane, Roach joined me in the den and gave me a guided tour of his mementos. I pointed to an oversized photograph of a scowling, bald man in a tuxedo and with his arms folded across his chest. The photo bore a lengthy but undecipherable inscription in white ink. "Mr. Roach," I said as I pointed to the picture, "I recognize this man, but I can't place him. Is this [pioneer film director and actor] Erich von Stroheim?"

Roach bent over and studied the photograph closely. Suddenly, his eyes welled with tears. He looked at me and said, "That was my dear friend—Mussolini! He was a very great man and a dear friend." The Italian Fascist dictator America had battled in World War II was Roach's dear friend? He caught me off guard with his warm feelings for a man whose countrymen so despised him that they hung him from his ankles in the middle of the town square and desecrated his corpse after they had killed him. "Mr. Roach," I said with a grin, "you are probably the only man alive today who not only can say you knew Mussolini as a friend, but who would admit to it!"

Roach shrugged off my comment and shared some insights into his relationship with *Il Duce*:

During my visit to Italy in the 1930s, I was summoned to meet Mussolini. I had only seen him in the newsreels, which depicted him as a ranting tyrant who would puff himself up like a big blowfish during his speeches. When I walked into his office, I entered a long room with only a desk and chair at the far end. He sat scowling at me as I approached. But he was full of crap and I knew it! He was acting for me, and I can always spot an actor. As I drew closer, my smile grew larger as his scowl grew deeper. Finally we were face-to-face. I had such a huge broad smile, and he had such a mean scowl! I knew he was a faker, and he knew I knew it. So he finally smiled and shook my hand, and from then on we were friends.

One night at dinner I sat next to Mussolini's wife. Mussolini sat across from me and next to his mistress. He kept fondling and groping his mistress during dinner. Mrs. Mussolini seemed oblivious to all this and showed no concern for her husband's behavior. Finally, I leaned over and said to Mrs. Mussolini, "Look,

I don't mean to pry, but doesn't it bother you that your husband is so intimate with this woman?"

Mrs. Mussolini appeared confused that I would even ask such a question and replied in great seriousness, "I am but a mere woman; he is Mussolini! How can one woman ever hope to please the great Mussolini? It is an honor just to be married to him."

When I told Roach that Mussolini obviously had his wife trained better than I could ever train mine, he laughed at my joke and slapped his knee. (Later that night I recounted this story to Christine. Without missing a beat, she looked me up and down, and then she replied dryly, "You're no Mussolini.")

Roach invited me to sit with him in the den. We settled into cozy armchairs as he reminisced about my favorite comedians, Laurel and Hardy. I asked him when he stopped making their films. He replied blandly, "When it wasn't worth it anymore."

Trying to interpret his comment and draw him out further, I suggested, "Oh, you mean their style of comedy had become passé after a while and was no longer marketable at the box office?" He leaned toward me, puffed his slender cigar, and then he corrected my misinterpretation:

No, that's not what I mean at all. I mean that when those two dumb bastards decided they knew more about making comedies than I did, that's when it wasn't worth it anymore, and that's when I stopped making their pictures! Neither one of them was any great brain. All Hardy liked to do was golf, and all Laurel liked to do was fish.

Spanky joined us and asked him why the Laurel and Hardy films have endured. "That one's easy," Roach chuckled:

Most producers who put together a comedy team had one funny guy and one straight man. With Laurel and Hardy, we had two comedians and no straight man. When Stan did something funny, we got a laugh.

Here I am with Spanky and The Boss, September 11, 1992. (Author's collection)

Then I had the camera cut to Babe [Hardy's nickname], and we got a laugh from his reaction. Then we cut back to Stan and got another laugh from his reaction to Babe. So you got three laughs for the price of one.

Roach told a story of taking a Catalina fishing trip with Stan on Laurel's yacht during their heyday:

This one's a little dirty. We were on the ship and Stan introduced me to a beautiful young woman. He said, 'She's the nicest woman I ever met. I met her at 6 p.m. and we were in bed having sex by 7 p.m.' Stan later married her. He married many times. Women were crazy about him for some reason. I never understood it. On screen he was such a little crybaby. Yet when Laurel and Hardy went on tour, the women went mad over him.

Switching subjects, Roach nodded toward Spanky and told me how he came up with the idea of making the *Our Gang* films:

One day I was listening to this awful audition of a little girl. She was heavily made up, and I only tolerated her because she was the daughter of a friend. When the audition was done, I told her the usual answer we gave people back then: "Don't call us; we'll call you." After she left my office, I wandered over to the window and looked out at the lumberyard across the street where a bunch of kids played. Two of them were having a life-and-death argument over a scrap of wood.

Later, I looked down at my watch and realized that I had been watching them for 20 minutes! I couldn't understand why I would be so interested in just watching a bunch of kids do what kids do. Then I started to think that maybe a film audience would like to watch kids just be kids. I told my employees to round up a bunch of kids and test them. We made the first film, Our Gang, and it was a huge success. The rest is history.

I did the same thing with Laurel and Hardy. People liked the Our Gang films because they got to watch kids being kids. They liked Laurel and Hardy because they got to watch adults be kids. It was the same formula.

"The funny thing about my career," he added, "is that everyone remembers me for the comedy shorts. Nobody remembers that I did some serious and great feature films too, like *Of Mice and Men, Topper, Captain Fury,* and *One Million Years BC*."

While we visited, the teenage son of Roach's cook played with a basketball in the rear yard. Roach urged me to go out and shoot baskets with the boy. He positioned his chair so he could watch our brief pickup game from the window. After ten minutes he called me back inside. "I'm tired today," he said, and then he pointed to his swimming pool. "I usually swim twice a day in the pool for exercise, but not today. I'm too damned tired."

Roach's nurse whispered to me, "The old man had been in pretty good shape until recently. He really did swim twice a day for exercise, but no more."

• • •

Our visit with Roach lasted over two hours. The conversation was fascinating, but I saw his energy fading. We returned with him to the living room when the time came to leave. Spanky kissed the old man on the forehead and said goodbye. They held hands and lingered for a couple of minutes and became teary-eyed at what both knew was a last farewell.

"Take care of my boy here, Judge!" Roach instructed me. He took my hand in his and patted it with the other. "It means a lot that you both came to see me."

"To our best Judge." Photo signed for me by Hal Roach during our visit to his home, September 11, 1992. (Author's collection)

• • •

Before we left, Roach asked me to send him a set of the pictures we had taken that day with my camera. A few weeks later, after I had the film processed and the prints made, I sent them to Don Aho. I asked him to give one set of pictures to Roach, and to ask The Boss to autograph two extras for me.

Aho returned my signed photographs bearing Roach's shaky autograph on them. His signature had deteriorated substantially since he had signed a picture for me during our visit. In his letter, Aho apologized for the poor quality of the autograph, explaining that the old man's health had declined significantly since Spanky's and my visit.

Hal Roach died two weeks later, on November 2, 1992, just short of his 101st birthday. While battling pneumonia, he suffered a fatal heart attack at his Stradella Lane home.

• • •

When I heard the news, I called Spanky to offer condolences. Sounding very down, he said he had been giving interviews to reporters all day, and that he was flying to California the next day for the funeral. He asked me to join him there.

We met for the service on November 4 at St. Paul the Apostle Church in Westwood. While waiting in the parking lot for Spanky, I ran into Don Aho. He told me that the old man had started slipping the very day we came over. Despite his increasing frailties, Roach had told him that morning, "Clean me up and make me look alive for Spanky's visit." Aho said that we were Roach's final visitors.

Hal Roach and me in his den, September 11, 1992. This was the last photograph ever taken of him, and it bears the last autograph he ever signed (he appears to have added his age—100). (Photo taken by Spanky McFarland; author's collection)

"More important than that," he said, "those photographs you took of Roach during your visit were the last ones ever taken of the old man. He never posed for another picture. Also, the ones he signed for you a couple weeks ago were the last autographs he ever signed. I brought them to him on his sickbed, and he insisted on signing them himself even though he could barely write any longer. He said he *had* to do it personally—he said that he didn't want the judge to hold him in contempt of court!"

Aho went inside the church with Roach's family. A few minutes later, I connected with Spanky in the crowded parking lot. One of the priests from the church asked me to take his picture with the former child star.

Spanky and I sat together during the service. He reminisced frequently about our meeting with Roach, and his eyes kept filling with tears as he talked about the man who gave him his start in movies. He also pointed out the other mourners with whom he had worked in the *Our Gang* movies: former child stars Dorothy "Echo" DeBorba, Tommy "Butch" Bond, Eugene "Pineapple" Jackson, and Mary Ann Jackson. One of early television's comedy pioneers, Sid Caesar, sat alongside longtime television talk show host Mike Douglas in the pew in front of us. "I was on Mike Douglas' show 20 years ago with Darla Hood [another Our Gang alumnus]," Spanky noted. "It was the last show she did before she died of a heart attack."

After the service, Spanky gave interviews and signed autographs on the front steps of the church. A slender, bald, elderly man approached us. "Spanky!" he said, "Don't you remember me?"

Spanky registered no recognition. "Uh, no, sorry."

The man smiled broadly: "It's me! Darwood Kaye—I played 'Waldo' in the *Gang* films with you!"

Spanky gasped. "Waldo! I haven't seen you in 50 years!" They hugged, laughed, and cried together. Waldo told us that he had spent his post-Hollywood decades in ministry as a Seventh-Day Adventist pastor. Their animated conversation grew somber when they noted how few of their costars still lived.

After the service, Spanky and I drove into downtown Westwood for dinner at Hamburger Hamlet. Since he never had the chance to have Roach sign the pictures we took during our meeting, I surprised him with one that I had Roach sign. He wept so much over the gift that I took it out of his hands.

"Geez, Spanky," I chided him, "get a grip on yourself—you're going to smear the autograph."

• • •

The following spring, Spanky came to Los Angeles to film an episode of the long-running television comedy sitcom, *Cheers*. After the shooting, he drove to my home in Glendale and spent the entire afternoon and evening with us. He said he enjoyed filming his cameo appearance. "They treated me well at the studio," he said. "I've

Our final visit: Spanky McFarland and me in the dining room of my Glendale, California home, March 14, 1993. He signed this photograph for me one week before his death on June 30, 1993. (Photograph by Christine Rogan; author's collection)

enjoyed being back before the cameras so much that I would like to pick up more studio work." He hoped that word of mouth around Hollywood might let people know he was available, but he rejected my suggestion that he get an agent. "They're all crooks," he snorted.

Christine and I sent him home to Texas with a suitcase filled with fresh avocados from our backyard tree. He said he planned another Southern California visit in the fall, and we put the date on the calendar for his return visit.

It wasn't to be. Three months after our last visit, Spanky suffered a massive heart attack at home and died at age 64 on June 30, 1993. He had survived The Boss by only seven months.

• • •

A year after *Our Gang* child star Darwood "Waldo" Smith and I met at Hal Roach's funeral, he served as a juror on one of my criminal trials in Division 3 of the Glendale, California courthouse. He died at age 72 on May 15, 2002 after a hit-and-run driver struck him.

Our Gang child star Dorothy "Echo" DeBorba died at age 85 of emphysema on June 2, 2010.

Our Gang child star Tommy "Butch" Bond died at age 79 of heart disease on September 24, 2005.

Our Gang child star Eugene "Pineapple" Jackson died at age 84 of a heart attack on October 26, 2001.

Our Gang child star Mary Ann Jackson died at age 80 of a heart attack on December 17, 2003.

Comedian and television pioneer Sid Caesar died at age 91 on February 12, 2014.

Talk show host and singer Mike Douglas died at age 86 on August 11, 2006.

26

Kennedy's Lincoln

In 1991, I brought Christine to Washington for her first visit to our nation's capital. Five years later, we moved there when I won a seat in Congress, but on that initial trip we remained tourists. Despite the vacation nature of our visit, the tug of history proved irresistible, and we enjoyed a memorable evening steeped in it.

On the 28th anniversary of President John F. Kennedy's assassination, I scheduled dinner with Evelyn Lincoln, who served as Kennedy's personal secretary for 12 years. She joined Kennedy's congressional staff when he ran for the U.S. Senate in 1952 and remained with him until his death in 1963. I began corresponding with Evelyn when I was a boy and we struck up a lasting friendship. She always sent cards on birthdays and anniversaries to my family and me, but we had never met. When Christine and I planned our trip, we made plans with Evelyn and her husband Abe.

Christine and I arrived at Duke Zeibert's restaurant and found the Lincolns in a corner booth enjoying cocktails. She wore her dyed jet-black hair in the same bobbed style of her early 1960s White House days; Abe wore his steel-gray hair long in the back and with bangs over his eyes. They both looked a bit eccentric for a couple in their eighties, but we hit it off immediately. Our conversation became so animated that the waiter tried unsuccessfully for over an hour to take our food order.

• • •

Evelyn and Abe spoke of their early years in Washington before she joined Kennedy's staff. Her father, a Nebraska congressman, was a close friend of William Jennings Bryan, the three-time Democrat presidential nominee. She and Abe married in Nebraska 61 years earlier, and shortly afterward moved to Washington for his patronage job: running an elevator in the Capitol. "The fellow running the elevator next to me was a Texas kid named Lyndon B. Johnson," Abe said with a smirk. "He was a phony then, and he died a phony."

Abe said his other patronage job was as a Capitol guard. They gave him a gun, a uniform, and he earned $135 a week: "It was one of the best-paying jobs in the world during the Depression. My only duty was to open each office of the Longworth House Office Building every night to make sure the windows were closed. Many times I caught a member of Congress having sex with his secretary, but I never revealed any of their names."

During these years, Abe befriended James Roosevelt, Franklin D. Roosevelt's eldest son. James once invited him backstage to watch one of his father's speeches: "Roosevelt was a cripple," he recalled. "He arrived for the speech in a wheelchair and wore leg braces. His son lifted him out of the chair with great difficulty. Once the curtain lifted and the crowd cheered, Roosevelt's face lit up instantly with such brilliance! It was amazing. He was like a superman. Yet the minute the speech ended and the curtain dropped, his smile disappeared instantly. His face shrunk and his body withdrew, and suddenly he looked like a shriveled old man that had aged 20 years in a matter of seconds. It was almost frightening to watch the transformation."

Evelyn needed little prodding to share memories of her many years working for JFK:

I first went to work for Kennedy by doing a research memo for him during his 1952 Senate campaign. I did it for free hoping he would like my work and ask me to join his staff. He never thanked me for the memo after I turned it in. After Kennedy won the Senate race, he called and offered me a job. I went up to the Senate gallery to watch him being sworn in. He looked so scrawny that day on the Senate floor, and he never did learn how to properly tie his necktie. There he stood, with the back portion of his necktie hanging lower than the front portion. He looked more like the elevator operator than a senator!

Years later, on Inauguration Day 1961, we walked into the Oval Office for the first time together. He looked at me and made a strange request: "For as long as I am president," he said, "you must never take a drink of alcohol." He was afraid I might inadvertently say something meant to be confidential. I promised him I would not drink, and I never did.

Kennedy's staff worked 18-hour days every day. He was a perfectionist. If you did something that was not his way, he would fire you just like that [snapping her finger]. But Kennedy never really "fired" anybody—he just wanted them gone. He would always have someone find you another job with better pay. He just didn't want the person around him anymore and it was our job to dispatch them.

I had a premonition he would die young. There was never any rest with him. Everything was done in such a hurry. He would read a book while he was shaving in the morning. He could never relax. Even when we would "vacation" in Palm Beach, when we would sit by the pool, Kennedy would dive in and swim a lap, then tell me, "Call Governor So-and-So." He would swim another lap and then dictate a letter. He would go like this for a long time: lap, dictate; lap, telephone call; lap, dictate. It never stopped. In all my years with Kennedy, I never took a vacation. We never stopped working. But if he were alive today, he would say this is a damned lie because he took me everywhere with him. But travel with him did not mean vacation. We never stopped working. Never.

As our waiter served dinner, Evelyn said that a major publishing house contacted her that morning to write a tell-all book on the Kennedy years. "They offered me a $2 million advance if I will write about the scandalous stuff," she said. "They want to know about Marilyn Monroe, the stories of Kennedy's womanizing, and so forth. I told them to forget it. They can keep their money. Some things will go with me to my grave."

During our dinner, Evelyn remained true to her word and never betrayed any secrets about Kennedy's promiscuity. However, as the evening wore on (and the cocktails accumulated), it became clear that she wasn't taking every secret with her into eternity—starting with her dislike for President Lyndon Johnson. At each mention of his name, her face tightened: "That man!" she muttered in a voice dripping with disdain. She recounted the behind-the-scenes maneuvering leading Kennedy to choose Johnson as his running mate in 1960. "You won't read this in the history books," she said. "All of the people present in Kennedy's hotel suite from that day are dead except me":

When Kennedy was a senator, Johnson was Senate leader. To Johnson, Kennedy was a nonentity and he treated Kennedy like a kid. Johnson never dreamed Kennedy would beat him for the Democrat presidential nomination in 1960. Johnson thought he had a lock on it. After Kennedy won, he followed the practice of being conciliatory to his defeated opponent. Kennedy asked me to call Johnson so he could congratulate him on running a tough race and to ask for his support in the coming election. I rang up LBJ's room and was told Johnson had gone to bed and was not to be disturbed.

Kennedy asked my husband, Abe, to bring a note down to Johnson's room. The note told Johnson that Kennedy wanted to meet with him the next morning. Meanwhile, Washington Post publisher Phil Graham learned Kennedy had sent a note to Johnson asking to meet, so the Post wrote an article saying Kennedy planned to pick Johnson as his running mate. The word spread like wildfire throughout the convention.

The next morning, when Kennedy read the article, he became frantic at the thought of having Johnson as his running mate. He huddled with Bobby [Kennedy] for over an hour in their hotel room over what he should do. Bobby was adamant that Johnson must not be the vice presidential nominee. Bobby couldn't stand Johnson and insisted that Johnson not be invited on the ticket even if the offer was nothing more than a courtesy. But events got out of hand. By the end of the meeting, Kennedy felt he would have to offer the position to Johnson if he was to hold Texas and not offend the delegates. Just before Kennedy headed out of the room to meet with Johnson, Kennedy privately told me not to worry. He was sure Johnson would not accept. Kennedy never, never intended to ask Johnson to be his running mate. His initial attempt to contact Johnson was just to mend fences. The man Kennedy really wanted as his running mate was Missouri Senator Stuart Symington. In fact, Kennedy had already told Symington he wanted him. Kennedy didn't believe Johnson would ever accept. But Johnson did accept and Kennedy was stuck with him. Kennedy was forced to call Symington and explain the situation. Symington understood, and as far as I know he never told anyone how close he came to the vice presidency.

After becoming president, Kennedy confided to me often that he was going to dump Johnson in 1964. Kennedy personally preferred North Carolina Governor Terry Sanford for the vice presidency in his second term.

If Evelyn still revered Kennedy's memory, she didn't grant the same degree of admiration to Kennedy's widow, Jacqueline:

There was no love between John Kennedy and Jackie. It was a loveless marriage. Old Joe Kennedy [JFK's domineering father] hand-picked Jackie to be his bride because of her breeding and family background. Joe recognized her for what she was: a woman who would make an excellent first lady. Kennedy dutifully went along with what his father told him to do. It was like watching the son of an ancient Chinese mandarin having his wife chosen for him—Kennedy was a son who let his patriarch pick a wife. Kennedy never loved her, but he knew he had to get married. He was afraid if he remained a bachelor for too long, people might think he was a homosexual or a playboy.

During the White House years, Jackie was having an affair with Aristotle Onassis and we all knew it. Kennedy knew it, too, but he didn't care. In fact, once he even sent Jackie down to Greece to stay with Onassis. Kennedy asked Franklin Roosevelt Jr. to go with Jackie so the press wouldn't think anything about it. But Kennedy knew full well what was going on. Onassis and Jackie loved each other even then and Kennedy didn't care. Kennedy told me privately several times that he intended to divorce Jackie after the 1964 election.

Abe agreed with his wife's assessment of the Kennedy marriage, but admitted he still fell under the spell of her charm. "Despite all her faults," he said, "Jackie was so attractive. She wasn't beautiful, but she was just so very *attractive*." He imitated how Jackie dropped her voice when she spoke to men: "She'd purse her lips into an 'O' shape, leaned forward, and in a sultry, breathy, exaggerated tone, said something like, [imitating her] *Governor, how do you do?*"

"Of course," Evelyn added, "that deep voice of hers was all for show. She was not like that at all. That breathy voice of hers was all a put-on. Behind the scenes she was a shrew. She constantly harped on Kennedy and harped about his family to him. She mocked his sisters for not knowing which fork to use at dinner. She kept calling his family 'shanty Irish.' She would screech at him, 'You're shanty Irish! You and your family are just shanty Irish!' There was no question but that he was going to divorce her after the 1964 elections."

Evelyn's cool feelings toward Jacqueline Kennedy didn't end with the young widow's stoic performance after his death in Dallas:

> After the shots rang out, we all rode over to Parkland Hospital. They were working on Kennedy in the emergency room, but we got the word early that there was no hope. After they declared him dead, I saw Jackie sitting in a waiting area of the hospital. She sat alone. I went over and hugged her. She gave me no response. She just sat there without emotion.

> After Kennedy's death, Jackie tried to evoke this phony "Camelot" myth. "Camelot" is a farce: there is no truth to it. If Kennedy were alive today and listening to all this "Camelot" silliness, he would laugh. Kennedy was flesh and bone. He was not a god or an idol the way Jackie and the family have tried to portray him since his death. Camelot was a creation of Jackie, along with historian Theodore White.

Another public figure that evoked her contempt was Kennedy's vanquished opponent in the 1960 election, Richard Nixon:

When Kennedy was in the Senate, Nixon's vice presidential office was near ours. I was always friendly with Rose Mary Woods, Nixon's personal secretary. When Kennedy was a senator, he had back surgery and was so ill that he was near death. The hospital priest administered the last rites of the Catholic Church to him. A Kennedy family member told me that he was going to die and that he probably would not last through the night. I went to the office to be there to answer the calls that would come once we got the word he was dead. Nixon strolled into our office that afternoon and said to me in a nonchalant fashion, "I hear your senator is going to die."

I became very angry with him. "No, he isn't," I told him. I was very offended by Nixon's callous attitude.[1]

Evelyn said she always liked former Vice President Hubert Humphrey, whom Kennedy defeated for the 1960 nomination. She felt sorry for Humphrey after he became Johnson's vice president following the 1964 election:

LBJ had his spies in government report on Humphrey. One of them told LBJ that Humphrey had privately commented that he disfavored Johnson's war policies in Vietnam. Johnson called Humphrey into the Oval Office. When Humphrey entered the room, Johnson ran up to Humphrey and screamed profanities at him. Incredibly, Johnson put his hands around Humphrey's throat, and in a mad frenzy began to choke him physically. Johnson screamed that if Humphrey didn't toe the line on Vietnam, Johnson would break Humphrey's career. Humphrey left the office in shock, but he stopped criticizing Johnson.

---

1   Syndicated columnist Chris Matthews, who wrote the book *Kennedy & Nixon*, disputed Mrs. Lincoln's account. He claimed that Nixon was deeply distraught over Kennedy's expected death following his back surgery.

I mentioned that Christine and I visited Kennedy's grave earlier in the day. Apparently, we had just missed seeing Evelyn there. "Today was my 56ᵗʰ visit," she noted sadly. "I go every year on his birthday and on November 22." She spoke with a heavy voice of that fateful day in Dallas, saying she rode a few cars behind Kennedy in the motorcade when the assassin struck. "As his car pulled out of Love Field for the ride through downtown Dallas, I saw him sitting in the backseat. He was waving his hand." Her voice cracked, and she elaborated no further. "After all these years, it's still too painful to discuss," she said.

"We have a dearth of leaders in America," she told me as we left

The Rogans dining with Evelyn and Abe Lincoln at Duke Zeibert's restaurant, Washington, November 22, 1991. (Author's collection)

the restaurant at the end of our evening. "We need another Kennedy today. You would have liked him, Jim, and I know he would have liked you. If I had known you back then, I could have brought you to the Oval Office to meet him any time you wanted. I'm sorry the opportunity never arose."

So was I.

• • •

Evelyn Lincoln and I continued our friendship until she died of cancer at age 85 on May 11, 1995. Her husband, Abe, died one month later.

27

The End of the Comparison

I n 1992, I received an invitation from Lodwrick Cook, chairman of ARCO, to a luncheon at the Ronald Reagan Presidential Library honoring former President Reagan and Mikhail Gorbachev, the last leader of the now-defunct Soviet Union—for a $5,000 contribution. The invitation to dine with Reagan and Gorbachev was enticing but prohibitive. I wrote Cook and thanked him for thinking of me but declined respectfully: Raising a family on a government salary, I told him, meant that if I spent $5,000 to dine with anyone, I would need to move to the Reagan Library permanently because I'd no longer be welcome in my current home.

A few days later, Cook's secretary surprised me with a phone call: "The Reagan event is sold out anyway," she said, "but Chairman Cook wants to invite you to a private lunch for Gorbachev at ARCO Towers in Los Angeles. He is having the lunch and reception so some of our executives and local government officials can meet Gorbachev during his visit to California." She advised me to get there an hour early because the Secret Service planned to secure the building.

I arrived for the event and found the surrounding streets swarming with activity. Police closed the traffic lanes closest to the building and security agents hovered everywhere. Hundreds of ARCO employees stood behind an outdoor barricade to get a glimpse of Gorbachev when his motorcade arrived.

A Secret Service agent escorted me to a private elevator to the 37th floor; another agent brought me into a large reception room where Los Angeles Mayor Tom Bradley and other local officials awaited Gorbachev's arrival.

At 12:15 p.m., spontaneous applause spread through the room. Gorbachev, accompanied by his wife Raisa and their daughter Irina, had arrived. Smiling broadly, he mingled freely during the reception and chatted with guests through a simultaneous translator.

Former Soviet President Mikhail Gorbachev, Los Angeles, May 5, 1992. (Photograph by the author)

When Cook introduced me to his honored guests, Mrs. Gorbachev extended her hand and greeted me in her best English: *E-e-e-t e-e-z n-i-z-e to meet you!*" Former President Gorbachev gripped my hand and pumped it vigorously.

As Gorbachev and I talked, I had the impression he was in no hurry to move on because (unlike everyone else) I didn't speak "at him" through the interpreter, meaning I didn't look at the interpreter and say things such as, "Please tell Mr. Gorbachev that I want him to know that I...." When communicating with him, I spoke to him directly and he did the same with me. He told me later that I was the only person he met during his California trip who knew how to speak through a simultaneous translation interpreter. I replied that I had an unfair advantage over others: As a trial court

With former Soviet President Mikhail Gorbachev, Los Angeles, May 5, 1992. (Author's collection)

judge in Los Angeles County, I dealt each day with criminal defendants through simultaneous translators, so the skill came naturally to me.

"I hope that is the end of the comparison!" he said as he laughed.

Ushers steered the guests into the main dining room. I found myself seated at the table right next to the honorees, with Raisa Gorbachev sitting behind me. During the luncheon, county and local government officials took turns presenting the Gorbachevs with gifts, certificates, and plaques. He acknowledged each memento with a smile and a bow before turning over the booty to an aide.

Between presentations, he continued to greet guests and sign autographs. Even my seatmate Tom Plate, editorial page editor for the *Los Angeles Times*, wasn't immune to the temptation. "It's not very chic for reporters to ask for autographs," Plate told me. I suggested this might be a once-in-a-lifetime opportunity to obtain a great memento for his grandchildren. He swallowed hard and approached the former Soviet leader with a pen and menu in hand. Gorbachev inscribed it in Russian, "To a great news editor."

In starting the program, Cook mentioned that Mrs. Gorbachev had a distinguished background as an educator, and that Gorbachev loves the ballet and opera. "And," he noted, "he can recite the works of [Russian author Alexander] Pushkin!" Gorbachev chuckled when he heard the translated claim and then called out a response from his seat: "I can't do too much of that anymore!" Cook presented the Gorbachevs with a handmade quilt from an Amish village in Pennsylvania. While Gorbachev admired the quilt, Mrs. Gorbachev climbed on top of her chair, pointed to the quilt, and said (in Russian), "That quilt is meant for me and not for my husband!"

Gorbachev received a standing ovation when introduced. He embraced his American host and then waved the room to silence. Speaking without notes (and with his interpreter at his side), he promised a brief impromptu speech. Noting that Los Angeles had been rocked by riots the previous week, he praised local officials for their handling of the violence. He said there had been speculation as to whether the unrest might force him to cancel his Los Angeles visit: "I had no intention of canceling," he said, which brought a rousing cheer.

His speech focused on expanding markets in the former Soviet Union. He encouraged the gathering of business leaders to expand commerce to Russia. "Your investments will help to make a free-market economy work there," the former head of the Communist Party implored the gathering of capitalists. It was ironic to hear the man given unprecedented power to hold together that dying communist regime now preaching the gospel of free markets. Yet Gorbachev showed no hint of discomfort at this new role. He expressed his hope repeatedly that Russia and the United States would work together to help modernize his nation through pro-growth policies and economic development.

• • •

Almost 30 years have passed since I sat in ARCO Towers and listened to the former president of the Soviet Union preach to an American audience the failures of socialism and the benefits of capitalism over a command economy. When reading the economic nostrums of some of our state and national leaders these days, I'm thinking we should invite Gorbachev back for another speech.

• • •

Raisa Gorbachev died of cancer at age 67 on September 20, 1999.

Tom Bradley served as mayor of Los Angeles from 1973 to 1993. He died of complications following a stroke at age 80 on September 29, 1998.

ARCO President Lodwrick Cook died at age 92 on September 28, 2020.

28

Mr. Television

I n 1948, only one in 150 Americans owned a television set. Then a brash comedian named Milton Berle became host of a new program called *The Texaco Star Theater*. Within a year, TV sales soared, largely because of viewer addiction to his outlandish antics. He so dominated the airwaves (the Nielsen ratings showed that 80 percent of every U.S. household with a set tuned in to him) that movie theaters and restaurants closed their doors on Tuesday nights, because they couldn't compete with the man dubbed "Mr. Television" and "Uncle Miltie." Years later, he related in his autobiography that one study showed Detroit's water reservoir level sank on Tuesday nights between 9:00 and 9:05: "It turned out that everyone waited until the end of the *Texaco Star Theater* before going to the bathroom," he wrote.

Berle's star power appeared so enduring that in 1951 Texaco signed him to an unprecedented 30-year television contract. However, with the new medium's exploding popularity, the comedy competition grew more potent. His popularity dropped as new programs challenged his supremacy, and in 1953 Texaco canceled his show. During the ensuing years, he remained a fixture in television, and he continued performing in feature films, on Broadway, and in nightclubs.

When I met him, he was decades removed from his early television success, but he remained very much a star and showed no signs of slowing down. Indeed, the *Guinness Book of World Records* claimed he performed the greatest number of charity benefit performances of anyone in show business history. It was at one such benefit that we met. In 1992, I attended a youth program fundraising luncheon at Burbank's Castaway restaurant where he entertained.

The audience rose and cheered for the 84 year-old comic legend when he appeared at the dais. Chomping on his cigar, he quipped, "Who am I, Ross Perot?" (At the time, Perot was a third-party presidential candidate.) He then launched into a rapid-fire Borscht Belt routine filled with ethnic humor for which modern standards of political correctness required frowns of disapproval in 1992 (and a far worse response these days). For him, political correctness gave way. "Hey," he asked the crowd as he pointed to the Hispanic waiter serving coffee at a front table, "How did that Mexican kid know I'm a Hebrew? Each time he waited on me, he kept asking [imitating a Spanish accent], *Jew want more chicken? Jew want more water?*" He then pushed his fist to his stomach feigning indigestion: "I've got so much gas that I'm being chased by the Arabs."

Other Berle gems:

- "I'm so unlucky. I loaned my friend $30,000 to have plastic surgery. Now I can't find the son of a bitch!"

- "Anytime someone goes into a deli and orders pastrami on white bread, somewhere a Jew dies."

- "At my age, I feel like Zsa Zsa Gabor's sixth husband. I know what I'm supposed to do, but I don't know how to make it interesting."

- "I recently married a woman who's 30 years younger than I. Three months ago we made love for one hour and three minutes. Of course, that was the night they turned the clocks back."

- "We owe a lot to Thomas Edison. If it wasn't for him, we'd be watching TV by candlelight."

- "Experience is what you get after you've forgotten her name."

And on it went: a repertoire of one-liners from an old vaudevillian who did the show without a note before him. After rocking the room with unrestrained laughter for 30 minutes, he finished to another standing ovation.

As people filed out of the banquet hall, the event producer, my friend Norman Mamey, invited me to meet Berle, who now wolfed down his untouched lunch before the waiters cleared the table. I felt awkward visiting with him while he tried to eat, but he insisted that I join him. He talked while chewing food, and pieces of broccoli kept falling from his mouth and onto his coat during our conversation. What the heck—at his age he deserved a little table etiquette slack. That minor distraction aside, he was delightful.

I gave Berle an old movie still from a film he made more than 50 years earlier. He thanked me as he studied the picture: "Now just one question," he asked: "Who the hell are these other people in it with me?"

When Mamey told Berle that I was a great public speaker, his eyes lit up. "If you speak in public a lot," he insisted, "then you need to buy my book *Milton Berle's Private Joke File*. There are over 10,000 jokes in it and it will be a valuable reference for you. It's only $20. Let's go—I'll give you a ride to the book store right now so you can buy it!"

Remembering that Berle had a reputation throughout his career for comedians suing him for stealing their material, I chided, "I'll buy your book if you will indemnify me if I get sued using your jokes."

"Buy my book and I'll give you a waiver!" he promised.

A photographer snapped a picture of us. Moments later, as we shook hands and said goodbye, he took a step back. His foot slipped from the stage, he reeled and began falling backward from the riser. I grabbed his arm and caught him just in time.

Just before the stumble: Milton Berle and me, The Castaways Restaurant, Burbank, June 25, 1992. (Author's collection)

He was unharmed, but the experience left him shaken. I helped him to his chair until he felt steady. After regaining his composure, he said somberly, "Thanks for saving me. That's how Bing Crosby died. Crosby fell backward off a stage and it led to his heart attack a few months later."

That instance was the only time during this Burbank appearance that Berle—and everyone else—didn't have a smile on his face.

• • •

Milton Berle died of cancer at age 93 on March 27, 2002.

Producer and Grammy Award winner Norman Mamey died at age 66 after a long illness on January 22, 2015.

29

Dream Team

As noted in previous chapters, on the last night of the 1972 Republican National Convention in Miami, I waited in line to shake hands with President Richard Nixon but my turn never came. In 1988, I came within a heartbeat of meeting him, but a faux Disneyland "guard" foiled my opportunity. Twenty years after Miami, my chance came finally. However, when I did meet Nixon, it wasn't over politics—it was over baseball.

In 1972, Nixon and his son-in-law David Eisenhower (grandson of President Eisenhower) collaborated in selecting their Major League Baseball all-time "dream teams." Twenty years later, they updated their selections and unveiled them at a fundraising event for Nixon's presidential library in Yorba Linda, California. Tickets for the luncheon cost $200 each; $500 donors received a special "Dugout Club" pass for a private reception with Nixon and his retired baseball player guests. After waiting decades to meet Nixon, I refused to let the opportunity pass. Despite the steep price, for the first (and last) time in my life I bought a $500 ticket to something.

• • •

On a table inside the Nixon Library I found the former president's private schedule left behind by an errant staffer. In flipping through it, I saw that he planned to depart Santa Barbara by helicopter at 9:30 a.m. and fly to Yorba Linda Middle School, where a car would pick him up and drive him to the "Eureka Entrance" of the Nixon Library. Once there, staff would escort him to the Marriott Room for makeup and rest before doing an interview. Whoever prepared the memo anticipated his comfort: handlers were directed to have Diet Pepsi, ice, yellow legal pads, and pens available for him in the room while he awaited the program's start time.

To Jim Rogan
With best wyst
Richard Nixon

Finally! Twenty years and $500 later, here I am with former President Nixon, Yorba Linda, July 15, 1992. (Author's collection)

After checking in, I went to the lower-level Olin Room for the Dugout Club reception. As I entered, I heard a familiar voice to my left. I turned and saw Nixon entering the nearby Marriott Room with library director John Taylor and several private security guards. Amazingly, none of the arriving guests recognized Nixon as he lingered in the doorway receiving a last-minute event briefing from Taylor.

A few minutes later, Nixon entered the Olin Room with David Eisenhower for the private reception. He addressed the guests briefly, saying that he preferred to reserve his remarks for the luncheon program. He thanked everyone for coming, and then he took his place in the receiving line.

I was one of the first people to meet him. When my turn came—finally!—Taylor introduced me to him as "Judge Rogan."

"Nice to meet you, Judge," he said as he gripped my hand. Then, looking at me closely, he said, "Are you really a judge? You look too young!"

"Bless you for that, Mr. President," I said, and then the photographer memorialized my $500 moment.

While welcoming guests, Nixon often wiped beads of perspiration from his brow and upper lip. Despite the uncomfortably warm temperature in the room, he smiled and greeted everyone, and he made a point to speak with each child moving through the line with their parents. Despite the "no autograph" rule printed on the reception and luncheon invitations, he signed every card, baseball, scrap of paper, and photograph thrust before him while ignoring library staff attempts to fend off the requests. I overheard one boy complain to his father that Nixon signed his baseball "RN" instead of penning a full signature. "That's the way he signs his name," the father growled, "so shut your ungrateful mouth and be glad you got it."

Following the private reception, ticketed luncheon guests assembled under an outdoor tent erected near the parking lot. American flags lined the stage decorated in red, white, and blue. A banner revealed the updated selections for the "Nixon–Eisenhower All Time Baseball Greats." A box of Cracker Jack served as each table's centerpiece, and the Los Angeles Dodgers organist played baseball-themed musical selections. Behind a rope line waited dozens of young boys in Little League uniforms, along with hundreds of additional spectators and fans hoping to see Nixon and the baseball stars when they entered.

As library director John Taylor introduced each current and former baseball player individually,[1] Nixon stood at the tent entrance awaiting his cue. When it came, a standing ovation greeted

---

1   The current and former Major League Baseball players attending were Johnny Bench, Bob Feller, Brooks Robinson, Harmon Killebrew, Johnny Mize, George Kell, Rollie Fingers, Maury Wills, Buck Rodgers, and Tony LaRussa. Also attending was Babe Ruth's daughter, Julia Ruth Stevens.

his entry while the USC marching band played a medley of patriotic tunes. He smiled and shook hands as he walked to his table. Once he took his seat, Roger Owens, the vendor famous for throwing bags of roasted peanuts with deadly accuracy (and with rocket-like speed) to customers at the Los Angeles Dodgers Stadium, threw a bag to Nixon from 100 feet away. Nixon caught it on the first attempt.

During lunch, a small ring of private security guards kept a watchful eye on Nixon as he chatted with his tablemates. During a break, John Taylor waved me over to Nixon's table. During our brief chat, I showed the former president a rare item from my political memorabilia collection: a campaign brochure from his 1950 U.S. Senate race against Helen Gahagan Douglas. It bore the caption, "Let's Elect Congressman Richard Nixon United States Senator— The Man who Broke the Hiss-Chambers Espionage Case."

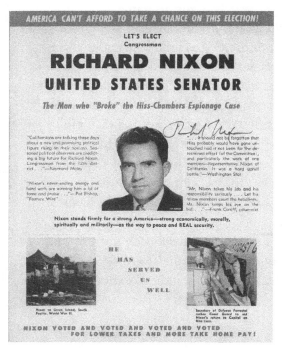

1950 Nixon for Senate flyer autographed for me by the former president at his library, July 15, 1992. (Author's collection)

"Where on earth did you get this?" he asked as he studied the vintage flyer. He pointed to the young picture of himself on the cover and looked at it for several seconds. When I asked jokingly if he had used his high school yearbook picture for it, he laughed. "It sure looks like it!" he said. "This pamphlet takes me back a long, long time." He picked up a pen and wrote his signature across the front of the brochure.

A sudden line of people wanting autographs formed behind me, and I don't think he enjoyed another bite of his food. He signed for fans throughout the rest of the luncheon. With him setting the example, the baseball players got into the signing act, too. Only Johnny Bench did so grudgingly, griping to fans about them breaking the no-autograph rule.

After lunch, David Eisenhower began the program by announcing the Nixon–Eisenhower picks for the greatest ballplayers, and he explained their reasons for each selection. Eisenhower then invited each visiting player to join him onstage for commentary.

Johnny Bench remembered playing one game in 1968 and seeing Eisenhower and his fiancée (later wife) Julie Nixon in the stands. "I only had eyes for Julie that day," Bench quipped.

Other players shared brief insights: Bob Feller described his lost playing time because of his military service in World War II ("At least we won that one!"). Rollie Fingers compared modern pitchers to those in his heyday, Tony LaRussa shared his philosophy of what it takes to keep a great team together, and George Kell talked about his years as a third baseman for the New York Yankees. Harmon Killebrew reminisced about meeting President Dwight D. Eisenhower at a baseball game in 1959. Turning to David Eisenhower, he said, "Your grandfather asked me to sign a ball for you that day. I asked him to sign one for me. We traded autographed balls, and I still have his."

"And I still have yours!" Eisenhower replied.

Maury Wills told of driving to Tijuana with friends in the mid-1970s. After a few drinks, he and his friends decided to stop by Nixon's San Clemente home and ring the bell. "Let's see if Dick is home," he said in jest. He had no expectation of seeing Nixon, but when the gates opened and a staffer ushered his group into the former president's study, they all registered shock. "Mr. President," Wills noted, "you were bigger than life then, and you still are."

Eisenhower asked Wills what it takes to win a baseball game. Before Wills could answer, Nixon walked to the stage and answered for him: "Steal!" he thundered.

When Nixon rose to speak, the 79 year-old former president received another standing ovation. Two aides removed the lectern that the previous speakers had used and replaced it with a stand-alone microphone. In his later years, Nixon eschewed notes and made a practice of speaking extemporaneously.

In his opening remarks, he mentioned the presence of Anaheim Angels manager Buck Rodgers and his recent injury while riding in the team's bus. "Now you know why I am opposed to busing," he quipped.[2] "And I want you to know I always root for the home team. I want the Angels to win the World Series while [owner and former cowboy star] Gene Autry is still around."

For almost 30 minutes, he reminisced about his love for baseball and sports. He said he attended his first baseball game in 1925 and became addicted ever since. His love of baseball even affected his thinking on signing autographs. "I signed lots of autographs today," he noted. "I try never to refuse a request, and I will tell you why. Back in 1942, I was eating dinner with my wife, Pat, in a restaurant in New York. Seated across the room from us was the legendary baseball star Babe Ruth. Pat went over to Ruth and asked him for his autograph for my little brother Eddie. As busy and as famous as the Babe was, he took the time to sign that autograph. When I came to a position in my life where people wanted my autograph, I have always tried to remember that if Babe Ruth had time to sign an autograph, then so do I."

Nixon said the first home run he ever saw hit in a baseball game was in the 1940s when Joe DiMaggio smashed one out near the stands where he sat. "But the greatest player I ever saw," he added, "was Jackie Robinson. In fact, Jackie was the greatest all-around athlete ever. He could have played professional football, basketball,

---

2   Court-ordered "forced busing," which mandated that school boards transport students from their nearby neighborhood schools and ship them off to attend out-of-district (and sometimes out-of-county) schools to meet classroom racial quotas, was a hotly charged political issue during Nixon's 1972 presidential campaign.

or been an Olympic athlete. One of my fond memories was in attending a UCLA–Oregon game with Jackie."

Nixon recalled attending another game with legendary New York Yankees manager Casey Stengel. "Had Casey lived," Nixon joked, "I might have made him Secretary of State. The first rule of politics is to confound the opposition. When Casey spoke, nobody could understand him! Only he could understand himself."

He noted that this year (1992) all the major presidential candidates (Republican George Bush, Democrat Bill Clinton, and Independent Ross Perot) were left-handed. "So it is settled," he concluded, "that our next president will be a southpaw. Any baseball man will tell you that left-handers tend to be a little wild. Our next president will be a left-hander, but we hope he isn't wild and that he will emulate one of baseball's best left handers and hit home runs for America the way Babe Ruth hit them for the New York Yankees!"

Former President Richard Nixon speaking at the "Nixon-Eisenhower All-Time Baseball Greats" luncheon, the Nixon Library, July 15, 1992. (Photograph by the author)

He returned to his seat amid another ovation. Jo Lasorda, wife of Los Angeles Dodgers manager Tommy Lasorda, presented him with one of her husband's jerseys. As the luncheon adjourned, he joined the players onstage for a group photograph. Guests surrounded Nixon, and he remained for another 20 minutes shaking hands and signing autographs.

With the event over, I went inside the library to tour a special exhibit of baseball-related presidential memorabilia. About an hour later, as I was viewing George H.W. Bush's first baseman's mitt from his days as captain of the Yale baseball team, someone tapped me on the shoulder and said, "I still say you look too young to be a judge!" I turned. There stood a smiling Nixon as he gripped my hand and thanked me for coming.

"Mr. President," I teased, "it's that sort of narrow thinking that kept you from becoming governor of California!"

He roared at my joke. "You might be right!" he replied.

Before leaving, he signed for me an engraved White House vignette with his famous "RN" initials. Unlike the little boy earlier in the day, I was not disappointed to receive the abbreviated version of his autograph—the in-person signature I waited 20 years to collect.

•••

Baseball Hall of Famer Bob Feller played from 1936 to 1956. He died of leukemia at age 92 on December 15, 2010.

Hall of Famer Harmon Killebrew played from 1954 to 1975. He died at age 75 on May 17, 2011.

Hall of Famer Johnny Mize, the four-time National League home run champion, played from 1936 to 1953. He died at age 80 on June 2, 1993.

Hall of Famer George Kell, the 1949 American League batting champion, played from 1943 to 1957. He died at age 86 on March 24, 2009.

Julia Ruth Stevens, daughter of Babe Ruth, died at age 102 on March 9, 2019.

30

Pat

Edmund G. "Pat" Brown became governor of California shortly after my birth. Serving two terms (1959–1967), he had the unique distinction of running for governor against two future presidents of the United States. In 1962, he won reelection by beating former Vice President Richard Nixon handily; four years later, he lost just as handily to political newcomer Ronald Reagan. Brown's gubernatorial legacy continued decades after he left Sacramento. His son Jerry succeeded him as California's 34th governor (1975–1983), and then he recaptured the governor's chair in 2010 and served two more terms. His daughter Kathleen served as California Treasurer and was the Democrat nominee for governor in 1994.

• • •

I first met Pat Brown in 1974 when his son ran for governor. Although I saw him a few more times at political gatherings over the years, we didn't become acquainted until I was a deputy district attorney and I introduced him as a guest speaker at a local function. He called me a few days later. After schmoozing about politics, he came to the point: the police had arrested for drunk driving the son of a major client of his law firm. "Jim," he asked, "can you do a favor for your old governor and make this go away for me?"

"Sorry, Governor," I told him. "Those days are long gone. You'll have to take care of this the old-fashioned way: plead him guilty or go to trial."

He chuckled. "Well, I thought you'd say that," he replied. "I'll plead him guilty and then you and I can go to lunch and talk politics some more."

We stayed in touch after that, and I liked him—a lot. He was a charming, backslapping pol of the old school. He never held it against me that I cut his drunk driving client no slack (or that I was a Reagan Republican). I never could bring myself to call him Pat, at least to his face, although almost everyone else did. The nickname fit: breezy, casual, affable.

• • •

We had lunch one afternoon in late 1992 at an outdoor bistro near his Los Angeles law office, which was a modest storefront suite across from the Century Plaza Hotel. Throughout our meal, I marveled at the number of people that recognized him and came over to shake his hand a quarter century after he left Sacramento. It was also clear to me that he delighted in the recognition.

During our visit, he complained that his weight had dropped from 185 pounds to 145 and that his right leg was troubling him. "It's hell growing old," he muttered. "I'm 87 now. I'm having trouble sleeping at night and then I get very tired during the day. I'm also having lots of trouble walking because of my leg. My muscles feel very stiff." Despite these infirmities, he told me that he still enjoyed playing golf.

As we dined, he recounted his early years in the law:

I was admitted to the bar sometime in the 1920s—I don't even remember what year it was anymore. I first worked for a blind attorney who gave me what he called the best advice in the world: stay out of politics! I didn't listen, of course, and ran for my first office shortly after law school. I don't even remember what that was for.

I had a real dilemma in those early years. My father-in-law was chief of police in San Francisco, and my dad ran a gambling operation. I lived in constant mortal fear that my father-in-law would arrest my father! Anyway, as you know, I later ran for district attorney of San Francisco, attorney general, and governor.

When I mentioned that we had more than 900 deputy district attorneys in the Los Angeles County DA's office, he shook his head in disbelief: "When I was district attorney of San Francisco, there were 27 deputy prosecutors working under me. I knew every one of them, I knew their wives and kids, and I had been to each of their homes for dinner."

During lunch, he shared these brief impressions of some leaders he knew during his career:

Harry S Truman: "A great president that I was proud to nominate at the 1948 Democratic National Convention."

Adlai E. Stevenson: "A wonderful man that I knew very well. He was witty, funny, and brilliant."

John F. Kennedy: "He was quite a fellow. In public, he was very urbane and polished. In private, he was very down-to-earth."

Richard Nixon: "He was pretty stiff and cold as a person. Still, over the years, Nixon and I have become friends and have remained in contact."

He reminisced about his campaign against Nixon for governor in 1962. With Nixon having been a U.S. senator from California, a two-term vice president, and coming within a whisker of defeating John F. Kennedy for the presidency (Nixon carried California that year), I asked if he feared Nixon would defeat him in 1962. "There was little doubt in my mind that I would lose," he said. "I thought Nixon would beat me for all those reasons."

"In fact," he continued, "Nixon's popularity coincided with a steady decline in my own. I had made some tough decisions that angered many people, such as giving Caryl Chessman a 60-day reprieve on Death Row.[1] I would go to speak at public functions and would be introduced as 'the governor of the great state of California' to a loud chorus of boos. So I thought Nixon would beat me. We debated several times that year. Nixon was a fine debater but very stiff. But in the end, I won. That was a very gratifying moment in my life."

I asked what he attributed as the key factor to his upset victory that year. He smiled: "I guess I just overcame Nixon with the sheer force of my personality and charm!"

He talked about the man who had defeated him for a third term four years later—Ronald Reagan. "You can't help but like Reagan," he said. "He is one of the most charming men I ever met." He said that he knew Reagan would be a difficult candidate to beat. "Many of the leaders of the Democratic Party felt Reagan would be a pushover, but I knew he would be tough. I had watched him on television and was reading the early polls very carefully."

Ironically, 25 years after they squared off for governor, former President Reagan's office was just a block down the street from Pat's law office. I pointed to Reagan's building, which was visible to us from our outdoor table, and I asked if they ever got together. "No, we don't socialize," he said. Then, after taking a long sip of water, he laughed and added, "You know, Reagan has made an entire career out of having us Democrats underestimate that son-of-a-bitch!" He said that his defeat by Reagan didn't surprise him: "It's difficult to run for a third term. You've probably accomplished all of the major goals you are going to be able to get through in two terms."

He asked the waiter to take our picture, and then he told me with a grin, "Jim, this picture of us together will get me reelected governor of California!"

"Governor," I teased in reply, "I have to run for reelection to the bench in conservative Glendale. If my voters see a picture of me

---

1   California's infamous "Red Light Bandit" executed in San Quentin's gas chamber during Brown's administration.

hanging out with Jerry Brown's dad, I'll be out of a job!"

He roared. "I guess Glendale hasn't changed much since I last ran!" he said. "Don't worry, Jim. I'll make sure Kathleen makes you her first pick for the California Supreme Court!"

Former California Governor Pat Brown and me at lunch, Century City, October 20, 1992. (Author's collection)

• • •

A few weeks later, Pat visited me in Glendale. I was presiding over a criminal jury trial when he entered the rear of the courtroom. I interrupted the proceedings to introduce him, and everyone in the courtroom stood and clapped (including the jurors and the in-custody defendant). Leaning on his cane, he made his way to the bench and greeted me.

Once we settled in my chambers, he complimented my décor, which consisted of vintage political campaign posters framed on the walls. "I love all these campaign posters. They give me a warm feeling," he said.

"Are you sure?" I asked as I pointed out a large 1966 Reagan for governor poster hanging in the corner.

"Well," he laughed, "maybe not *that* warm!"

At his earlier request, I had brought several trays of old Democrat campaign buttons from my collection to show him, including one displaying items from his own election campaigns. Looking at a 1946 campaign postcard from his race for state attorney general, he said, "Boy, I sure looked young then!" He laughed—hard—when he spotted a badge that the Nixon campaign had put out in their 1962 race. It read, "SOB—Sweep Out Brown."

Recently he and his wife Bernice had signed for me a family photograph depicting them with their two children in the family business, former Governor Jerry Brown and California State Treasurer Kathleen Brown. I told him that I had sent the photo to Kathleen with a note warning her that he had promised she would make me her first appointment to the California Supreme Court: "Governor, I told your daughter that my legal research had uncovered an ancient legal maxim. It is the doctrine of *Ex Governis Promiso Patricae*, which legally binds a governor's daughter to the promises of her father. I promised to release her from the obligation and save her the embarrassment of having to appoint a conservative Republican if she would simply sign the photograph. She returned the picture with this inscription: 'Judge Rogan, The doctrine of *Ex Governis Promiso Patricae* has just been declared unconstitutional by the Republican-appointed Supreme Court. Whew!'"

He loved the punch line, and then he turned serious. "I really think Kathleen will be the next governor of California," he said with obvious pride. "Then we will be the first family in history where a father, son, and daughter have all been governor of the state."

"Governor, as a Republican, may I just say this—thank God you've stopped having kids!"

We drove to the Oakmont Country Club for lunch. The day was especially clear and brisk outside, which showed off the nearby mountain ranges. Admiring the view, he said, "I had no idea how pretty Glendale is."

"Of course you didn't," I told him. "When you ran for governor, Glendale was one of the state's most conservative cities. This is the first time you ever came through here without cover of darkness!"

When we arrived at the club, I helped him out of the car. He gripped my arm as we made our way slowly to the table reserved for us. It was wonderful listening to him reminisce about his career and family:

> My daughter Kathleen is a great kid and she will make a great governor. And Jerry was a good son. He was in the seminary for many years before he decided to study law and politics. He was a good governor, but didn't always make good [political] decisions.

> The paper recently reported he now is thinking of running for mayor of Los Angeles, but that won't happen. Jerry just says things like that because he likes to get his picture in the paper. In 1970, I thought about running against Reagan again and settling the score for him defeating me. But my wife told me no. She said it was Jerry's turn to make his name and I had to step aside for him. Just as I did so for Jerry, now it is Kathleen's turn to run and Jerry will step aside for her. He won't run for mayor.

I asked him what thoughts went through his mind that morning in 1959 when he took his first gubernatorial oath of office. He took a sip of wine, smiled, and said, "Just that I am going to be a damned good governor!"

He said that Republican Governor Earl Warren (later chief justice of the United States) became his good friend. "In fact," he noted, "Earl didn't campaign for my Republican opponent when I ran for attorney general. Earl was a great big guy with a warm smile. He wasn't a great legal scholar, but he had great instincts."

When it was time to go, he presented me with a present: an inscribed copy of his book on capital punishment, *Public Justice, Private Mercy*. He took my arm and I escorted him across the dining room toward the exit. He leaned even more heavily upon me than earlier.

Some distraction from across the room caught my attention and I turned my head away from him momentarily. In that instant, I felt his arm slip off mine. "Oh, God, no," I thought—he must have fallen. As I turned quickly to grab him, he was gone.

Growing frantic, I spun to look behind me and I saw him walking away at such a brisk clip that I had to hurry to catch up. When I reached him, I offered my arm for support. He waved me away. I didn't know it at the time, but as we were leaving, he noticed an occupied banquet room with a sign outside announcing the monthly meeting of the Glendale Federated Republican Women. When he saw it, he let go of my arm, straightened up, and charged across the dining room and into their meeting.

"Good afternoon, ladies!" he called out cheerfully as he bounded inside. "When you go home today, I want you to tell all your husbands that you had lunch with the governor of California!"

"Oh my!" one of them exclaimed. *"It's Pat Brown!"*

He shook hands and kissed each of the surprised and delighted women. He signed autographs, posed for pictures, told jokes and stories, and charmed every single person in that room. "Governor," one Federated lady told him solemnly, "as you know, we are all Republican women. To be honest, we didn't care too much for Jerry, but we love you!"

"And I love you, too!"

With that, he turned to me and winked. *"Now* we can go," he whispered.

He blew the ladies a kiss, gave a little bow as they applauded, and walked away jauntily. Once we cleared their sightline, he took my arm, leaned on it, and re-aged the 50 years he had shed for a few minutes when he strode into that banquet room.

• • •

I kept in touch with Pat, but our contacts became less frequent because of his failing health. He died of a heart attack at age 90 on February 16, 1996.

I still miss him.

31

Sissy Picture

Rand Brooks was a fixture in our local Glendale business community. A loyal Republican, he came to political events often when I spoke. We became good friends, and when I ran for office later I had no more reliable supporter.

For almost 30 years, Rand owned and ran Professional Ambulance Service. Many of his acquaintances never knew that this was a later-in-life career. In the 1930s, he worked as a trick-riding cowboy in a Wild West show where his partner threw knives at him. Later he tried his hand at acting in movies and early television. But he had one role that guaranteed his place in motion picture history: he played Charles Hamilton, Scarlett O'Hara's first husband in the immortal 1939 film classic, *Gone with the Wind.* Whenever I urged him to write a memoir of his Hollywood experiences, he would tell me that nobody would be interested. When I suggested he tape his stories, he demurred: "I'll do it only if you are the one asking me all the questions."

I never taped an interview with Rand, but occasionally I coaxed from him stories of the old days. Once, when I expressed concern over lunch that my questions took him away from business, he laughed: "I'm 75 years old," he said, "so I'm in no hurry for anything. Besides, I don't do any work around here anymore. I just come in when I feel like it. Now, in the early days of the business, things were different. I was the dispatcher *and* the ambulance driver."

As long as Rand wanted to talk, I wanted to listen.

Rand once showed me the stacks of fan mail piled on his desk. Fifty years after making *Gone with the Wind* (or, as the fan clubs call it, GWTW), he still received 25 or more letters a day asking for an autographed picture. Although he accommodated every request, he said he tried for years sending back signed photos depicting him in western gear and riding a horse. Regrettably, that wasn't what the fans wanted, so his autographing chores focused almost exclusively on GWTW mementos. When I asked why he preferred signing cowboy photos, he said, "Because in *Gone with the Wind* I looked like a sissy. They made me up to look like an orange-haired sissy in that damned picture, but that's the photo everyone wants. I like people to know I made other movies besides that one."

The "Sissy Picture": Scarlett O'Hara (actress Vivien Leigh) marries Charles Hamilton (Rand Brooks) in *Gone with the Wind*, 1939. (Author's collection)

I told him that I suspected he only pretended to dislike fans remembering him for GWTW since it cemented his place in movie history. "I guess you're right," he said. "But I still hate to see how they made me up like a sissy for that part!"

He continued:

I'll never forget going to that damned beauty parlor every day to be made up with curly orange hair. They did the same thing to Leslie Howard [who played "Ashley Wilkes" in the film]. We used to sit under the big hair dryers together each morning and shoot the breeze.

When we were filming, news reached our studio that the great international actress Ingrid Bergman was coming to the United States to make a picture. Both Leslie Howard and I were dying to meet her. We kept pestering the producer, David O. Selznick, to bring her to the studio.

One morning Leslie and I were in makeup for a full day of shooting. We were sitting with curlers in our hair under those damn hair dryers with orange dye all over our heads. Selznick walked in with a big smile on his face. "Boys," he said, "I have a surprise for you!" In walked Ingrid Bergman. She looked at Leslie and me sitting there under those hair dryers and laughed at us.

"We girls should get together some day and go shopping," Bergman said with a smile, and then she walked away. I never forgave Selznick for that!

Rand had fond memories of GWTW's star, Clark Gable: "He was a man's man in every way," he recalled. "Gable could hunt, fish, drink, gamble, cuss, and laugh with the best of 'em." He shared this little-known story about Gable from the filming:

Gable absolutely didn't want to make Gone with the Wind. He knew there would be great expectations about his performance, and he had just been trashed by the critics for making a dog of a picture called Parnell. Gable was no "actor" in the traditional sense. He was just Gable playing himself. He didn't think he could do the job, and he didn't want to do it.

After he signed on, he was great, but one scene threw him. It was the scene when his little daughter died, and he was supposed to cry. Gable just couldn't do it. He didn't know how to "act" out a cry, and he felt his fans would think he was a sissy. Directors and coaches spent a long time trying to get Gable to cry, but nothing worked.

Finally, the director, Victor Fleming, called a break in shooting. Fleming was like a father to Gable. He was much older, tougher, and experienced. Gable thought of him as a second father. Fleming put his arm around Gable and said, "Let's go get a drink." As they left, Fleming turned and signaled to the crew to stay put. "Nobody leaves," Fleming whispered to a cameraman.

Gable and Fleming went out and for three hours got drunk. When they returned, they were laughing, singing, and carrying on. They were almost falling down. Suddenly, Fleming pretended that Gable somehow offended him. "You're no goddamned actor," Fleming growled at Gable. "You're just a no-good, goddamned pretty boy. You make me sick. Look around, King,[1] at some real actors—Vivien Leigh, Olivia De Havilland, Thomas Mitchell, Leslie Howard—they're actors. You're nothing! You've held up this production and we've all wasted our time with a worthless piece of shit named Clark Gable."

Gable was stunned and was really shaken up. Fleming persisted in his insults. "You're bringing down this whole picture, you sorry son of a bitch. You're a no-talent pretty boy asshole. You can't act worth a shit, and you make me sick."

---

1   A 1930s fan magazine contest named Gable the "King of Hollywood," and the nickname stuck.

With that, Fleming shoved Gable onto the crying scene set. He
ordered Olivia to join him. "Come on, King, let's see you act.
Let's have a good laugh at the pretty-boy King who isn't worth
a shit."

Fleming ordered the lights on, and then he whispered to the
cameraman, "Roll it." Suddenly, Fleming was no longer drunk!
He was cold sober when he called out, "Action!"

Gable filmed the scene and sobbed all the way through it. He
shot it in one take. It was one of the tenderest scenes in the
entire film. When Gable finished, the crew gave him a standing
ovation. Gable didn't know what had hit him. Fleming threw
his arm around Gable. "You are the King," he said with a smile.

As for the female leads in GWTW, Rand had fond memories
of each. Vivian Leigh, he said, was a great actress: "She was very
nice, but she was also very serious. During the day she was being
directed on the set by Victor Fleming, and she was intimidated
by him. Fleming was a man's director. There was nothing subtle
or gentle about him. So at night she would go to the home of her
director-friend George Cukor, who coached her in preparation for
the next morning's shooting."

He and costar Olivia De Havilland remained friends over the
decades,

Although she's mad at me right now. Olivia knows my wife and I
are good friends with Ann Rutherford [who also was in GWTW
and played the role of Scarlett's younger sister] and go out to
lunch often with her. Well, I think Ann was once involved with
a man married to Olivia's sister, actress Joan Fontaine. In fact, I
think Olivia was once involved with the man herself. Anyway,
I called Olivia in Paris a couple of weeks ago and asked her for

some traveling advice. She grew very haughty with me. Olivia is a sweet woman, but she still is the 'queen bee' and she snapped at me: 'Why don't you call Ann Rutherford for advice?' I got mad at her and got off the phone. But I guess it's time for me to call her and make up."

Rand once put me on the phone with Olivia De Havilland, and she and I corresponded a few times thereafter. Rand even warned my wife jokingly: "Be on your guard! Olivia's very fond of the judge. She always asks about him and says, '*James Rogan—James Rogan*, that's a fine Irish name,' and she always pronounces it with a thick brogue."

On another visit, he reminisced about his good friend and fellow actor from their early Hollywood years, President Ronald Reagan:

I used to go on publicity shoots with Ronnie when we were both young. In those days, the studios would set up things for us to attend on weekends, and the photographers from the different magazines would come and take our pictures. I remember one Saturday the studio sent Ronnie and me to the opening of an ice cream shop on Sunset Boulevard. They dressed us up in turn-of-the-century clothes and had us dispensing ice cream to a young starlet for the photographers.

Nothing pleased him more than talking about his early days as a cowboy in the Wild West shows. He told me that for ten years he roped, rode, and stood against a wooden backdrop while his partner threw long knives at him. He once showed me a picture of him standing against the wall with knives circling him and another blade sailing through the air toward him. "My partner was amazing," he remembered. "If he threw one knife at me, he threw 20,000 of them. He never drew blood and only once pierced my shirt." When I asked him how he could stand there for three shows a day and let someone throw knives at him, he replied, "Because I had to feed the kiddies."

To Chris + Jim —
After meeting your family...
you're a good judge of everything. Best always
Rand Brooks "Charles Hamilton"
AKA "Sweaty" — Cpl. Boone"

The Rogan family with Rand "Charles Hamilton" Brooks in his ambulance company office, Glendale, December 10, 1993. (Author's collection)

Besides his acting career in early Hollywood, we had another link that drew me to him. For many years, his wife was Stan Laurel's daughter Lois. As an old Laurel and Hardy fan, I delighted in listening to him reminisce about my favorite comedy duo:

Babe [Oliver Hardy's nickname] gave Stan all the credit for their success. Babe always said, "Stan was a genius, and all I did was do what he told me to do."

Although Stan could be funny in private, he was basically a very serious man. He was sweet but serious. We had a wonderful relationship.

Stan was married many times. One of his wives, Lois, was a bitch. She was cheap as well as mean. I was married to their daughter

Lois for 28 years. The first 20 years were good ones. My ex-wife, Lois, was a good lady, but her mother did everything possible to destroy our marriage.

The guy that owns the merchandising rights to Laurel and Hardy, Larry Harmon, is a crook. He stole the rights from Stan. I was going to handle all that for Stan and Stan would have made money. Instead, Harmon did it and cheated him. Stan's attorney, Ben Shipman, was also a crook. He kept Stan broke while he lived high off the hog from Stan's money. Stan kept Shipman around because Shipman was always able to get Stan out of trouble.

Rand offered a brief insight into another Hollywood legend, his onetime costar, Marilyn Monroe: "I got a call from a guy in New York recently who wanted me to talk about Marilyn for a scandal magazine. I told him to go to hell. I made a low-budget movie with

GWTW signed photograph of Olivia De Havilland. She surprised me with this treasure for my birthday in 1993. (Author's collection)

Marilyn many years ago [*Ladies of the Chorus*, 1948] when she was first getting started. There was no scandal there. Our relationship was friendly and pleasant. There was nothing sensational. Marilyn was just a sweet, naïve, and insecure girl."

I'm sorry that Rand never wrote his book. He had more than enough wonderful stories of the Golden Age of Hollywood to fill a volume. He was a great guy and a great friend.

• • •

Rand Brooks sold his ambulance company and retired to his ranch in the Santa Ynez Valley to breed horses. He died of cancer at age 84 on September 1, 2003.

Olivia De Havilland died of natural causes at age 104 on July 26, 2020.

32

Woooo–Hoooo

Our family friend Peggy Grande worked as former President Ronald Reagan's assistant chief of staff in his Los Angeles office for many years. The year following the birth of our twin daughters, Peggy offered to set up a meeting with President Reagan so they could have their picture taken with the great man. Is there more than one answer to an offer such as that?

After we arrived at their suite of offices in the Fox Plaza Building, she introduced us to the staff before leading us to Reagan's private office for our 11:00 a.m. appointment. She stepped inside and announced our arrival, and he came from behind his desk to welcome us. He wore small hearing aids in each ear and moved a bit slower since I last saw him, but he still stood arrow-straight for an 82 year-old man. Besides, there was nothing elderly in his firm handshake.

His private office had changed little since we last visited. His desk was framed with cases filled with books, photographs, and political mementos. The desk set I saw in 1989 (a gift from his Secretary of Defense) was now replaced by a large swiveling block with "Yes," "No," and "Maybe" carved on it. A pillow with the Reagan brand stitched on it rested on the sofa.

As he greeted Dana and Claire with a "finger" handshake, the girls appeared captivated by the grandfatherly statesman. Peggy, with camera in hand, suggested we pose for a group photograph. Reagan initially began to put Christine in the center, but I asked him to be in the middle so the girls would be next to him in the picture. I held Dana in my arms while Peggy readied her camera. He looked at Dana and leaned in closer while telling her she was a beautiful little girl. In a flash, she grabbed his nose and began to twist it! He laughed as I pried loose her fingers from the presidential proboscis.

Just before Peggy took our picture, Claire began wiggling in her mother's arms and kicked off her right shoe. I bent to retrieve it. Despite his advancing years, he beat me to it. He bent down quickly, scooped up her shoe, and put it back on her foot.

With Claire again fully dressed, and his nose free from groping fingers, we smiled for Peggy. She tried the shutter but it didn't work. "Mr. President, I'm so sorry," she said. "There's no film in the camera. This will just take a second."

While Peggy fiddled with the camera, he turned to me: "You know, Jim," he said, "from what I hear you'll end up in politics yourself. And when you're in, you'll take lots of these group pictures like we're doing here, with the politician standing in the middle of the shot. I want to teach you a little trick that the actor Fredric March taught me when I first started making pictures in Hollywood."

I paid close attention to the advice he shared: "When the photographer poses a group picture like this, and you're the guy standing in the middle, get the photographer to count for you *one—two—three* before taking the picture." As he told this story, he looked serious while imparting the suggestion. I listened just as intently as he continued: "Now, when the photographer is counting for you, when he gets between the numbers *two* and *three*, here is what you do." With that, he got up on his tiptoes, wiggled all ten of his fingers down by his sides, and sang in a warbling falsetto voice, *"Woooo-hoooo!"*

With the demonstration completed, he nodded his head affirming the wisdom of this suggestion. My expression doubtless betrayed my suspicion that he was pulling my leg, but his earnestness never wavered, I broke down: "Mr. President, I'm sure there's a really good reason you want me to count *one—two—three* and then wiggle all my fingers, get up on my tiptoes, and say, *Woooo-hoooo*, but I'll be darned if I can figure out why."

Still looking at me with great intensity, he gripped my arm and said, "Because, Jim, when you wiggle your fingers, get up on your toes, and go *Woooo-hoooo*, everyone will look at you like this." He slackened his jaw and made a vacant expression with his face, which added to my puzzlement.

"Mr. President, why do I want people to look at me like this?" I asked, and then I mimicked the dim-witted face back at him.

Reagan beamed. "Because," he said, "when they look at you like this [he again made the dopey face], in the photo it will look like this!" He then opened his mouth and eyes wide and looked at me as if in awe and admiration. "You can't get people to pose like that naturally!" he exclaimed. "It makes you look like Superman in the picture."

To Jim & Chris Rogan — With Best Wishes.
Ronald Reagan

Woooo-Hooo! Former President Ronald Reagan with my family, March 29, 1993. (Photograph by Peggy Grande; author's collection)

Because I still thought he was putting me on, I said, "Mr. President, you've been famous for 50 years. You've been a movie star, a TV star, a governor, a four-time candidate for president, and a two-term president. You've probably taken a million group photos. Are you telling me that in all those poses, you've had the photographer give you a *one—two—three* count, and then you got up on your toes, wiggled your fingers, and trilled *Woooo-hoooo*?"

Reagan patted me on the shoulder paternally, leaned in, and whispered in my ear with a big grin, "Damn near!"

When Peggy returned with a roll of film, I winked at Reagan and nodded my head toward her to signal that I wanted to play a joke on her. He nodded his assent silently: "Mr. President," I said, "my wife really wanted this photograph to have a homogenous look to it. So that you can match our daughters' outfits, we brought you a large, floppy polka-dotted cap to wear like the one the girls are wearing!" I pretended to rifle through the diaper bag for the nonexistent hat.

Reagan reached out his hands anxiously. "Oh, that's great1 Give it to me!" We laughed at Peggy's shocked reaction to the anticipated loss of her boss' dignity.

Peggy loaded the film, but she still had trouble getting everyone to look at the camera because Reagan kept kidding throughout the session. When he said that he babysat for a reasonable fee, I handed him Dana and told him that Christine and I were going to the movies and that we'd pick up the kids in a few hours.

"Take as long as you like!" he replied as he held Dana.

With the photo op completed, he asked if we had visited his new presidential library, and then he showed us his framed copy of the "five presidents" photograph taken at the dedication. He told us it was the first time in history that five chief executives came together for such an occasion.

I asked if he had any plans to invite newly inaugurated President Bill Clinton to a similar event and make it a six-president picture. He broke into a wry smile and shook his head. "No comment," he said dryly. (In a break with protocol, Clinton had failed to invite the Reagans to his presidential inauguration ceremony two months earlier. The White House later claimed it was an oversight.)

Reagan told me that he had reread my 1988 article explaining why I had switched from the Democrat to Republican Party. He said that as an ex-Democrat himself, he became a Republican for many reasons. "But the thing that really did it for me was a radio address by Al Smith that I heard in the 1930s. Smith was the 1928 Democrat nominee for president and former governor of New York who had been a big Franklin Roosevelt supporter. Smith broke with Roosevelt and declared the Democrat Party had abandoned its leadership role during Roosevelt's term." As he shared this account, his humor and vigor disappeared momentarily. He lost his train of thought and stood in uncomfortable silence groping for the words to finish. Fortunately, I was up on my FDR trivia, and I helped him complete the story by filling in the details of Smith's break with Roosevelt. The uncomfortable moment passed.

We had scheduled only a brief photo op with the girls, but, as usual, he prolonged our appointment by telling stories. Not wanting to impose on him further, I thanked him for making time to see us, and Christine assured him that our daughters would grow up treasuring their photograph with him. He thanked us for the visit, we bid him goodbye, and he escorted us out the door.

In exiting his private office, we encountered a half dozen secretaries and assistants waiting outside. Word had spread throughout the office that twin baby girls were here, and they had waited to see them. The charming staffers surrounded us, with each wanting a turn holding one of them. Reagan remained standing in his office doorway watching the commotion Dana and Claire had caused. After passing the girls around and sharing a few "new father" stories, I chatted with Dottie Dellinger, his longtime secretary.

Twenty minutes later, someone handed Dana back to me as I turned to collect my family and leave. When I looked back, I noticed that Christine and Claire were nowhere around. I asked Peggy what had happened to them. "They're back inside with the boss," she said. "They've been in there all this time."

I peeked inside his office and saw Christine deep in conversation with Reagan while Claire nestled quietly in her mother's arms. Rapping on the door, I stuck my head inside and asked, "Do I need to be jealous about this?" Christine told me later that when we left his office, she held Claire so that she was facing backward toward Reagan. When the secretaries intercepted us, and unbeknownst to me, he had followed Christine out the door while wiggling his finger and playing with Claire. When the secretaries took turns holding Dana and as I chatted with Dottie, he invited Christine and Claire back inside his office. During their second visit he showed them the artwork on his office walls, including a horse and pasture scene painted by his barber's 12 year-old daughter. He handed Christine his binoculars and gave her a tour of the Los Angeles landscape.

Reagan asked Dana and me to rejoin him in his office, where he showed us paintings and photos of his ranch near Santa Barbara. He said he had bought the ranch many years ago and had done much of the brush clearing himself. He still went up there to work on the roads and to clear brush because he worried about a series of recent hill fires.

Christine told him that we had stayed stayed at the Alisal Ranch near Solvang, which abuts a portion of his property, and that we rode horses near the common border. An avid horseman, he replied that he knew almost every tree and rock on those paths. He told us the next time we were riding up there to come get him and he would join us.

Reagan said that Peggy had told him the story of our adopting our twin daughters. He told us that he and his first wife (actress Jane Wyman) had adopted their son Michael, and that the adoption had proved a great blessing to his family. "But then," he added as he patted the cheeks of our twins, "you don't need me to tell you that."

Christine, Claire, and President Reagan share a private moment in his office, March 29, 1993. (Photograph by Peggy Grande; author's collection)

• • •

As we approached the elevator, a young Boy Scout with a sash full of merit badges arrived for his photo op with the former president. The young scout looked up at me and said excitedly, "I'm going to shake hands with President Reagan and get his autograph!"

Remembering my own youthful enthusiasm when I first met him, I understood how he felt—perhaps better than most.

33

Nixon at Twilight

I may have only met Richard Nixon once (once and a half, if you count the time that the Disneyland fake Secret Service employee shooed me away), but I did get to hear him speak several times in his twilight years.

In early 1993, I received an invitation to attend a policy conference on US–Asian relations in the post–Cold War era, which featured a luncheon address by former President Nixon. More than 1,000 people crammed into the Biltmore Bowl in Los Angeles to hear him. I had a good seat: at the tables next to me were former Secretaries of State Henry Kissinger and Lawrence Eagleburger, former Treasury Secretary William E. Simon, former Japanese Prime Minister Toshiki Kaifu, former National Security Advisors Robert McFarlane and Brent Scowcroft, and California Governor Pete Wilson.

In introducing the former president, Wilson said that he began his political career as a young assistant during Nixon's unsuccessful 1962 race for California governor. In 1966, Nixon offered him a permanent staff position as he geared up to run for the presidency. Wilson demurred, telling Nixon that he wanted to run for the California legislature that year. "Pete," Nixon told him, "if that is how you feel you can best serve your country, then run." Wilson ran and won, and it started a career in elective office that spanned three decades.

When Nixon took the stage, he joked about giving Wilson his

start in politics: "Pete, I'm sorry I got you into so much trouble so long ago!"

The former president had aged physically since I saw him last. His hair looked grayer and his voice had grown more gravelly. His mind, however, remained razor-sharp, and he delivered a lengthy discourse on Asian policy without any notes before him. He said that if peace and stability are to continue there, the United States must remain involved in that region along with the other major players. "We are the only power that is not considered to be a potential threat to any other nation," he said. "The unanswered question is whether the United States has the will to rise to the challenge. America responded magnificently to the threat of the Cold War when it began. The question is, with the Cold War over, can we respond to the promise of peace?"

Nixon recalled his first visit to Japan shortly after World War II, when the prime minister had told him that America had done his country a favor by destroying Japanese factories. "We are now building better ones to compete better," the minister told him long ago. "And," he added, "he was right. Japan's gross national product is one-half the size of America's, and they are gaining."

Regarding China, Nixon quoted Napoleon: "China is a sleeping giant. Let him sleep. For when he wakes, his size will be felt throughout the world."

"China," he added, "no longer sleeps. The Great Wall [of China] is very thick. It is difficult to be heard from the inside, but it is impossible to be heard from the outside."

Turning to Russia, he urged the United States to continue sending economic support there to encourage democracy and establish free markets. Without the United States making this investment, "the peace dividend will go down the tube." That, in turn, would force America to rearm at previous levels. He praised President Clinton for supporting aid to Russia and insisted that a market economy there would eventually strengthen the American economy and create thousands of domestic jobs. Noting that Kissinger, his former Secretary of State, dissented on this point, Nixon laughed and said, "I hate to disagree with Henry on anything!"

Former President Richard Nixon, the Biltmore Hotel, Los Angeles, April 21, 1993. (Photograph by the author)

"It is almost cliché to say the Cold War is over and the West has won it. That is only half-true," he argued. "It is true the communists have lost the Cold War, but the West has not yet won."

President Nixon was 80 when he delivered his speech at the Biltmore Hotel on April 21, 1993. He had one year and one day remaining to him.

• • •

On January 20, 1969, the day Richard Nixon took the oath as the 37th president of the United States, I was an 11 year-old boy who cut school to watch the ceremony from start to finish on our rabbit-eared black-and-white television. Using my Christmas gift—an old reel-to-reel tape recorder—I draped the microphone over the channel knob and made an antiquated recording of the event. For months thereafter, I replayed my tape of Nixon's inaugural address until I could recite it almost by heart. I never dreamed that a quarter century later I would attend the silver anniversary of that historic event with him.

Nixon commemorated the 25th anniversary of his inaugural by hosting a reunion for his cabinet and senior administration officials at his presidential library. The ceremony was by invitation only, but my friend Bob Finch (a former Nixon cabinet member) gave me two tickets. I brought along Walt Lewis, my former boss in the Los

Angeles County District Attorney's office (and a lifelong registered Democrat) as my guest. A perennial Nixon hater, I thought he might find the event intriguing.

The morning was beautiful, with a warm sun and light breeze blowing. Folding lawn chairs faced the reflecting pool with American flags encircling it. Scores of police, Secret Service agents stood watch as guests enjoyed refreshments at the garden reception.

Ushers invited everyone to take seats for the ceremony. Walt and I found chairs in the front row of the non-reserved area (with reserved seats saved for the Nixon Administration officials). A bell choir played *America the Beautiful*, library director John Taylor introduced the dignitaries, which comprised a *Who's Who* of Washington power brokers during the four previous Republican administrations. Seated nearby were former Secretaries of State Henry Kissinger, William P. Rogers, and George Shultz; former Secretaries of Defense Caspar Weinberger, James Schlesinger, and Donald Rumsfeld; former Secretary of the Treasury William Simon; former Secretaries of Housing and Urban Development George Romney (father of 2012 GOP presidential nominee Mitt Romney) and Samuel Pierce; former Budget Director Roy Ash; former Postmaster General Winton Blount; former Secretaries of Education Terrel H. Bell and Lamar Alexander; former Secretary of Transportation Claude Brinegar; former Secretaries of Labor Peter Brennan and James Hodgson; former Secretaries of Commerce Ann McLaughlin, Maurice Stans, Barbara Franklin, and Peter Peterson; former Secretary of Health, Education, and

Former Presidents Richard Nixon and Gerald Ford, the Nixon Library, January 20, 1994. (Photograph by the author)

Welfare Bob Finch; former Secretary of the Interior Walter Hickel; and former Ambassadors Leonard Firestone and Walter Annenberg. The biggest round of applause went to Kissinger, the final cabinet member to arrive. While awaiting their introductions, I saw Nixon, former President Gerald Ford, and former First Lady Betty Ford standing together along the corridor from the library leading to the outdoor stage.

William Simon opened the program by recalling the mood in America 25 years earlier on that blustery 1969 Inauguration Day: "America was rocked by Vietnam and civil unrest. Richard Nixon challenged us to overcome these difficulties. He led America out of Vietnam, led our prisoners of war home with honor, and led the way to better relations with the Soviet Union and China. Despite the pounding he received, Richard Nixon would not let the tragedies of his life or of his presidency destroy him. He was truly the last casualty of the Vietnam War."

George Shultz spoke directly to Nixon, asking, "Do you remember when I was your Secretary of Labor, when we did the 'Philadelphia Plan' and the full-employment budget?" As Nixon nodded, Schultz added, "I tried to think of something nice to say about your wage and price controls! At least we showed that if a great cast of characters—John Connally, Don Rumsfeld, and I—couldn't make them work, nobody could!" When the laughter and applause subsided, he said, "And Bill Clinton still hasn't gotten the message!"

Former Secretary of State Henry Kissinger, the Nixon Library, January 20, 1994. (Photograph by the author)

In his remarks, Henry Kissinger referenced the faint chants heard from a small group of protesters across the street: "[In 1969] protesters believed that ending the Vietnam War was as easy as changing television channels. We knew the logistics would be a difficult, heart-breaking task. But Richard Nixon's position was one of highest morality: that those who relied on the word of his predecessors and threw in their lot with democracy would not be abandoned. The honor of the United States was an element of the peace process. By becoming the architect of peace, Richard Nixon served the children of those who protested against him."

Kissinger also directed a personal observation to Nixon: "As a refugee from totalitarianism, and speaking with a foreign accent, and having always supported your political opponents, it is a tribute to your generosity that you gave me the opportunity to serve our nation. Our country will always remember you for your policies and legacies."

Nixon's first Secretary of State, William Rogers, walked to the stage slowly and fumbled for his reading glasses before sharing these early impressions of his future chief:

> I first met Richard Nixon during the Hiss-Chambers case.[1] He was the only member of the Congress who wanted to continue investigating Alger Hiss. Nixon's philosophy was simple: if Chambers lied when he said he knew Alger Hiss during his communist activities, then we should say so and exonerate Hiss. If Hiss was lying, then America needed to know. This determination led to the successful case against Hiss because Richard Nixon refused to quit.

---

1   During the Truman Administration, *Time* magazine news editor Whittaker Chambers admitted having been active during his youth in the Communist Party and claimed to have known Alger Hiss—a high-ranking government official—as a member of the same communist "cell." Hiss denied the allegation and said he never met Chambers. Then-Congressman Nixon pressed a congressional investigation, and Hiss eventually went to prison for perjury. After the publication of the Venona Papers in 1995, as noted by Ted Morgan of the Claremont Institute, Hiss' guilt became indisputable.

Next was the "Fund Crisis."[2] Many people on Eisenhower's campaign train wanted Richard Nixon off the ticket. But Richard Nixon refused to resign until he had the chance to address the nation. This was before the era of political damage control teams. Richard Nixon spoke without notes or a prepared text. Yet after his speech, the crowds grew bigger for him than appeared for [Democrat presidential nominee] Adlai Stevenson.
Finally, Rogers recalled the defeats and the victories:

When Richard Nixon lost the presidency to John F. Kennedy in 1960, it was the closest election in history. Many Nixon supporters demanded a recount, but Richard Nixon refused. He was too concerned about the stability of the American government. He lost again in 1962 when he ran for governor of California. But this quality of resilience led to his election to the presidency in 1968 and his huge reelection victory in 1972. It was a tribute to his leadership, and his activities over the last 20 years since he left the White House are a testimony to his determination.

It fell upon former President Gerald Ford to introduce Nixon. Speaking from three-by-five note cards, Ford remembered:

When I first went to Congress in 1949, Richard Nixon had already emerged as a leader from the Alger Hiss case. He exposed the dangers of communism around the globe, and it now becomes my job to sum up Richard Nixon in five minutes!

2   Shortly after Dwight D. Eisenhower selected Nixon as his 1952 running mate, Democrats accused Nixon of accepting a "slush fund" from wealthy businessmen to cover personal expenses. With pressure mounting for Eisenhower to drop him from the ticket, Nixon appeared on live television and delivered his famous "Checkers" speech in which he denied any impropriety. Eisenhower retained Nixon and they sailed to victory in November.

When thinking about President Nixon and how he helped to meet and win some of our greatest public challenges of all time, and how he met and prevailed in a myriad of personal challenges as well, it comes down to two words in my opinion: resolve and resilience—the resolve to stay the course against all odds, and the resilience to outlast, and sometimes even outlive, his critics in one personal crisis after another.

The audience stood and cheered as Ford presented Nixon. They embraced and waved while library assistants mounted the stage, removed the lectern, and replaced it with a lone microphone on a pole. Once again, Nixon planned to speak extemporaneously.

When the crowd fell silent, Nixon clasped his hands behind his back and thanked Ford for the generous introduction, and then he paid tribute to his White House successor: "I have known Jerry Ford for many years. Jerry was a football star center at the University of Michigan, and I couldn't earn a letter at Whittier College! I once asked Jerry if he made the All-American football team. He told me, 'No, I wasn't that good.' Although Jerry Ford did not make the All-American team in football, after 33 years of service to his country, he sure made the team for America."

Mentioning the small group of chanting protesters across the street, Nixon chuckled and said to the audience, "I hope you haven't been distressed by some of that background noise we've had here. I remind our young people out there that I've been heckled by experts!"

Commanding the attention of the rapt crowd with a voice raspy with age, he spoke of his Inauguration Day 25 years ago, and he compared it to the state of the world today:

During my 1969 inaugural parade, I was disappointed when the Secret Service insisted we ride in a closed car from the Capitol to the White House. They told me there were too many protesters along the parade route waiting with eggs and other overripe substances. Things are so different in the world today than they were in 1969. One hundred million people are now liberated in Eastern Europe while communism is collapsing in China. And in America, there is a different spirit. When I last met [Chinese communist dictator] Mao Zedong shortly before his death in 1976, he asked me, "Is peace all you want?" I told him we want peace, but we want peace with justice. That simple answer would not be sufficient today.

Today America's heritage of freedom is being spread around the globe. This idea of freedom must be our focus for peace.... Can the West provide to these searching peoples the freedoms they seek? That is the challenge of today: the challenge to peace.
As to the future, Nixon offered this prediction:

As we look into the next century, I see a very exciting prognosis. We will see a century where enormous progress will be made in health. Political freedom will be the rule rather than the exception, because the communications revolution has had the effect of making dictatorships unviable. They cannot stand having their closed societies opened up.

As we approach the day of a new millennium, I would say you could not possibly think of a day in which one would be more fortunate than to live in the United States of America on this day and in this time. The reason for that is what we can achieve in the future. In the next century, the role for the United States will be to provide leadership. If we refuse, who will do it? The United Nations? De Gaulle once said that parliaments can paralyze policy; they cannot implement it.

Looking across the courtyard to the modest house where he was born 81 years earlier and where his beloved wife, Pat, was laid to rest in the garden recently, Nixon ended his remarks with a simple analysis of the incredible ups and downs of almost 50 years in public life:

Is politics worth it? I remember in 1973 when we entertained a choir from a South Central Los Angeles church at the White House. At the end of the performance, a young black man said to me, "It's a long way from Watts to the White House." Today, standing in the shadow of the simple home my father built only a few feet from here, I can tell you it was a long way from Yorba Linda to the White House, too. Politics is never going to be heaven, and sometimes it is hell. But it was worth the trip.

The final speech of a long career: former President Richard Nixon, the Nixon Library, January 20, 1994. (Photograph by the author)

• • •

After hearing Nixon's speech at the library that day, I asked Walt Lewis about his impressions. He told me, "You know, I supported John F. Kennedy over Nixon in 1960 and I grew up despising him. I always supported *anyone* that ran against Nixon. In fact, one of the happiest days of my life was the day he resigned the presidency. That's why I still can't believe I'm saying this, but when I sat listening to him, I hung on his every word. He has a charisma that I've never seen before. Maybe it just doesn't come across on TV. I don't know how else to express it—*I was drawn to him.*"

Not long after, Walt became a Republican.

• • •

At the end of Nixon's remarks that day, his administration alumni joined him onstage for a group photograph. When the program adjourned, Nixon stood at the side of the stage greeting guests and signing autographs. I was in his receiving line and (yet again) just about to meet him when Bob Finch called me aside to introduce me to some of his former White House colleagues. While I spoke with Bob and his friends, Nixon's security detail led him away.

Although my habit of just missing the chance to meet Nixon was growing monotonous, today I didn't mind because Bob gave me some great news. He said that he had talked to Nixon about me earlier that morning and of my oft-frustrated desire to meet him, discuss his career in politics, and seek his advice. Bob said that Nixon planned to return to the library for an intimate dinner with a few friends on June 16, and that the former president had invited me personally to join him. "Nixon told me to tell you that at your dinner, you can ask him questions until you get bored!" Bob said.

Finally, my chance to spend time with Richard Nixon and seek his advice would come, and the opportunity couldn't be timelier. A little more than a month after this Nixon Library reunion, I stepped down from the bench and announced my candidacy for the California legislature in a special election to fill a vacant seat. My time had arrived.

Former Presidents Richard Nixon and Gerald Ford, former First Lady Betty Ford, and alumni of the Nixon Administration, January 20, 1994. (Author's collection)

• • •

When Richard Nixon left the stage on that 25th anniversary of his inaugural, he walked to the nearby courtyard to visit his wife's grave before departing the library. Three months later, he rested beside her. He died at age 81 on April 22, 1994 of complications following a stroke.

The speech Nixon delivered at that anniversary celebration was his final public address. Sadly, our dinner never occurred.

Once again, I had missed him.

• • •

Former Secretary of State William P. Rogers died at age 87 of congestive heart failure on January 2, 2001.

Former Secretary of State Lawrence Eagleburger died at age 80 of pneumonia on June 4, 2011.

Former Secretary of Defense Caspar Weinberger died of pneumonia at age 88 on March 28, 2006.

Former Secretary of Defense James Schlesinger died of pneumonia at age 85 on March 27, 2014.

Former Secretary of the Treasury William Simon died of pulmonary fibrosis at age 71 on June 3, 2000.

Former Secretary of Housing and Urban Development George Romney, the former governor of Michigan, died of a heart attack at age 88 on July 8, 1995.

Former Secretary of Housing and Urban Development Samuel Pierce died at age 78 on October 31, 2000.

Former Budget Director Roy Ash died at age 93 of Parkinson's disease on December 14, 2011.

Former Postmaster General Winton Blount died at age 81 on October 24, 2002.

Former Secretary of Education Terrel H. Bell died at age 74 of pulmonary fibrosis on June 22, 1996.

Former Secretary of Transportation Claude Brinegar died at age 82 of natural causes on March 13, 2009.

Former Secretary of Labor Peter Brennan died at age 78 of cancer on October 2, 1996.

Former Secretary of Labor James Hodgson died at age 96 on November 28, 2012.

Former Secretary of Commerce Maurice Stans died at age 90 of congestive heart failure on April 14, 1998.

Former Secretary of Commerce Peter Peterson died at age 91 of natural causes on March 20, 1998.

Former Secretary of Health, Education, and Welfare Bob Finch died at age 70 of a heart attack on October 10, 1995.

Former Secretary of the Interior Walter Hickel, the former governor of Alaska, died at age 90 on May 7, 2010.

Former Ambassador Leonard Firestone died at age 89 on December 24, 1996.

Former Ambassador Walter Annenberg died at age 94 of pneumonia on October 1, 2002.

Former National Security Adviser Brent Scowcroft died at age 95 on August 6, 2020.

34

I Don't Do Trash

In early May 1994, I won a special election to fill a vacancy in the California State Assembly. The day after taking office, I flew to Los Angeles to attend a fundraiser for California Attorney General Dan Lungren and his guest speaker, former Secretary of Defense Dick Cheney.

A popular national figure in 1994 because of his leading role in helping direct U.S. forces during the Bush Administration's Persian Gulf War, Cheney now traveled America as an undeclared candidate for the 1996 Republican presidential nomination. At a private reception, Lungren introduced me to the balding, bespectacled Cheney, who congratulated me on my victory and asked to get together

Former Defense Secretary (and future Vice President) Dick Cheney with me, Century Plaza Hotel, Los Angeles, May 10, 1994. (Author's collection)

with me in Sacramento soon to discuss his White House plans.

• • •

During his introduction of Cheney, Lungren said that he had argued his first case before the United States Supreme Court recently. Later that evening, at a cocktail party in Washington, he saw Associate Justice Ruth Bader Ginsberg, who said she remembered him from his oral argument. "It isn't often," she told him, "that we get many tall, good-looking men arguing before our Court."

"Can you imagine," Lungren asked, "if I had said something like that to her?"

Cheney's physical appearance belied his speaking skills: the dour-looking man had a polished style and wonderful comedic timing. He began his remarks with this story:

When I first won election to Congress in 1978, my best campaign worker was Mrs. Johnson, my high school English teacher. She would return all my campaign flyers and mailers with the grammatical errors corrected. Mrs. Johnson liked to call me from time to time, and when I was Secretary of Defense she somehow managed to get the personal telephone number that rang directly on my desk in the Pentagon.

In August 1991, we were in the midst of an international crisis with an attempted coup against Soviet leader Mikhail Gorbachev. I was in a high-level strategy meeting with the chairman of the Joint Chiefs of Staff, the Secretary of State, and many other officials. Suddenly, my private telephone rang. It was Mrs. Johnson calling from Jackson Hole, Wyoming.

"Hi, Dick," she said. "How are you?"

I told her I was very busy, that we were in a big meeting, and that there was a coup going on in the Soviet Union. I asked if I could call her back.

"No," she said. "I've got a big problem now." I asked her what was wrong.

"Dick, they're not picking up my trash."

I told her, "Mrs. Johnson, right now I have generals and admirals in my office, the Soviet Union is collapsing, and we are facing a military coup against Gorbachev. I'm Secretary of Defense now, not a congressman. I do war and peace—I don't do trash."

Mrs. Johnson said, "Dick, you were in Congress for ten years. Don't tell me you don't do trash."

I asked why she didn't call old Joe Sullivan, the city maintenance worker who lived down the street from her. "I didn't want to go that high up," she replied.

• • •

Five months later, Cheney's office called and invited me to join him at a GOP luncheon at the Quiet Cannon Restaurant in Montebello. There I met with Cheney privately before the event. He asked if he could visit me in Sacramento after the 1994 midterm elections to discuss his 1996 presidential plans, and to have me introduce him around to my Republican colleagues to lay the early groundwork for a California primary effort. We agreed to set a date for the visit after Thanksgiving.

During the luncheon, I sat with Andrew Goldman, a member of Cheney's staff. Goldman said Cheney had been campaigning for Republican candidates for the past 18 months and would announce his own presidential candidacy before Christmas. "We'll have about a month to rest after the November elections," he sighed, "and then we are in for two years of hell."

Following his introduction, Cheney began his speech by crediting his marriage to a Republican election:

> My wife and I met after the 1952 presidential campaign when I moved to Wyoming. As a result of Eisenhower's victory that year, my father moved our family out there to accept a position in the new administration. I once told my wife that if Eisenhower had lost the election in 1952, we never would have met in Wyoming and she would have married another man. She replied, 'Yeah, and he would have become Secretary of Defense instead of you!'

Cheney focused his remarks on what he saw as the likely prospect of upset Republican victories in the 1994 midterm elections. Since I always heard GOP leaders make similar predictions every cycle (only to see the claim fall flat each November), I gave this commentary little weight. After all, Democrats held uncontested control of the U.S. House of Representatives for 40 uninterrupted years. Still, Cheney saw a different horizon:

> Nineteen ninety-four can be one of the defining elections, just like 1980. In that year, President Jimmy Carter endured military failure. Our defense rescue helicopters crashed in the Iranian desert and he couldn't get our hostages out. Later that year America elected Ronald Reagan. After 12 years of Republican rule, nobody questioned the credibility of U.S. military forces. Our friends knew they could count on us, and our enemies knew not to cross us.

He said that he has been campaigning for Republican candidates for the last a year and a half and had driven alone in his car across the country over 8,000 miles. "I wanted to reconnect with the American people," he said:

> When I was Secretary of Defense, I spent a lot of time on international problems and Soviet issues. Now I wanted to do like I did when I was in Congress. I hit all the truck stops and McDonalds' along the way. It reminded me that America is really all of us. There are 250 million people who get up each morning and contribute to our nation. I believe the Republican Party of 1994 is about America. People have had a belly full of government in their face. We are spending too much money and allowing government to interfere too much. The good news is that in November of 1994, we will see a new phenomenon—a national Republican victory in state and federal races.

Cheney predicted that after the 1994 elections, Republicans would hold more than 200 House seats: "We will have the greatest number of Republicans in the House of Representatives than we have had in over 40 years," he promised. "And Bill Clinton's worst nightmare will come true: waking up the Wednesday morning after the election and finding Newt Gingrich as the new speaker of the House!"

• • •

In October 1994, Dick Cheney saw a tsunami coming that few others recognized or believed. He was right. That November, Republicans swamped Democrats in the midterm elections and seized control of Congress for the first time in four decades.

The one thing Cheney didn't see that day was his own change of heart. After spending two years prepping for a White House run, he backed out of the 1996 presidential contest. However, he didn't remain sidelined on the bench. Four years later, George W. Bush picked him as his running mate. He went on to serve two terms as vice president of the United States before returning to private life in 2009.

35

Before the Storm

I encountered President Bill Clinton a couple of times during my state legislative tenure and before I went to Congress, where I crossed swords with him during our impeachment duel.

The first time was in December 1994, when I was in Washington to attend the American Legislative Exchange Council conference. While there I visited my friend John Emerson at his White House office, where he worked as a special assistant to the president. I first met John when I was a deputy D.A. for Los Angeles County and he worked as the chief deputy for the Los Angeles City Attorney. John invited me to attend President Clinton's signing ceremony for the General Agreement on Tariffs and Trade (GATT) treaty, designed to cut global tariffs and abolish trade barriers between the signatory nations.

On the morning of the ceremony, I arrived at the Organization of American States building on Constitution Avenue. A Secret Service agent escorted me into the ornate second-floor chamber. On a center-stage table rested the treaty, bordered by a neat row of a dozen bill-signing pens for Clinton's use. A lectern framed by the United States and presidential flags was to the right.

The Marine Band played as the guests filled the hall. Dignitaries on the stage included Senate Minority Leader Bob Dole (two years away from becoming Clinton's 1996 Republican White House opponent), outgoing Speaker of the House Thomas Foley, Commerce Secretary Ron Brown, and Treasury Secretary Lloyd Bentsen (the 1988 Democrat vice presidential nominee). The audience cheered the arrival of Bentsen, who had announced his retirement two days earlier.

With everyone seated, the band played *Ruffles and Flourishes* and *Hail to the Chief* as Clinton and Vice President Al Gore entered the room together. Clinton smiled and nodded as the audience rose and applauded.

Gore opened the meeting by thanking those responsible for helping to pass the treaty. "But the person who helped the most,"

he added, "was the president of the United States." With that simple introduction, Clinton joined Gore at the lectern and credited his vice president for the treaty's passage: "If [Gore] hadn't gone on television in that national debate on NAFTA and refuted the theory of the 'giant sucking sound,' I'm not sure we would be here today."[1]

At the conclusion of his remarks, Clinton sat at the table as the dignitaries gathered behind him. He signed the treaty

President Bill Clinton at the GATT Treaty signing, Washington, December 8, 1994. In the background are (from left) Commerce Secretary Ron Brown, House Speaker Tom Foley, and Senator Bob Dole. (Photograph by the author)

---

1 GATT's companion treaty was the North American Free Trade Agreement (NAFTA) that Congress passed the previous year. Prior to its passage, Gore debated former presidential candidate Ross Perot, who claimed that Americans would hear a "giant sucking sound" as we lost domestic jobs to Mexico if Congress enacted NAFTA.

Senator Bob Dole, GATT Treaty signing, Washington, December 8, 1994. (Photograph by the author)

using various pens, and then he passed them out as souvenirs to those who helped secure passage.

Clinton greeted our group briefly before heading to his waiting motorcade. It was the first time I had seen him since our Memphis encounter almost 20 years earlier.

Dole welcomed me to Washington and said that he would like to visit with some of my Assembly GOP colleagues and me about his planned presidential race against Clinton in 1996. We agreed to meet in Sacramento later. While we talked, a White House aide rushed over and handed Dole one of the treaty-signing pens. "Oh, I almost forgot this," Dole said as he slid the memento into his coat pocket.

• • •

A few months later, I returned to Washington for the annual bipartisan legislative trip hosted by the speaker of the California State Assembly. For three days, administration and congressional leaders briefed us on issues of state and national interest. On our final day, we boarded a chartered bus for a meeting with President Clinton at the White House.

An aide greeted us at the North Gate and escorted us up the circular driveway to the West Wing, where a Marine sentry stood guard. Our delegation settled into the Roosevelt Room (next to the Oval Office). On the mantel rested Theodore Roosevelt's Nobel Peace Prize alongside a sculpted bust of Eleanor Roosevelt and portraits of the Presidents Roosevelt (Theodore and Franklin).

Shortly before 9:00 a.m., California Assembly Speaker Willie

Brown advised us that Clinton and White House Chief of Staff Leon Panetta were on their way. "When the president gets here, I will introduce him," Brown said. "The president will then speak. There will be no time for questions." Moments later, the door opened and Clinton and Panetta entered. The delegation rose and applauded. Brown, in an uncharacteristic loss for words, could only come up with, "Ladies and gentlemen, the President of the United States of America, William Jefferson Clinton."

"You did that well," Clinton cracked to Brown as he stepped to the lectern. Looking tanned and dapper in a dark blue suit and black onyx cuff links bearing a gold presidential seal, Clinton scanned the room at the collection of Republican and Democrat legislators currently engaged in a protracted speakership battle after the midterm elections left our chamber in a 40–40 tie. "Well," he joked, "y'all look like you're gettin' along okay!" The legislators laughed as he added, "Maybe the press reports coming out of California are as wrong as the press reports coming out of Washington."

He spoke for 20 minutes about federal issues related to California, but he also confronted his Party's recent loss of the U.S. House of Representatives for the first time in 40 years. As to new GOP Speaker Newt Gingrich's "Contract with America" upon which Republican House candidates ran and won, he claimed that the GOP saw it as a cure for America's problems. "I agree with some of the things in the Contract," he added, "for example, prison policies and tort reform. I want a smaller government, but I want a more effective government. I want a government that is lean but not mean. We need to empower the people to make do in their own lives. We need to worry about the security of our own people on their own streets. The great debate in America now is this: what should government be doing, and who is going to pay for it. In the federal government, we want you to tell us what we can do to help you, so that you can do what needs to be done."

Clinton introduced Panetta (a former California congressman) who discussed administration policies for disaster relief in California. While Panetta spoke, Clinton stood off to the side with Speaker Brown. Because of my proximity, I could hear Clinton ask Brown in a whisper which GOP member was his "nemesis" in the ongoing speakership battle. Brown whispered in Clinton's ear, and then he and Clinton looked over at Assembly GOP leader Jim Brulte, who was seated in the rear of the room.

After taking questions, an aide signaled that Clinton needed to leave. Brown stepped to the microphone: "Just so everyone knows," he said while pointing to Clinton, "it was his idea to take questions, not mine! So staff, please don't be mad at me!"

As the legislators stood and applauded, Clinton approached those of us seated in the front row and shook hands. I handed him a document signed for me by his five predecessors I had met over the years and asked him to autograph it. "How long did it take you to get all of these on here?" Clinton asked as he inked his signature to the collection.

"Too long!" I replied as I thanked him for the courtesy.

President Bill Clinton with (from left) me, Assemblywoman (later Congresswoman) Barbara Lee, unidentified White House staffer, Assemblyman (later Los Angeles Mayor) Antonio Villaraigosa, Assemblywoman Sheila Kuehl, the White House, March 15, 1995. (Official White House photograph)

• • •

When I ran for Congress in 1996, Clinton came to my district that June to campaign—not for my opponent or against me, but on his own behalf. I hadn't planned to attend his speech at Glendale Community College, but the Republican National Committee called the night before and asked me to go and rebut everything he said that the GOP didn't like. Of course, a lowly state legislator trying to compete with the president of the United States for press attention was something of a silly notion, but I was game for the challenge.

On the morning of his speech, ushers showed me to a reserved seat with the other local elected officials. As usual, Clinton ran behind schedule, so we all sweltered under a hot sun awaiting his arrival (reporters called this "Running on Clinton Time").

A formation of three Marine helicopters circled overhead, with the last in line emblazoned with the presidential seal on its side. A few minutes later recorded music blared *Hail to the Chief* and Clinton emerged onstage amid the cheers of a very enthusiastic crowd.

After delivering a stump speech extolling what his political advisor Dick Morris called "small bore" campaign issues (tax breaks for college students, more educational programming on television, mandatory school uniforms in public schools, and teenager curfews), Clinton climbed off the stage, shed his coat, and dove into the crowd. While he shook hands along the rope line, I searched for reporters who might be interested in my rebuttal to the president's nanny-state remedies. When it became clear there weren't any wanting to hear my alternate vision for America, I abandoned my RNC assignment and invited my staff to join me for lunch at the Rocky Cola Café in nearby Montrose.[2]

When we arrived at the diner, I noticed a couple of Secret Service agents outside but I paid them little attention. I assumed they were

---

2   Now closed, the Rocky Cola Café was located at 2201 Honolulu Ave, Montrose, California.

now off duty following the president's Glendale departure. Once seated in a booth with our food orders placed, the teenage waitress returned to our table looking flustered: "President Clinton will be arriving in a few moments," she announced. "The Secret Service has asked that everyone remain seated at their tables, and please make no sudden movements." As she spoke, patrons at the far end of the diner began applauding.

Clinton strolled around the restaurant greeting the surprised customers. When he reached our booth, I introduced myself, welcomed him to my district, and introduced my staffers to him. He took the time to speak to each of them individually. He laughed when he shook hands with my chief of staff, Greg Mitchell, who had financed a recent trip to Europe with the cash he made as a professional comedic Bill Clinton look-alike. When Greg told Clinton how he earned his mad money, Clinton joked that Greg was stealing the cash: "You're a lot younger and a lot handsomer than I am!"

My campaign coordinator, Jeff Lennan, asked for an autograph and handed Clinton the blank side of a business card. "Will you write on it, *Good luck Jim?*" Jeff asked. As Clinton obliged, Jeff gave me a mischievous wink. After Clinton returned to his booth to munch down his buffalo

Rogan for Congress campaign card (obverse and reverse) signed by President Clinton, Rocky Cola Café, Montrose, California, June 11, 1996. (Author's collection)

burger, Jeff handed me the card: "Here's a little gift for your memorabilia collection." When I looked at the "Good luck, Jim" inscription, Jeff told me to look on the other side. It was a Rogan for Congress campaign card. It was tempting, but I refused my staff's plea to show the press President Clinton's expression of "luck" in my congressional race.

Surprise lunch meeting: Here I am (trying to stand, but wedged tightly between the booth and the wall—and not wanting to make any sudden moves!) welcoming President Clinton to the 43rd Assembly District, Rocky Cola Café, Montrose, California, June 11, 1996. (Official White House photograph)

A few days later, I ran into a few local Democrat operatives who were pals of mine. They told me the only thing that galled my congressional opponent more than Clinton snubbing him during the visit was the headline the local papers ran the next day: "Rogan Ends Up Having Surprise Lunch with Clinton."

• • •

Later that November, voters returned Bill Clinton to Washington, and they sent me there to join him. When next we met, it would be under drastically different circumstances.

36

Bobby's Friend

As some of my earlier stories noted, I had mixed experiences meeting President Jimmy Carter. Truthfully, whenever I encountered him over a 20-year period, I usually found him moody (interspersed with moments of transitory friendliness). When I was a member of the California legislature and he visited my district, I hoped the experience might be more pleasant than others, but I'll let you be the judge.

By 1995, Carter (out of office almost 15 years) had become a prolific author, with eight books to his credit since leaving the White House. Carter's newest effort, *Always a Reckoning*, was something different: a collection of his poetry. While on his book promotional tour, he scheduled a book signing in Glendale, which was the heart of my Assembly district.

My staff called his office in Atlanta and asked to set up a brief photo op for my infant daughters and to allow me to present him with the customary resolution of welcome from the state legislature. His staffer asked if I was a Democrat or Republican. When told that I was GOP, he denied the request summarily. My assistant gave me the news. I told her not to worry—I would take this to a higher authority. I called to my pal Bobby Salter, who ran the only gas station in Plains, Georgia (Carter's hometown).

As told in an earlier chapter, Bobby grew up in Plains with the Carter family. Some years earlier, Bobby purchased the town gas station from Billy Carter, the president's brother. I knew that each week Bobby hosted a fish fry for Carter's Secret Service detail at the filling station, and he always fed them well. When I called Bobby and explained my problem, he responded, "Jim, don't you worry none. I'll take care of my ol' Yankee cousin! Consider it done. You just show up to that event and tell the head of Carter's Secret Service detail that you're a friend of ol' Bobby's!"

With nothing more than Bobby's assurance in hand, I flew home from Sacramento on the appointed day and drove my family downtown to the bookstore. Carter was inside signing books while a huge crowd of people wrapped around the block waiting their turn. I asked a security guard to give my card to the head of the Secret Service detail. Within minutes the agent in charge approached with an outstretched hand: "You must be Bobby Salter's friend!" he said with a big smile. Before I knew it, a swarm of agents had lined up to say hello: "Always glad to meet a friend of good old Bobby!" they told me.

The agents ushered us inside the store and made a path through the crush of bodies. I found the scene humorously ironic: that I was the elected representative for the district meant nothing, but because I knew the guy who owned the local gas station in Plains, the welcome mat rolled out.

Carter sat at a table in the midst of all this activity, scrawling "J. Carter" in machine-gun fashion on books thrust before him. He rarely looked up from his signing task. There were too many people waiting to buy a book to allow for idle conversation.

Agents escorted us into the stockroom at the rear of the store, now used as a temporary Secret Service post. Ladders, shopping carts, and scores of shipping cartons cluttered the room alongside piles of books stacked all over the floor. A small wooden table with bottled water awaited Carter. When he finished signing for customers, he was to come inside the stockroom and sign additional books for the employees and police assigned to his detail.

"The president will probably keep signing for all the customers until the books are gone, or until everyone lined up around the block gets one, so it may be a while," the agent advised me. "He doesn't like to be disturbed while he is signing, so I'm sure he won't stop to meet you until he's done. Please make yourself at home, and when the president is through, we'll bring him in for a picture with your daughters. President Carter is pretty good about signing books. He wants to make sure everyone gets one. He canceled the rest of his schedule tonight so he could sit here and sign."

That was admirable on Carter's part, but it turned out to be a long evening: he signed books for every patron in line—more than 2,000 of them. In the meantime, Christine and I tried keeping our two year-old twins engaged by reading stories, playing games, and taking them for walks around the nearby stores. Directly outside the exit door of the stockroom was the parking lot (sealed off with police tape) where Carter's limousine awaited. Secret Service agents let our girls take turns climbing on the backseat and playing inside the luxurious car.

As the evening wore on, I took Claire for a little walk through the bookstore to keep her occupied. She broke free of my grasp momentarily, ran around an aisle, and headed straight for Carter. The former president still sat at the table signing books with his back to us. I caught Claire just as she ran up to Carter, who looked over with a smile when he saw my cackling girl running from her daddy. Still, her sudden commotion startled the Secret Service and police, but everyone relaxed quickly when they realized the cause.

It was 10:00 p.m. when Carter signed the last book. He then came back to the stockroom where the agent in charge introduced us: "Mr. President," he said with great formality, "allow me to present Assemblyman and Mrs. James Rogan. Judge Rogan represents this district in the California legislature."

"I understand you're a friend of Bobby Salter's," Carter said as we shook hands. Christine nudged me in the ribs to accentuate my own lack of clout; I replied that I knew Bobby well.

"And you admit to it?" he asked with a grin.

"Only for tonight, Mr. President," I responded.

That exchange ended the small talk. His staffer told him he would be taking a picture with our family. Carter said, "I'll get in the middle," and stepped between Christine and me as we held the girls. "Come on," he called to the photographer. "Let's get this over with."

Ouch.

The photographer, Bill LaChasse, snapped a couple of quick pictures. "Okay, that's it," Carter announced, and then he

"Let's get this over with." Former President Jimmy Carter with (from left) Christine, Claire, Dana, and me, Super Crown Books, Glendale, California, February 8, 1995. (Photograph by William LaChasse) (Author's collection)

walked away. Christine later told me how annoyed she felt by his curtness, especially after she waited over three hours to meet him. After seeing him many times before, the potential for abruptness didn't surprise me.

The Glendale police officers working on his security detail formed a receiving line. Again, Carter was all business. He walked down the line shaking hands quickly, but he didn't pause to speak with any officers. He then sat at the wooden table and signed a waiting stack of books. As he was signing, I slipped out to the customer counter, bought three of them, placed them in the stack, and he signed them for my family. With the last book signed, he walked out the rear exit to his waiting limousine without bidding anyone goodbye.

Dana and Claire, up long past their bedtime to meet the former president, slept soundly in our arms before we made it back to the car.

37

Always Looking the Part

I n late 1995, I attended the annual "Sons of the Desert" banquet at the Hollywood Roosevelt Hotel. These dinners always proved a delight for us old film buffs, because the program consisted of the ever-thinning ranks of movie actors from the 1920s–1940s, who entertained and shared memories of their Tinseltown heyday at these affairs. Among those participating in this program were sisters Lassie and Peggy Ahern, who told stories about making their first silent film with humorist Will Rogers in 1923; Eugene "Pineapple" Jackson (who made his silent movie debut with Mary Pickford in 1925) sang and danced as he played the ukulele; Frank Coghlin, the only child star under exclusive contract to director Cecil B. DeMille, talked about appearing in *Gone with*

"The Lollipop Kid" Jerry Maren and me, Hollywood Roosevelt Hotel, October 28, 1995 . . .

the Wind; Dick Jones told the story of how Walt Disney picked him, at age ten, as Pinocchio's voice for the 1940 animated feature.

A particular favorite was my friend Jerry Maren, one of the handful of surviving Munchkins from the 1939 film *The Wizard of Oz*. That night Jerry sang the song he had warbled to Judy Garland as he handed her a lollipop before she embarked down the Yellow Brick Road: "We represent the Lollipop Guild . . . and in the name of the Lollipop Guild [he bowed from the waist], we wish to welcome you to Munchkin Land!"

. . . and Jerry (center Munchkin), as he presented Dorothy (Judy Garland) her lollipop in *The Wizard of Oz*. (Author's collection)

Seated at the table next to me was Ellen Corby, who began her career as a script girl for Laurel and Hardy and later became a film and television star in her own right. She appeared in dozens of movies, including Frank Capra's classic *It's a Wonderful Life* (1948). That same year she won an Academy Award nomination for her performance in *I Remember Mama*. In later years, she charmed a new generation of fans as the beloved grandmother on the long-running 1970s television series *The Waltons*. Although confined to a wheelchair and with fingers crippled by arthritis, her sweet smile greeted each of the scores of fans approaching her at the banquet.

I was thrilled that evening when I learned that my dinner partner was Anita Page. The frail, elderly, and utterly charming woman is remembered today only by serious film scholars—all of whom agree that Anita was the last of the great silent movie stars and one of Hollywood's first international sex symbols. Considered in her day as one of the most beautiful women to grace the silver screen, she made her movie debut in 1925, and then she signed a long-term contract with MGM. By 1928 she had rocketed to fame and eclipsed Greta Garbo as the star receiving the most fan mail, averaging more than 50,000 letters per month. She appeared opposite such leading men such as Lon Chaney Sr., Buster Keaton, Ramon Novarro, Douglas Fairbanks Sr., Walter Huston, and a young newcomer named Clark Gable. She created an international incident in the early 1930s when the Italian dictator Benito Mussolini publicly declared Anita his favorite actress and asked MGM executives to get him an autographed picture. Despite heavy lobbying by the studio and the U.S. State Department, Anita flatly refused to sign for the fascist. She remained a top box office draw until 1934 when she retired from films.

My dinner companion and the last of the silent screen stars: Miss Anita Page, the Hollywood Roosevelt Hotel, October 28, 1995 (Photograph by the author) . . .

When we met over dinner, Anita was almost 90. She dressed with the overstated elegance of the "Norma Desmond" character from *Sunset Boulevard*: heavy makeup, a vintage gown and mink stole, and silver opera-length gloves that kept falling down her withered, slender arms. When she walked (she needed assistance on each side), her shoes kept slipping off her feet. But none of these sartorial difficulties took away from her saucy tone and the mischievous gleam in her eye.

Despite our prodding during dinner, Anita talked little about her long-ago days in Hollywood. She showed more interest in discussing life in the present. She did make an exception when someone at our table mentioned that we dined in the historic ballroom where the Academy Awards held their first presentation ceremony in 1927. "You're right," she nodded in agreement, "It was held here. I had a starring lead in a picture that year and I was nominated for an award, but I didn't win." Our tablemates looked at one another in amazement: Anita had not only attended the first Oscar ceremony, but she was a nominee. We were impressed greatly, but to Anita it was no big deal.

"That night everyone looked so elegant," she recalled. "I wore a long, white, beautiful gown. Back then, the Academy Awards ceremony was just a dinner dance:

. . . And in her prime: Anita Page, 1928. (Author's collection)

nothing big or too special. We never expected it would grow to the degree it has."

"I remember they had a wonderful dinner served that night," she reflected, "but someone at a nearby table yelled at his waiter an accusation that the cook was serving canned peas. Although the waiters and chefs denied it angrily, it became a big joke, with everyone asking their waiters about the canned peas." It was a pleasure meeting and having her as my seatmate that night. We became friends and stayed in touch.

• • •

Eventually, Anita moved to a retirement home in Burbank located in my legislative district. The administrator invited me to attend their annual Christmas banquet where I planned to present Anita with a resolution from the state legislature proclaiming "Anita Page Day" in California.

At the banquet, and before Anita came down to the dining hall for the award, her nurse pulled me aside. She confided that she had started helping Anita get ready for the dinner more than eight hours earlier because the retired actress required that much time to be "presentable" (as Anita termed it). "This is the first time Miss Page has ever come down from her room to join the other residents," she told me. "She never wants to leave her room and join in any community activities because she says it takes too long to get ready. I keep telling her, 'Miss Page, you don't need to go to all this trouble! Just come down and meet everyone. They'd be delighted to get to know you.' But she always refuses politely."

Later that evening, after I presented the legislative scroll to Anita, we had dinner together and I raised the issue. "Anita," I told her, "don't worry about getting dolled up just to go downstairs to a meal. Go as you are—nobody cares. They have movie and bingo nights, regular entertainment, parties, and lots of other social activities. You need to come down and mingle more often and don't worry about how you look."

She gave me a long gaze, and then she put her small hand atop mine. "Dearie," she said politely, "that might do for everyone else, but it would not do for me. You see, I'm a motion picture star, and I must *always* look the part."

And she always did.

Looking the part: Anita Page and me at dinner following the presentation of the state legislature's "Anita Page Day" resolution, Burbank, California, December 15, 1995. (Author's collection)

• • •

Anita Page started getting out more. Sixty years after she retired from films, she returned to acting and made a couple of low-budget thriller movies. She also started appearing at nostalgia shows signing autographs and greeting new generations of fans until ill health forced her to curtail her activities. She died at age 98 of natural causes on September 6, 2008. She was the last surviving major star of Hollywood's silent film era, and the last known survivor who had attended the first Academy Awards ceremony.

Jerry Maren died at age 98 of heart failure on May 24, 2018.

Lassie Ahern died at age 97 of complications from influenza on February 15, 2018.

Peggy Ahern died at age 95 on October 24, 2012.

Eugene "Pineapple" Jackson died at age 84 of a heart attack on October 26, 2001.

Frank Coghlin died at age 93 on September 7, 2009.

After suffering a fall at his home, Dick Jones died at age 87 on July 7, 2014.

38

"What Doin'?"

I n early 1995, former President George Bush invited my family to his welcoming ceremony at a private hangar when he flew to Los Angeles Airport. At the last minute, Assembly Republican leader Jim Brulte needed me in Sacramento because of votes on a key piece of legislation. He promised that if I skipped the Bush meeting he would make sure my family got a rain check, and he made good on the pledge when Bush flew into Mather Air Force Base outside Sacramento for a speech a few months later.

Mather stood nearly deserted when we arrived. The Pentagon had shuttered the base a couple of years earlier due to budget cuts. A lone security guard at the entrance waved our car through the gate without checking our identification or inquiring as to our business. We drove past rows of empty barracks and down silent streets to the rear of the property, where we parked in front of the Trajen Air Support hangar. A dozen former Bush staffers, along with a couple of Secret Service agents, stood along the tarmac awaiting his arrival.

At 5:50 p.m., a small private jet landed on the airstrip behind the building. It taxied slowly and came to rest 20 yards from the hangar. A Secret Service agent waited at the end of the red carpet now rolled out to greet the former chief executive. The pilot raised the hatch, and George Bush appeared at the door shaking hands with the flight crew and presenting each of them with a souvenir presidential tie bar identical to the one that he wore.

Bush stepped from the plane and waved to the small welcoming reception. Other than having more gray in his otherwise dark hair, his appearance had changed little since leaving the White House a few years earlier. He grinned and walked over to us. "This looks like it's going to be a *real* family picture," he said as we shook hands.

Before his arrival, I had rehearsed Dana and Claire in saying, "Hello, President Bush." They had developed some proficiency in enunciating the phrase (minimal complexity for three year-olds, I supposed). Now I prompted Claire to convey her greeting: "Claire," I asked as Bush shook her hand, "can you say hello to President Bush?"

Her eyes lit up. "Hi, Bush!" she called to him, "what doin'?" With that, she lunged out of my arms toward Bush, wrapped her arm around his neck, pulled him cheek to cheek against her, and then planted a big kiss on his lips! Bush roared with laughter as Christine apologized for Claire's aggressive affection. "I'm sure you understand little girls, Mr. President," she said. Turning to Claire, Christine told her, "President Bush is a daddy, too."

"And a grandpa!" he added.

To Jim & Christine Rogan with best wishes, G Bush

Claire Rogan releases her chokehold from the neck of the 41st president of the United States: George Bush with the Rogan family, Mather Air Force Base, October 6, 1995. (Photograph by William LaChasse)

After visiting with my family, he pulled me aside for an update on my congressional race. He expressed his longstanding regard for my predecessor, Congressman Carlos Moorhead, and told me that I would love Congress. "It's a great honor to serve there," he said. Then, turning to Christine, he asked her how she felt about my running.

Christine's smile belied her initial reservations. "I'm behind his decision," she said.

"Good," Bush added. "I know about your last Assembly race, Jim. You had a tough one, but it sounds like you went through the worst of it. You'll do just fine from here on in."

Before leaving, I asked Bush to autograph for me an engraved vignette of

"You'll love Congress": with former President George Bush, Mather Air Force Base, October 6, 1995. (Photograph by William LaChasse)

the White House signed by the previous presidents I had met. Bush studied the abbreviated signature of President Richard Nixon, which he had signed *RN*. "Old RN," Bush said. "I've seen that version of his signature many times in the past when I worked for him. This will be a nice memento to pass along to the girls someday."

Bush grasped Christine's hand. "Hang in there," he told her. "We need good people in government like your husband."

• • •

After winning a seat in Congress, I had the honor of getting to know President Bush. He showed great interest in my career and he helped in many ways—including hosting a campaign fundraiser (with his wife Barbara) for me in Houston during my final reelection effort. By the end of that race, one might have thought that I was a member of his family by the concern and interest he showed in my campaign. I'll save these stories for a future book.

Although conservative Republicans generally don't rank George H.W. Bush as among our great presidents, there is no denying he was one of his generation's great patriots, and one of my generation's great gentlemen.

39

Losing Stinks

Back in the early 1990s, a reporter doing a profile piece on me asked for my list of contemporary politicians that I admired. She expressed shock when my list included one of the leading liberals in the Democrat Party: former Massachusetts governor and 1988 Democrat presidential nominee Michael Dukakis. When asked why I included a man whose name was anathema to Republicans of that era, I replied, "Because Dukakis is one of the few men I can name in politics prepared to lose an election because he stood by his principles. I may have disagreed with those principles, but I admire his integrity greatly." I cited as examples some positions he took in his race against George Bush that he knew were political losers. Because of it, Bush beat Dukakis handily.

Although I had met Dukakis a couple of times during his White House run, I didn't know him personally. That opportunity came after he returned to private life. When the newspaper published the interview I gave, I sent him a copy with a note expressing admiration from a Republican who, I regretted telling him, was a former Democrat who changed parties during his donnybrook with Bush.

Coincidentally, a few days later, I attended a judge's conference in Boston. A student intern working for Dukakis called me at my hotel and said that the former governor had received my letter and tried to call me at my courthouse. When he learned that I was in Boston, he wanted to invite me to his speech at the Kennedy

"To Jim: I still don't understand your philosophy, but keep slugging and keep serving!" Governor Michael Dukakis campaigning for the 1988 Democrat presidential nomination, the Sportsmen's Lodge, Los Angeles, California, August 25, 1987. (Photograph by the author)

School of Government at Harvard. I accepted the invitation and asked if I needed to contact any Dukakis staff member at the site. He laughed at the suggestion: "I'm his 'staff,' and I won't be there. I have a midterm tomorrow."

Here again was a lesson of politics I've seen repeated frequently: a national leader going from the pinnacle of power to commanding a staff (in this case) consisting of a grad student working for extra credit.

• • •

I arrived at the Kennedy School 90 minutes early, which got me a front row seat for Dukakis' speech in the ARCO Forum for Public Affairs. The room filled quickly, with late-arriving students finding standing-room-only spots in the balcony two floors above. Sitting there in a pinstriped suit and wing-tip shoes amid hundreds of college students in T-shirts, shorts, and flip-flops, I felt out of place.

Governor Michael Dukakis addressing students at the Kennedy School of Government, Harvard University, Cambridge, Massachusetts, July 15, 1993. (Photograph by the author)

When Dukakis arrived, his apparel did nothing to alleviate my self-consciousness. He wore an open-neck Hawaiian print shirt, khaki slacks, white gym socks (with a big hole in one ankle), and sneakers. Obviously, I didn't get the wardrobe memo.

The audience applauded when he arrived and settled into a chair on the platform. A student offered a brief introduction before he stepped to the lectern. Using no notes, he kept his talk as casual as his dress. "Let's get something straight at the outset," he warned with a grin. "I do not claim to be an expert in politics. If I knew anything about politics, we would be having this meeting in the East Room of the White House!" The audience laughed and applauded. He promised to stay until five o'clock: "That's when I have to go to my favorite Greek barber down the street and get a haircut."

Although he covered a range of domestic and international issues, his primary theme was encouraging young people to enter politics at the ground level. "When I was a law student down the road," he recalled, "I remember a young U.S. senator named John F. Kennedy coming to talk with us and saying he wanted to run for president. Kennedy uplifted and encouraged us. And aside from myself, who later went on to become governor and a presidential candidate, my other classmates included Senator Paul Sarbanes, our first EPA director Bill Ruckelshaus, and United States Supreme Court Justice Antonin Scalia. By the way, Scalia was as conservative in law school as he is now on the Court. But he made it onto the Supreme Court, for better or for worse!"

Dukakis urged the students not to fear starting at the bottom by running and losing, citing as examples his own experience as well as that of President Bill Clinton:

Clinton came home from law school at Yale and ran for Congress unsuccessfully. In politics, you have to be prepared to lose. Clinton and I were both young governors with good national notices who were nonetheless thrown out of office after one term. We had the distinction, along with Minnesota Governor Rudy Perpich, of being the only governors defeated for reelection that came back and later won. We called ourselves "The Retread Club."

Keep in mind that "Dukakis" was not a household name when I first ran for statewide office. I served in the legislature for eight years before I decided to seek the 1970 Democrat nomination for lieutenant governor. One of my aides said I needed name recognition, so we made up 10,000 bumper stickers saying simply, "Dukakis 70." My aide slapped one of those on his car and drove across the state. He pulled into a gas station (in those days the attendant pumped the gas for you) and the guy asked my aide, "What the hell is a Dukakis?" My aide replied, "It's a rare bird. There are only 70 of them left in existence."

During the question period, a student asked if he had any future political plans. "I doubt I will ever be a candidate for office again," he responded. "New York Governor Mario Cuomo likes to say, when he is asked similar questions, that 'Bill Clinton will be reelected in 1996, so by the year 2000 guys like Cuomo and Dukakis will be on Medicare.' After 12 years as governor and a prior run for the presidency, what is there left to run for? This doesn't mean I won't stay active in politics and try to help when I can."

When asked about the man that vanquished his White House effort five years earlier, he said, "Truthfully, I thought George Bush would be a better president than he was. I say that with all due respect. He just never seemed to connect with the people. I don't think he had a clue what ordinary Americans needed."

When a student suggested that the kind of programs a Dukakis Administration might have created have been implemented by President Clinton, he replied, "Let's just say I'm sleeping a lot better with Bill Clinton in the White House than I did when George Bush was there. And I'm sleeping a hell of a lot better than I did when Ronald Reagan was there!"

As the program neared its end, I raised my hand (without identifying myself when he called on me). I mentioned that I read a few years ago that during a discussion between two losing Democrat nominees, Walter Mondale had asked George McGovern how long it takes until the pain of losing the presidency goes away; McGovern had replied, "I'll let you know." I asked how he dealt with the loss personally.

He paused for a moment before answering: "Look, losing stinks. Aside from the deep personal disappointment, you're damned tired after an 18-month national campaign. Plus, millions of people who believed in you feel let down. I received thousands of letters after the election from people saying they cried themselves to sleep. You feel a tremendous sense of disappointment, but you can't dwell on it. You move on. A friend said that losing an election builds character;

I'm just sorry I couldn't let my character-building end after my 1970 loss for lieutenant governor!"

Dukakis closed his speech with this final observation about running for the presidency:

> When you run for president, people recognize you wherever you go. Last year I visited my son and grandchild in Venice, California, where my wife Kitty and I stayed at a bed-and-breakfast near the beach. If any of you have ever been to the Venice boardwalk early in the morning, you know there are lots of strange people who hang out there. One morning I went out for a power walk. Two guys who looked like they hadn't slept in a real bed for months were eyeing me up one side and down the other. One guy finally said, "I know you! You ran for president!" I kept walking by and nodded in agreement. He turned to his friend and said, "Do you know who that guy is? That's Jerry Dukakis!"

At the conclusion of his talk, students surrounded Dukakis to shake his hand, get autographs, and pose for pictures. Dukakis tarried happily and demonstrated his multilingual talents by chatting at length in Spanish with one student from Mexico, and even greeting a Korean student in his native tongue.

When I introduced myself, he winced: "Jim," he said, "I'm so sorry. I didn't know that was you when you asked the question." He put his arm around my shoulder and pulled me off to the side for a private chat. He asked about my judicial conference, what I had seen in Boston—even details regarding the recent birth of my daughters. His patient graciousness overwhelmed me, especially since so many students remained waiting to meet him.

I insisted he get back to business. As we shook hands, he said he wanted to keep in touch. When we returned to the waiting assemblage, a student handed me his camera and asked me to take his picture with Dukakis. While I aimed the camera, Dukakis pointed to me and told his young admirer, "You don't know who is taking that picture? That's Jim Rogan—a very important judge in California."

Appreciating the greatly exaggerated sentiment, I told the student, "I have to do things like this when I'm asked. I'm up for reelection next year!"

Dukakis remained surrounded by fans and showed no signs of breaking away when I left the Kennedy School. I looked at my wristwatch: it was almost 5:30. His Greek barber would have to wait for another day.

• • •

That day at the Kennedy School was almost 30 years ago, and Mike Dukakis and I have remained friends since. From grabbing an occasional lunch at UCLA when he comes west to teach, to me speaking to his class, and from taking congratulatory calls from him when I won elections (and getting a much-appreciated cheer-up call when I lost a big one), to him cooking left-overs for me one late night in his Brookline kitchen, I've come to know Mike as a man of great kindness and personal charm. There isn't a touch of imperiousness in his genetic code. Behind the scenes he's a regular guy. He's nothing like the stiff and emotionless drone that some in the press (and everyone in my Party) portrayed during his presidential race.

My favorite memory of him shows both his humility and his sense of humor. It occurred in March 1996, when I was Assembly Majority Leader in the California legislature and running for Congress. A couple of months earlier, I had received a note from him telling me he would be teaching at UCLA for the winter semester and suggesting we get together. One morning he called my office manager, Denise Milinkovich, and asked if I was free for breakfast the next day. When she told him she would clear my schedule, he said, "Great—I'll drive out from L.A. to Glendale to meet him."

"Oh, no, Governor," she protested, "that won't do. He'll insist on driving out to see you. He won't want you driving all this way to see him."

Mike cut her off. He told her it was his choice and that he didn't mind driving. Under protest for the protocol lapse, she set up breakfast the next morning in the coffee shop of the Glendale Red Lion Hotel (now the Hilton). Mike then asked how much time we'd have; she said we could meet for breakfast at 7:30, and my schedule was clear until my late morning meeting with local school board members. "Sounds great," he told her. "And if Jim doesn't mind, maybe I can tag along with him to the next meeting and give him a quiet boost with the teachers."

Would I mind? I couldn't pay for that kind of help.

The next morning, I stood in the hotel lobby talking with a couple of our local city council members when I saw the elevator doors open. Mike stepped out (again dressed casually) and crossed the lobby. Many patrons gave him a surprised double take or approached and asked if it really was him. He greeted each person, and then he joined me.

A waiter seated us at a rear table. We ordered coffee, split an English muffin (neither of us were big breakfast eaters), and had a chance to catch up in many areas. As usual, he was disinclined to talk much about himself. He filled our time with questions about my congressional race, my experiences as majority leader, my family, and how politics had affected them.

My curiosity about his presidential campaign couldn't wait. I steered the conversation to it by mentioning that Christine and I had crashed his Biltmore Hotel party in June 1988 on the night he won the California primary (and his delegate count put him over the top for the presidential nomination). He reminisced about that night in the Biltmore and said that it held a special meaning for him. Twenty-eight years earlier, he and some of his buddies had hitchhiked across the United States to reach Los Angeles for the 1960 Democrat National Convention. In that same ballroom he heard his fellow Brookline native John F. Kennedy speak to delegates the day before he defeated Lyndon Johnson for the presidential nomination.

"Jim—you're the best, despite your Party!" Breakfast at the Red Lion Hotel: Governor Michael Dukakis and me, Glendale, March 1, 1996. (Photograph by Greg Mitchell)

As for his own White House run, he said that after winning reelection to the governor's office in 1986, he gave no thought to running for president. However, after the Iran-Contra scandal rocked the Reagan–Bush administration, it got him thinking: "I told my staff I would look at running for six months and then make a decision. Ultimately, I decided to give it a try."

"The night I accepted the presidential nomination at the Democrat Convention in Atlanta was a thrill," he added. "It was a great night, but by the next day it was back to work." What surprised me most about his experience in seeking the presidency was that he found the overall process less than exhilarating. He described being on the go constantly for almost two years and giving thousands of interviews on the same subjects repeatedly. "After you've tried to answer the very same questions 50 different ways, you grow incredibly bored," he said. But the worst part for him was the sense of isolation while running. When he became governor, he declined all security and often rode the subway alone to work. "But once you sign on to the Secret Service as a presidential candidate," he lamented, "your life as you know it ends. You are surrounded by a huge wall that nobody can penetrate. It's terrible."

When discussing his defeat, he showed a dispassionate frankness: "I hated to lose the White House, but you don't brood about it. You get over it. In '88 we were way ahead of Bush. After my convention, I decided to run a campaign on the high road and not engage in character assassination–type politics. As you now know, my strategy failed. The Bush campaign tarred me with Willie Horton wherever I went.[1] They did their best to work me over at every opportunity. I didn't respond properly, and that cost me the election."

As the time drew near for me to head to my meeting with the local school board members, he volunteered to accompany me. I concocted an idea for a great practical joke and called my chief of staff, Greg Mitchell, who moonlighted as a professional Bill Clinton impersonator. I told Greg to rush over to the Red Lion with his Clinton makeup.

Soon Greg arrived, and we all piled into Greg's beat-up red Mustang for the drive over to the Burbank Department of Water and Power. We arrived about 15 minutes late for the meeting, where the increasingly impatient board members waited for me in the conference room. I had Mike and Greg stand just outside the door while I entered the room alone and apologized for my delayed arrival.

"This meeting is so important to me that I decided to swing by my district office and pick up my chief of staff and my legislative director," I said. Then I called my coconspirators into the room one

---

1   In the 1980s, Horton was a prisoner serving a life sentence for murder in Massachusetts, where state law provided for weekend furloughs for inmates. After obtaining a pass, Horton assaulted, robbed, and raped a victim. Dukakis didn't create the program (in fact, it began under a Republican governor in 1972), but he had supported it. The Bush campaign used the Willie Horton case in an unending barrage of blistering negative attacks against Dukakis.

by one as follows: "You all know my chief of staff, President Bill Clinton." With that, Greg entered the room to laughter. Everyone there knew Greg and knew that he worked on the side as a Clinton impressionist.

Now came the payoff: "I don't think any of you have met my legislative director, Governor Michael Dukakis." Mike then rounded the corner and entered the room dressed in his casual shirt, khakis, and sneakers. For a moment there was silence as the board members studied my "staffer." Then they all laughed.

"Hey!" said one board member, "you actually do look a little bit like Dukakis. But you're too short—and your nose is too big!"

Now it was our turn to laugh, and nobody laughed harder than did Mike Dukakis. As he started speaking in his distinctive baritone voice, I watched the faces of our prank victims change from mirth to confusion to shock. After a few moments, they understood that as unlikely as this far-fetched scene appeared, here stood the real McCoy.

"I just wanted to come by and say hello with my pal Jim Rogan," he said. "You have a great guy in your assemblyman, but I still don't know where he gets his politics!"

After the shock: Governor Michael Dukakis and me with the Glendale and Burbank school board members, Burbank Department of Water and Power, March 1, 1996. (Photograph by Greg Mitchell)

"From being left out in the sun too damned long!" I answered.

As the jolt wore off, the board members lined up to meet him. He posed for pictures and signed autographs for them before it was time to head back to UCLA to teach his class. We packed him back inside Greg's old beater Mustang, I said goodbye, and then I returned to my meeting with the board members. They were still in such shock that it took a while before anyone remembered why they had requested the meeting with me!

• • •

Governor Mike Dukakis continues teaching college courses and he continues inspiring new generations of students. I can think of no better example of public service than the one set by their professor.

40

Man Talk

After meeting for the first time the new governor of Texas, George W. Bush, I gave my legislative staff an assessment of the former president's eldest son:

1. He was very amiable.

2. Unlike his father, he was a serious supply-side/limited-government Reagan conservative.

3. If he ever ran for president, he would never win.

Today, conservative activists think I got two out of those three predictions wrong. So sue me. Besides, who'd trust my political judgment? Back then I also thought I could win a U.S. Senate race from California—as a conservative Republican!

It was early 1996. George W. Bush was the recently-elected governor of Texas, and I was the new majority leader of the California State Assembly and also a GOP candidate for Congress. I received a call from the California Republican Party office asking me to introduce Bush at a breakfast organized in his honor. Bush's staff wanted him to start making connections with members of the Southern California GOP donor base.

The day before the event, I received a somewhat panicky call from a Party staffer: "We're charging a nominal $50 for a reception and breakfast with Bush and his wife, but we have almost no takers. We want you to bring about 30 people—we'll comp them. We just need to have more bodies in the room so that it won't be an embarrassment." In later years, when hordes of people spent tens of thousands of dollars to rub elbows briefly with President and Mrs. George W. Bush, I remembered how we couldn't give away tickets to an intimate breakfast with them.

The organizers held the breakfast in the penthouse of the Regency Club in the Westwood section of Los Angeles.[1] The Bushes arrived ahead of schedule that morning (a hallmark during his presidency; he rarely never kept an audience waiting). He must have seen my picture in a briefing file, because when he got out of his car he walked over and greeted me with a cheery, "Well, hello, Mr. Majority Leader!" His wife, Laura, was both warm and gracious.

I escorted the Bushes to the foyer and introduced them to the assembled guests (both paid and comped). We mingled for half an hour, and then he and Laura joined me at the reserved table for breakfast, along with Los Angeles Dodgers owner Peter O'Malley. A fitness buff who ran seven miles daily, Bush passed on the fare of greasy sausage, hash browns, and eggs, and instead asked for a fruit plate.

It didn't take long for Bush (a former part-owner of the Texas Rangers) and O'Malley to become engrossed in a lengthy (and exclusive) discussion relating to baseball team ownership. During their two-man powwow, I tried to crack into their conversation by interjecting my own ballpark experiences ("Hey, I've been to a few Dodgers games," or "I sure love those big Dodger Dogs they sell at the park. Hey, Peter, do you guys use Gulden's or French's mustard on them?"), but after a while I gave up and let them have their fun. Still, I felt that my grandfather who raised me—a longshoreman on the San Francisco docks for 45 years—would shake his head in

---

1   Located at 10900 Wilshire Blvd in Los Angeles, the Regency Club closed in 2011.

dismay at the sight of the menfolk talking baseball while Laura and I shared stories and swapped photographs of our twin daughters.

On that topic, we had a semblance of commonality. When Laura drew her husband into our discussion of the challenges of raising twin girls from a dad's perspective, I told him I appreciated his pain. My girls were only three, and his were 14. "Mine won't want a driver's license for years," I said, "and yours are almost there."

"I'm not worried about the driver's license," he said as he sipped his coffee. "I'm worried about the boys that are starting to call for them."

During the Man-Talk: Texas Governor George W. Bush and me, Regency Club, Los Angeles, April 19, 1996. (Author's collection)

Bush and I settled into a political discussion. He called me crazy for leaving the bench for the rough world of politics. I replied, "Look who's talking—you left *baseball* for politics!"

He chuckled: "Yes, that's true, but I'm having the time of my life as governor. I really get to make an impact on people's lives." He then brought up my recent legislation, Assembly Bill 888 (signed into law as California's Sexually Violent Predator Act). He asked many questions about what I put in the draft and how I got it passed. He said that he wanted to propose a copycat bill to the Texas legislature, so I had one of my staffers retrieve a copy of my bill and legislative analysis for his later review.

He asked about my current congressional race, and I gave him the lay of the land insofar as I was running as a Republican in a Democrat district (which grew increasingly Democrat each day). I told him the national and state Democrat Party had targeted me for defeat and that I would have an uphill climb to keep it in the Republican column. He said he would be back to California several times between now and November 1996, and he offered to come out and help me. Of course, I was delighted to accept.

• • •

After the program began, I introduced him for his speech. He returned the favor by urging everyone to help me go to Washington in November to join the great GOP revolution led by House Speaker Newt Gingrich. Speaking from a prepared text, he expressed optimism that presumptive GOP presidential nominee Bob Dole had a strong chance to win the White House that November: "Bob

Dole is so strong in Texas that he should abandon Texas. He has it won. He should focus his fire on California where he can win." He concluded with a brief synopsis of his goals for moving Texas forward economically by adopting free-market conservative principles.

Reliving 1992: Texas Governor George W. Bush and Greg Mitchell, Regency Club, Los Angeles, April 19, 1996. (Photograph by the author)

When the meeting

adjourned, I introduced Bush to my legislative and campaign staff. When he met my chief of staff, Greg Mitchell (the Bill Clinton professional look-alike), he laughed heartily: "Hey, let's get a picture together!" he insisted. "We can relive the 1992 election [when Clinton beat Bush's father for the presidency]." After Greg posed with him, Bush made me promise to send him a copy of the photo. "I want to show this to Mother and Dad," he said.

I walked the Bushes to his car. He thanked me for coming and for introducing him around. "I'll be back to help you later this year," he promised as he gripped my hand.

• • •

During the course of my 1996 congressional campaign, we contacted Bush's office many times trying to set up an event with him. His staff never returned our calls. I didn't take it personally. Governors have bigger issues on tap than helping with out-of-state House races.

• • •

Despite my confident prediction in 1996, four years later voters elected George W. Bush the 43rd president of the United States. And, of course, California voters never elected me to the U.S. Senate. When it came to my political prognostications that day, as they say in baseball, I was 0 for 2.

41

One for the Team

In 1972, U.S. Senator Bob Dole gave me his autograph when I was a boy. In 1996, as the Republican presidential nominee, he flew to California and campaigned for me when I was my district's GOP congressional nominee. His running mate, former Congressman Jack Kemp, did the same. No appearances they did meant more to me than those in the closing days of the race when both showed up even though my home state was a lost cause for the national ticket.

Elected to the House of Representatives in 1962, Dole advanced to the Senate in 1968. When I first met him, he served as chairman of the Republican National Committee during the Nixon Administration; later he became President Gerald Ford's 1976 GOP vice presidential running mate. He ran for the presidential nomination unsuccessfully in 1980 and 1988, but in 1996 he secured the prize and faced off against incumbent President Bill Clinton. Despite enormous odds and trailing badly in polls, he barnstormed the country gamely.

A former college and professional football player, Jack Kemp entered Congress in 1970 and became a darling of the conservative wing of the GOP. He ran unsuccessfully for the 1988 Republican presidential nomination. After the dust settled, President George Bush selected him as his Secretary of Housing and Urban Development. Dole picked him as his 1996 vice presidential running mate to help unite his Party's right flank.

I thought Dole's selection of Kemp was smart politics, but I found it curious personally. Two months before the nominating convention, I spent an afternoon with Kemp in Sacramento when I introduced him at a Republican rally. In private, he expressed to me great dissatisfaction with Dole as the GOP's

Former Congressman Jack Kemp and me after we addressed a GOP campaign rally, Crest Theater, Sacramento, California, June 5, 1996. (Author's collection)

presumptive nominee: "Here goes the Grand Old Party again," Kemp said. "They're gonna pick the guy whose turn it is instead of a candidate who can win this damned thing."

• • •

I bumped into Kemp at Dulles Airport in Washington one week before the start of the 1996 GOP National Convention. Since we both were between flights, we hung out while waiting for our planes to arrive. I told him I was a Dole delegate and asked him if he planned to attend the convention. "I'm not even going," he snapped. "This will be the first one I've missed in decades." When I asked why, he said he planned to attend a charity fundraiser hosted by former NFL quarterback Roger Staubach. "Besides," Kemp said with growing irritation in his voice, "Dole's people didn't even invite me to speak there. I've spoken at all of them for the last 25 years. So I'm not even going." He went on again to denigrate Dole's candidacy, saying it was telling that the soon-to-be nominee couldn't gain traction against a guy in the White House (Clinton) who is scandal-plagued and has no morals.

Less than a week later, after Dole announced Kemp as his surprise running mate pick, Kemp addressed a breakfast meeting of the California GOP convention delegation only hours before delivering his formal nomination acceptance speech. When he arrived at the breakfast in triumph, the audience jumped to their feet and cheered madly for California's native son. I stood in the front row, looking at him with my arms folded across my chest, shaking my head and with a big smirk on my face. He smiled and waved to the fawning crowd. When he looked down and saw me, a sheepish look crossed over his face. He grinned at me and shrugged his shoulders in mock surrender.

Whatever tensions (if any) existed behind the scenes with the two nominees, it never showed publicly. They both ran hard to win, and they ran hard to help down-ticket candidates like me on the ballot with them.

• • •

Less than three weeks before the election, my family and I arrived at Burbank Airport's Mercury Aviation terminal to greet Dole when his campaign plane arrived. Shortly after 3:00 p.m., a sleek jet emblazoned with "Bob Dole for President 1996" on the fuselage touched down. Secret Service agents escorted us to the end of the red carpet. A few minutes after the plane came to rest, the door opened. Dole smiled and waved, then flashed a thumbs-up to the cheering supporters assembled. He looked tanned from weeks of outdoor campaigning, and his broad smile belied any trace of late-in-the-race fatigue.

Dole greeted Congressman Carlos Moorhead, his old friend and House colleague (and the

Welcoming Senator Bob Dole to California's 27th congressional district, Burbank Airport, October 17, 1996. (Photograph by William LaChasse)

man I hoped to succeed).
Moorhead introduced us.
"I know Jim," he said, and
then he greeted my family.
I gave him a Dole-Kemp-
Rogan trigate campaign
button that we made for
our upcoming rally. I told
him that despite the troubling polls, we produced
these because I was proud
to run with him.

He climbed into a
limousine for the ride
to our Glendale rally. I
joined Congressman

Campaign volunteers passed out this trigate Dole-Kemp-Rogan
badge at our Glendale Rally, October 17, 1996. (Author's collection)

David Dreier, GOP state party chairman John Herrington (Secretary
of Energy under President Reagan), and Dole's California campaign
manager Ken Khachigian in the follow-up car. The motorcade
wended its way slowly through downtown Glendale, where people
lined the streets smiling and waving as the procession passed.

Once at our destination, we entered City Hall, where Dole
greeted local officials and posed for pictures before his campaign
staff led us to the holding area to await our rally introductions.
While backstage, he asked how my race was going. As I gave him an
abbreviated analysis, he pulled from his coat pocket the campaign
button I had given him at the airport. "Jim," he asked, "will you
pin this on my lapel? I want to wear it for our rally." Dole couldn't
accomplish the simple task without asking for assistance, because
this hero lost the use of his right arm 50 years earlier from wounds
received by German machine gun fire in World War II.

While awaiting the introductions, he paced back and forth
and sprayed throat lubricant into his mouth repeatedly. "As this

campaign nears its end," he said, "I fear my voice won't hold out."

When the rally began, escorts led us from the holding area to the front of City Hall. I stood with Dole awaiting our cues. His campaign coordinator gave me my directions: once everyone assembled on the platform, I was to kick off the proceedings with my campaign speech, and then he wanted me to introduce California Attorney General Dan Lungren (who would introduce Dole).

The crowd roared loudly at each introduction of the various dignitaries. I was one of the last to take the stage before Dole. When the announcer called my name, Dole patted me on the back. "Okay, Jim," he said encouragingly, "let's go do it!" I stepped out into sunshine and cheers. A sea of American flags, pom-poms, and Dole and Rogan posters waved across the crowd of more than 3,000. Two large banners proclaimed, "California is Dole Country" and "Dole's Golden Rule: You Earned It, You Keep It." Secret Service and police sharpshooters were atop the roof of the courthouse across the street (the same courthouse where I once served as the presiding judge). Dozens of television and still cameras trained on the stage from a riser erected nearby. As the band played and the crowd's enthusiasm grew, Lungren told me how impressed he was by the energy: "This is great. He's been getting crowds like this all around the state."

A deafening cheer rang out when Dole appeared and walked to the stage, His coordinator rushed over and told me to hold off introducing Lungren: "We've had a change of plans," he said. "Don't do anything until I go check. I'll be right back." Meanwhile, the band's music pulsated as the crowd's roar grew. Dole stood onstage flashing a thumbs-up and waving. Amid this electricity, Lungren leaned over and asked, "Aren't you supposed to introduce me?" I told him that Dole's aide had called a signal change and said not to start until he returned. "Oh, forget him!" Lungren said. "There's too much excitement going now. We need to keep it going!" With that, he gave me a shove toward the lectern.

Standing at the microphones, I saw two smoky teleprompter

screens before me with Dole's prepared remarks ready to scroll for him. A three-ring binder with his speech typed in large font rested on the lectern. I was surprised that at this late stage of the game, Dole relied on a prepared text to give a stump speech to the Party faithful.

After motioning the crowd to silence and welcoming everyone, I made a brief pitch for my congressional campaign before introducing Lungren, who in turn presented the nominee.

Dole began by urging my election to Congress, and he graciously referenced my campaign several times during his speech. He hammered on President Clinton's lack of ethics and the growing number of White House scandals. Deriding Clinton's 28 visits to California since becoming president, he said, "Clinton comes to California and drops money from the federal treasury the way you and I leave tips at the restaurant!"

While he spoke, I noticed Christine standing behind the security barrier directly below the stage holding Dana and Claire by the hand. I walked offstage, gathered the girls in my arms, and carried them back with

"Shameless—Shameless": Here I am holding Dana and Claire while Bob Dole rallies the faithful, Glendale, October 17, 1996. (Photograph by William LaChasse)

me so they could be part of the rally from the best seat in the house. The twins joined in the spirit. Each time the crowd cheered, they waved pom-poms. Soon I noticed the photographers turning their lenses away from the candidate and on the happy girls in my arms. When Lungren saw this press diversion, he whispered to me with a chuckle, "Shameless—you're shameless!"

"I'll rent them to you when you run for governor in '98," I told him.

Bob Dole and me at the conclusion of our campaign rally; on his lapel is a large Dole-Kemp-Rogan campaign button, October 17, 1996. (Photograph by William LaChasse)

Dole wound up his speech with a call to arms: "California is not Bill Clinton country. It's still Reagan country! And on November 5, it's going to be Dole–Kemp country!" Several loud pops from confetti guns showered the crowd with a thick, heavy stream. Dole called over to me: "Come on, Jim," and raised my arm in a victory pose before we climbed down to shake hands with the crowd.

Dole signed scores of autographs and posed for pictures. At one point, he got ahead of me and a Secret Service agent asked me to catch up to him: "The senator is talking to your nieces and nephews and he wants a picture with all of you."

As our procession moved down the rope line, I noticed my young nephew, Andrew Apffel, back in the crowd with tears in his eyes. I walked back and asked him what was wrong. "All of my brothers and sisters got an autograph except me," he said. When I told Dole that Andrew got overlooked, Dole went back and turned Andrew's tears into a smile. (If a very proud uncle may brag for a moment, that teary-eyed boy became Corporal Andrew Apffel, United States Marine Corps.)

• • •

Back in the holding area, I thanked Dole for coming out and giving my campaign this huge boost. "Jim," he replied, "you can repay me by winning this election. I'll see you in Washington."

• • •

With only five days before the election, the national GOP campaign arranged a hastily scheduled rally in my district with vice presidential nominee Jack Kemp at Woodbury University in Burbank. When I arrived at the site, orga-nizers told me I would be introducing Kemp to the large crowd of supporters assembling despite the threatening rain clouds forming overhead.

Here I am introducing 1996 GOP vice presidential nominee Jack Kemp, Woodbury University rally, Burbank, October 31, 1996. (Photograph by William LaChasse)

I was already onstage with the other candidates and local officials when Kemp's motorcade arrived shortly after 2 p.m. Jack and Joanne Kemp, along with television and motion picture actors Chad Everett, Billy Barty, and Bo Derek, emerged from the lead bus and made their way to the platform.

I drew a laugh from the audience when I introduced the nominee by recalling, "The first Republican National Convention I ever attended was in 1972 when I was just 14. I remember listening to one of the most dynamic speakers of the convention. He was a freshman congressman from Buffalo, and I'll never forget the stirring speech he gave—seconding the nomination of Spiro Agnew for vice president!" As the audience roared over Kemp nominating Agnew (who later resigned the vice presidency in disgrace), he called out from his seat,

"Your memory's too good, Jim!"

Like Dole before him, Kemp urged the crowd to send me to Congress. He also talked about growing up in Los Angeles and meeting his wife Joanne at nearby Occidental College when both were undergraduates.

After bashing the Clinton administration for its unending scandals, he closed with this summary of the entrepreneurial differences between the two Parties: "We are the party of civil rights. The Democrats want minorities to ride in the front of the bus, which is their constitutional and God-given right. We want to unlock the capital and credit to let minorities own the bus—and the hotel—and the restaurant!"

When he finished, he reached into a box filled with foam "Dole–Kemp" footballs and tossed them to the crowd. He locked arms with the candidates on stage for a victory pose, and then he jumped off the stage to shake hands with people along the rope line.

• • •

On election eve, Kemp and I repeated this drill at a Long Beach rally. I finished out the evening going to multiple campaign events.

Finally, on November 5, the long race ended and the balloting began. That afternoon, as America voted, Kemp called me at home from his campaign plane to wish me luck. "This time tomorrow, Jimmy, you'll be the next congressman from the 27th district," he told me optimistically.

I returned the positive cheer. "More importantly, Jack, by this time tomorrow you'll be the next vice president of the United States."

He snorted. "Yeah, well, hmmm, anyway...." He returned to wishing me luck on *my* campaign.

Kemp knew.

• • •

Bob Dole and Jack Kemp failed in their bid to unseat Bill Clinton by almost nine points. They lost my county by a whopping 20 points. Meanwhile, I won election to Congress that same day by squeaking out 50.1 percent of the vote in my Democrat-heavy district.

After I moved to Washington, I saw Bob and Jack occasionally, and both did several events for me when I ran in each of my reelection efforts. Whenever I needed any help from either man, politically or advice-wise, they always were there. I asked both in later years why they came to California repeatedly so late in the 1996 race to do rallies like the ones with me when they knew they couldn't win California.

Both told me the same thing: if they couldn't win there, at least they could try and help the down-ticket candidates like me. Most nominees running behind would have blown off the loser states—and us.

When it came to California in 1996, both Bob Dole and Jack Kemp took one for the team. Because they did, I went to Congress. I'm forever grateful to them.

Home stretch rally (from left: Joanne Kemp, 1996 vice presidential nominee Jack Kemp, me, State Senate candidate Paula Boland, Congressman Howard "Buck" McKeon), Woodbury University rally, Burbank, October 31, 1996. (Photograph by William LaChasse)

• • •

After the election, Bob Dole and Jack Kemp returned to private life. Bob joined a prestigious Washington law firm as a political and legal consultant—and he also popped up occasionally as a TV pitchman.

Jack served as chairman of his Washington-based Kemp Partners consulting firm and continued his involvement in charitable and political work until his death from cancer on May 2, 2009 at age 73.

42

Bad Rap

We conservatives always accuse the mainstream news media of having a double standard when covering Republicans and Democrats. Until Donald trump came along, nowhere was this imbalance more evident than in its treatment of Vice President Dan Quayle (1989–1993).

A veteran of both houses of Congress, Quayle had built a solid reputation among his Senate colleagues when George Bush tapped the 41 year-old as his 1988 running mate. Almost from the moment Bush announced the selection, the press pounced on Quayle, claiming that his Vietnam-era U.S. Coast Guard service was akin to draft-dodging, and that his 12 years in Congress showed a lack of experience for the job. Once elected, they magnified every minor verbal gaffe as proof of their collective assessment. Of course, when the Bush–Quayle ticket ran for reelection four years later against Democrats Bill Clinton and Al Gore, these same press complaints evaporated despite Clinton dodging the draft during the Vietnam War and Gore having the same amount of congressional service that Quayle had when Bush had picked him.[1]

After the Bush–Quayle ticket lost reelection in 1992, Quayle

---

1   The mainstream media's total lack of interest in these same "qualifications" became evident when Senator Barack Obama declared his candidacy for president with barely two years of congressional service under his belt (one-sixth of the amount of time Quayle spent in Congress) and with *no* military record.

returned to his native Indiana and contemplated his future. He made no secret of his interest in a Clinton rematch in 1996, but a serious illness placed his White House ambitions on hold. Instead, he relocated to Arizona and hoped to establish a Western political base to strengthen his chances for a later presidential run. This move coincided with my first congressional race, and I was delighted to receive his offer to campaign for me in my district.

With only two weeks to go until Election Day, my campaign staff and I drove out to Mercury Terminal at the Burbank airport to pick up Quayle, whose small private plane taxied and landed at 1:45 p.m. He climbed out with his jacket slung over his shoulder. When I thanked him for coming to help, he laughed. "Don't thank me, Jim. I should thank you. You've done me a big favor. My family and I just moved to Arizona and the moving vans arrive today with the boxes. So Marilyn [Mrs. Quayle] gets to unpack them while I come to Southern California!"

Welcome to Burbank: greeting former Vice President Dan Quayle at Burbank Airport, October 19, 1996. (Photograph by William LaChasse)

We hit it off immediately. He was friendly, warm, engaging, and very unpretentious.

Our first stop was Barron's Family Restaurant in Burbank, where reporters and a group of fans with cameras waited outside. Dan hopped from the van, tossed his jacket on the seat, and rushed across the street to greet each person there. Once inside, he sipped coffee, shook hands with customers, posed for photographs, and signed autographs. His surprise appearance delighted owner Connie Barron and her customers.

• • •

During the ride to my Glendale fundraiser, I asked Dan when he had learned that he was under serious consideration for vice president by George Bush in 1988. He said it was a few weeks before the GOP convention:

I was at a golfing tournament with my daughter. My secretary called me on my car phone and said George Bush called twice that day. I told her to tell him to call me when I got to the office. A few minutes later my secretary again called to say Bush had called for the third time. When we finally spoke, he said he wanted to consider me. I asked for a day to discuss it with my wife, Marilyn.

Former Vice President Dan Quayle campaigns with me at Barron's Family Restaurant, Burbank, California, October 19, 1996. (Photograph by William LaChasse)

I called Bush the next day and told him it was okay. I knew it was serious because there was no other reason for him to call me. I hadn't even endorsed him for president. I didn't know him all that well. I had been to his home a few times with other members of Congress, but to be candid, we weren't friends. We were from two different generations.

As the Republican Convention grew closer, I knew it was between Bob Dole and me. One morning I heard Dole interviewed on TV and popping off about how undignified the whole process was of being considered for the second spot. When I heard that interview, I turned to Marilyn and said, "Well, that's it. I guess it's us." Bush called me and said he wanted to introduce me to a national audience in New Orleans [the GOP convention site]. Marilyn and I were unprepared for how our quiet lives were about to change. Suddenly, hordes of Secret Service agents and reporters surrounded us.

I wasn't nervous about standing before the convention to deliver my acceptance speech. I was more pumped up than nervous. It was quite a night in my life. The rest, of course, is history.

The van parked at the former home of my in-laws (1521 Melwood in Glendale). This afternoon it would serve as the location of our event, but it also held another special memory for me. In 1988, my wife Christine and I exchanged our vows in the rear yard of that house.

Local Republican officials awaiting our arrival welcomed Dan. We made our way through a thick crowd of supporters. When I introduced him to my family, he told Christine how important it was for me to run and win: "But you need to know how very different your lives will be once you go to Washington," he cautioned.

After a 45-minute photo-op line, Dan and I went out to the rear yard where a couple hundred

Former Vice President Dan Quayle campaigning for me, Glendale, California, October 19, 1996. (Photograph by William LaChasse)

supporters cheered when we emerged from the house. I introduced him, and he gave a rousing speech on my behalf. His off-the-cuff remarks were light, fun, and very complimentary in urging my election to Congress.

• • •

Driving back to the airport, we continued our conversation about his career. I asked if on the day he became a freshman congressman he had ever considered the possibility that he might be vice president one day. "No," he said. "But after two terms in the House, I grew bored. We were in the minority and didn't get to do very much. I decided to run for the Senate and move up or out. I ran against a very popular three-term incumbent, Birch Bayh. I beat him in the 'Reagan Revolution' of 1980, and then we Republicans were in the majority. It was much better. If you keep the Republican majority in the House in 1996, you will see what I mean.

"You'll find once you get to Congress that there is not a lot of raw talent back there," he told me. "You may wonder for the first few months how you ever got there, and then you'll spend the rest of your life wondering how most of them got there!"

When we arrived at the airport, he gave me his new home telephone number: "Call me if I can do anything else for you. Also, have Christine call Marilyn. She'll tell her what to expect as a congressional wife." When I told him Christine would balk at picking up the phone and calling the former vice president's wife, he took my home number. "Then I'll have Marilyn call her," he said. A few days later, she did.

I walked him to his plane and thanked him again for all the help. "I'll see you in Washington, Jim," he called out as he climbed aboard. "You're in for the greatest time of your life."

• • •

Once I got to Washington, I stayed in touch with Dan. He not only helped my races with a personal appearance and a fundraiser, but he also contributed financially to my campaign.

After my work as a prosecutor in Bill Clinton's impeachment, when the national Democrats made me their number-one target for defeat in the 2000 election, he came out and addressed the California Republican State Party convention. He opened his keynote dinner speech by signaling me out in the audience, calling me a hero for fighting for the rule of law. He then led the hall in giving me a standing ovation.

Later that year, he called to tell me he planned to run for the presidency in 2000 and asked for my support. My heart sank. I had committed already to Texas Governor George W. Bush. I told Dan I had endorsed Bush because I thought he could win the White House, and I didn't think Dan could overcome the obstacles he inherited by the mainstream media's unrelenting tarring of him. He was gracious and said he understood.

In later years, I've often thought about that phone call. I don't think my political analysis was wrong, but I've wished I could relive the moment. If it were possible, I would have endorsed Dan. I know my endorsement back then didn't mean much of anything, but it meant enough for him to call and ask for it.

As I noted in the opening chapter of my book on Clinton's impeachment (*Catching Our Flag*), after being one of the first House members to endorse Bush, I met with him in Washington one week after the Clinton impeachment trial ended. Putting his arm around my shoulder, he filled me with praise: "You did a great job in the impeachment trial, Jimmy, and I'm really proud of you. I'm going to do all I can to help you win in 2000 and keep your seat." To cement our connection, he pulled me in closely and whispered in my ear, "You avenged my father," a reference to candidate Clinton defeating President George H. W. Bush in 1992. When we met again a few months later, Bush repeated the same theme with the same arm thrown around my shoulder. "I'll be there to help you," he pledged to me. "We'll have a great campaign. We'll campaign a lot together in your district."

During the 2000 general election campaign, Bush (by now the GOP presidential nominee) brought his campaign to my district twice. Both times my political team organized the rallies and turned out the thousands of volunteers for him. Both times his campaign called at the last minute with a message from the governor: he respects you deeply for your role in impeachment; you did the right thing; thanks for putting together the rally, but don't come: "We don't want you at the rally, on the stage, or in the photograph," I was told. I honored each request, assuming it came from staff rather than from the grateful candidate who pledged to help me for doing the right but unpopular thing. Still, it stung like hell to learn that at each of those rallies Bush stood on the stage and looked out upon a sea of hundreds of "Rogan for Congress" signs waving in his face. In his speeches and press interviews in my district, he never once mentioned my name or asked anyone to help me. As one reporter told me later, "It was like he came into the district of a congressman under indictment."

When Dan Quayle pledged his support to help me, he followed through on every level. He stood by me.

When he asked, I should have done the same for him.

43

Vignettes from the Mailbox

When I was a boy, I pestered famous politicians for autographs, advice, and information about their careers when we met in person. When I couldn't meet them, I pestered them through the mail. Back in 1968 (when I was 11 years old), I wrote President Lyndon Johnson and asked for an autograph. I never thought a president would write back to me, but he did. Soon the postman delivered mail to me almost daily from someone who at one time was a major player in Washington.

I took advantage of these opportunities to ask my subjects to share memories of the people and events from their past. I donated most of the hundreds of responses I received over the decades to archivists at the U.S. Capitol, the Richard Nixon Presidential Library Foundation, and to Hillsdale College. Writing this book now gives me a chance to impart these stories, some of which came from people alive when Ulysses S. Grant was still considered presidential timber.

• • •

Over the years, I asked a number of former political leaders to share their recollections of the various presidents they knew and with whom they served.[1]

---

[1] I left the capitalization and punctuation in these letters as the various authors used it.

Senator John Sparkman (D-AL) (1899–1985), the 1952 running mate of Democrat presidential nominee Adlai E. Stevenson, served in Congress from 1937 to 1979. He offered these insights of President John F. Kennedy's inauguration; he had presided as the co-chair of the 1961 Presidential Inaugural Committee:

> I have very clear memories of the Inaugural of President Kennedy. On the morning of the Inaugural Day, I went by the home of Speaker Rayburn of the House of Representatives and he and I went together to the home of President-elect and Mrs. Kennedy in Georgetown. We took them in the car with us to the White House for a courtesy call on President Eisenhower, after which we went to the Capitol together.
>
> At the Capital Mrs. Sparkman and I gave a luncheon for the new President and Mrs. Kennedy and others closely connected with the inauguration. Following the luncheon we went to the Inaugural Stand, where first Vice President Lyndon Johnson was administered the oath of office, followed by the Chief Justice of the United States administering the oath to President Kennedy. Following the inauguration President Kennedy delivered the Inaugural Address. It was one of the most beautiful speeches I ever heard in which he pronounced that lasting statement "Ask not what your country can do for you, ask what you can do for your country."
>
> Following the luncheon and the Inaugural, I escorted President and Mrs. Kennedy to the White House for the Inaugural Parade.
>
> I knew President Kennedy quite well, having served with him in the Senate. We were good friends and I respected him highly. President Kennedy sent me a large photograph in color showing our ride together in the parade. The photograph was signed by

both President and Mrs. Kennedy. The President wrote on the photograph: "John, you got us into all of this."[2]

Senator Burton K. Wheeler (D-MT) (1882–1975), the 1924 running mate of Progressive Party presidential nominee Robert M. LaFollette, served in the U.S. Senate from 1923 to 1947. When I received letters from him, his secretary paper-clipped a little note to them and apologized for his signature. She said Wheeler was blind and in his nineties. He dictated his letters to her, and then he insisted on signing them for me personally. She said she had to place his hand on the paper so he would know where to pen his name:

> I knew a good many candidates for the Presidency, but not too many Presidents. I met Harding in Butte, Montana when he was on his way to Alaska. I was introduced to him as a newly elected Senator. He said, "I don't know whether to congratulate you or to commiserate with you!" He died on that trip. He was a weak President.

> I knew Calvin Coolidge. He was honest and made a good President considering the problems that he had to face at that time, which were somewhat minor compared to those of today.

> I knew Herbert Hoover. He was an able individual, but a very poor politician, and as a result wasn't a very successful President. I talked with him as I did with President Coolidge on a number of occasions.

> I knew President Roosevelt. I was the first Senator to come out publicly for his nomination. He was a master politician and knew how to manipulate various groups and play them like a master

---

2   April 14, 1970.

musician. He advocated some very fine legislation. I handled quite a good deal of it including the Utility Holding Company Bill which I put through the Senate with one vote. I handled the Wheeler-Case bill, the Wheeler-Howard Bill and the Transportation Act of 1940, in addition to some other minor bills for him. A great many people said I hated him because I disagreed with him on the Court fight [Roosevelt's attempt to pack the U.S. Supreme Court with additional members] and on the war issue [isolationist Wheeler had opposed U.S. entry into World War II prior to the Japanese attack on Pearl Harbor]. I didn't hate him. Personally I liked him. He had a charming personality. On one occasion William Randolph Hearst was criticizing him to me and I said, "Why don't you go to see him." He said, "I am afraid to. Everybody who goes to see him gets taken right in."

I was selected by the Democrats and Republicans who were opposed to Roosevelt's program of packing the Supreme Court, and I led the fight against it, and we succeeded in defeating the legislation. That was his most serious defeat during the time he was President. After that in 1939 he sent for me and asked me to handle the Railroad Transportation Act. I finally agreed to do so and it became known as the Transportation Act of 1940. After that I disagreed with Roosevelt on the war issue. I said that I was opposed to getting into the war unless we were attacked. Of course when Japan attacked us, I said we would have to lick them. There was no question but what Roosevelt wanted to get us into the war. Even Churchill, in some of his memoirs, said that in his conversations with Roosevelt, Roosevelt assured him that we would get in even if he had to create an incident.

I knew Truman intimately. I was Chairman of the Senate Interstate and Foreign Commerce Committee and he was a new member. And he would tell you today if he were alive that I helped him when he first came there more than anybody else. He was a close friend of mine at all times. He was not a great Senator but was looked upon as one who belonged to the lower echelon.

I knew Eisenhower. He had a wonderful personality and I felt he made a good President, not a brilliant one.

I knew Nixon but only casually. I think he did right in resigning. It was hard for me to believe much that was said about him until after his admission that he had lied to Congress, to the people and to his own lawyers. I know President Ford just casually. I know very little about [Ford's nominee for vice president, Nelson] Rockefeller except that he is a very rich man, and that he was elected and reelected as Governor of New York. I don't know of any reason why he shouldn't be confirmed.[3]

Senator Claude Pepper (D-FL) (1900–1989) served in the U.S. Senate from 1936 to 1951, when he lost a primary for reelection. Pepper returned to Congress in 1963 as a member of the House of Representatives, where he served until his death in 1989:

I came to the Senate at the beginning of the second term of President Roosevelt and enjoyed a close and warm friendship with him. I think he was one of our few greatest Presidents. What he did to save our country from economic collapse, to build the forces of freedom in the world, and to win World War II, was a monumental achievement. It could not have been excelled by anyone. His impact upon our government and nation will long endure.

President Truman, as Churchill said, deserves much commendation for his ability to make decisions and to take and maintain

---

3   April 5, 1974, and October 7, 1974.

firm positions. He did not accomplish in the domestic field as much as Roosevelt or Johnson, but in general he pursued a wise and aggressive course. He made some mistakes in foreign affairs, as when he, after World War II, failed to support the efforts of many people in Southeast Asia to keep the French from going back into Vietnam as a colonial power. If that had happened, we might not have had the tragedy of Vietnam that we are lamenting today.

President Johnson achieved more in domestic policy than any other President except Roosevelt, his friend and mentor, but he made a tragic mistake in enlarging the war in Vietnam and in fighting it—or allowing the generals to fight it the way we did.

President Eisenhower was an honorable man, but having no experience in politics did not achieve, as President, comparable to his achievements as Commander of the Allied Forces in World War II.

President Nixon's record and character are well known to you without my having to make any comment. His influence upon public life in America has been vastly contaminated. President Ford is an honorable and candid man who means well. It's too early to make an appraisal of his Presidency.[4]

Senator Margaret Chase Smith (R-ME) (1897–1985) served in Congress from 1940 to 1973, becoming the first woman to serve in both houses. She ran unsuccessfully for the 1964 Republican presidential nomination:

4   April 30, 1975.

My first opportunity to meet a president was when I visited Washington as a graduate from Skowhegan High School in 1916 and was introduced to and shook hands with President Wilson. I also met President Coolidge but I knew Mrs. Coolidge personally.

It was my privilege to have dinner with President Herbert Hoover at his home in the 1960s. He called personally one day and asked if I would do this as he would like to talk with me. The only other person present was one of his assistants. I was a great admirer of President Hoover and this meant a great deal to me.

As you know, the Roosevelts spent a great deal of time in Maine at their summer home in Campobello, now a part of the international conference center. He gave us much to be thankful for when he showed the vision and courage necessary to bring us out of that deep, deep depression.

President Truman, a longtime member of the U.S. Senate and an historian, gave us much to be thankful for in as much as he was an historian, studied issues confronting him, making decisions that remained with him.

President Kennedy was an attractive young man; but because of his assassination, had too little service to be judged. President Johnson was one of the outstanding leaders of the U.S. Senate.[5]

Senator Charles McC. Mathias (R-MD) (1922–2010) served in Congress from 1961 to 1987:

About my recollections of presidents, I might start with the first I met, Calvin Coolidge. In February 1929, when I was six years old,

---

5   July 1, 1981.

my father drove from Frederick, Maryland, to pay a farewell call on President Coolidge before he left the White House on March 4th. It is a commentary on the changing times that presidents then had the leisure for such social courtesies. He took me with him and on the trip tried to explain why we were going to visit. When I heard that the President was moving I asked if his furniture was packed. No, my father replied, a president took only his "wardrobe" when he left the White House. To me, at that age, a wardrobe was a massive mahogany cupboard and I pictured the President struggling with it. When we reached the Oval Office the early spring sunlight was flooding the green carpet, which I can still see with the inward eye. I do not recall the conversation except that when we were leaving my father started in the wrong direction. I can plainly hear Coolidge's clipped Yankee voice saying "Please go out the other door."

My introduction to President Herbert Hoover took place a relatively short time later under very different circumstances. The President's full name was Herbert Clark Hoover and the Clark family had lived on a farm in Carroll County, Maryland. Since the site was a short distance from Washington the President wanted to visit the house of his ancestors which he had never seen. My father had helped to make the local arrangements so he was invited to join the President's party. We met the White House limousine at the designated rendezvous where Mrs. Hoover invited me to ride with her and the President to the Clark farm. Sometime later the President sent me one of the then new, smaller size dollar bills which he had autographed and which I still have.

Because Frederick, Maryland, is situated between Washington and Shangri-La (now Camp David), I had occasional glimpses of President Roosevelt and President Truman. Beginning with President Eisenhower, I have had substantial contact with every succeeding president up to George Bush. Those stories will have to wait, however, for another occasion.[6]

Senator Charles Percy (R-IL) (1919–2011) served in the U.S. Senate from 1967 to 1985, when he lost a bid for reelection. Often mentioned as a potential presidential or vice presidential candidate, Percy never sought national office. He wrote me of two presidents with whom he was intimate (Eisenhower and Ford), and then threw in for good measure his recollections of meeting the legendary prime minister of Great Britain, Winston Churchill:

In 1958, I was President of Bell & Howell Company, and I was the Illinois state finance chairman of the Republican National Committee. The election year of 1958 had not been a good one for the Republican Party, and we were concerned about what we could do to rebuild our party. Following the election, I decided I needed a vacation, so I was skiing in Sun Valley, Idaho when I received a telegram from President Eisenhower asking me to attend a meeting of Republican leaders at the White House early in 1959. Our group met with the President, and when he asked for suggestions, I proposed that we set up a Commission on National Goals. The Commission would be headed by a prominent person, and the members would be selected from both Republican and Democrat parties. Once the goals were outlined, the Republican Party could establish a committee that would indicate how Republicans thought they might achieve those goals. I also hoped that the Democrats would do the same. I thought that this would be good for the country and that the committees could come up with an answer to the question "Where should we be as a nation by 1976—our bicentennial?"

---

6   July 3, 1991.

President Eisenhower was enthusiastic and invited me back to the White House the next day. It turned out that he was working on his State of the Union message and wanted to add to it a request to set up the Commission on National Goals. We spent the day working on this part of his speech, and after we had finished, he invited me back to the White House residence section for a friendly chat. I'll never forget that talk we had together, because it was then that I became aware of the President's humility and learned of his loyalty. He was talking about his brother Milton Eisenhower, who was President of Johns Hopkins University. President Eisenhower put his arm around my shoulder and said, "Milton is the brightest of the Eisenhower brothers. He was the one who really should have been President, not I." He also made me an offer, and over the years I learned of his loyalty. He told me that he hoped that I would run for public office myself one day, and that he would support me "be it the highest office in the land." He truly meant it and did indeed support my political career through the years.

The State of the Union message was given, and it included a request for the Commission. President Eisenhower asked me to head the Commission, but I had to refuse. I was too much of a Republican to head a non-partisan group such as this, though I gladly accepted his invitation to be the Chairman of the Republican Committee on Programs and Progress. This was the group that published a report on what we thought our party ought to do to achieve the goals of the Commission. After nine months of work, our report, Decisions for a Better America, was published. I have always thought it was my work on this Committee that caused me to be named Chairman of the 1960 Platform Committee of the Republican National Convention which led to my full-time entry into politics.

I first met Jerry Ford in Peoria, Illinois in 1949, when we were both elected as two of The Ten Outstanding Young Men of the Year by the United States Junior Chamber of Commerce. He has proved the wisdom of their choice since then. His 1976 campaign theme of candor, honesty and openness is exactly the theme that I think deserves high priority.

Both Jerry and I look upon a swimming pool, lake, ocean or river as the best possible place for exercise, and both of us would like to be able to swim every day of our lives. The exception was when Jerry became President and had to leave his home, which had a pool, to move to the White House where President Nixon had removed the pool. While he was waiting for a new White House pool to be completed, I mentioned to Jerry that as I swam in my own small pool in Georgetown, I said to myself, "Now, if I lived at 1600 Pennsylvania Avenue, I wouldn't be able to do this."

Winston Churchill was the most impressive foreign politician that I ever met. I never knew him during his term in office, but I met him later in Washington when he came to visit President Eisenhower. I also once found myself seated next to Churchill on a plane flying from London to the south of France. I told him that years before, a London collector of rare books had put together a complete set of all of the writings of Winston Churchill, from his earliest work to his latest, and had bound these in red leather. I had bought the complete set which was my most treasured possession, because as a public official it inspired me. But, I admitted to him that the stories of his early difficulties in school had also been a source of great satisfaction to my son Roger, who early in life was not particularly a good student either. I recalled that he had told of doing so poorly in school that he was not permitted to continue in Greek. He was required instead to continue his courses in English. I mentioned that he had concluded his autobiography with the words "Thank God I was forced to learn how to speak and write the English language." I told him that many of us were also appreciative of this. A smile settled over his face as he seemed to reflect upon his love of the English language and what he had done with it over the years to advance his own political cause and to save his beloved England.[7]

Stansfield Turner (1923–2018), a retired admiral and former director of the CIA, shared this recollection of his mentor and former Annapolis classmate, President Jimmy Carter:

In December of 1974, I was passing through Atlanta on Navy business. I asked for and had an appointment with then-Governor Jimmy Carter, who had been a classmate at the Naval Academy many years before. What impressed me first about our meeting was that it took him only about one minute to dispense with the normal pleasantries of "How are you" and "What have you been doing." For the next 29 minutes he interrogated me up and down about the state of our military preparedness. What he was doing was stretching my thinking into areas I had not considered, but which would be of concern to a president. It was an exciting and challenging experience for me, one that left me mentally drained at the end.

At the completion of my 30-minute interview, the Governor led me to the door, and as we parted said he wanted me to know that in two days he would be declaring his candidacy for the presidency. I said "Good luck, Jimmy" and left with very little thought that he would actually become president. Nor did I have the slightest idea that his becoming president would change my life in the dramatic way it did—from Admiral to Chief of the CIA.[8]

---

7   August 30, 1991.

8   July 31, 1991.

• • •

I corresponded over the years with many former presidential candidates and their running mates. A few recollections of historic campaigns of bygone days follow.

As noted earlier, Senator Burton K. Wheeler ran as the 1924 vice presidential nominee of the Progressive Party along with presidential candidate Robert M. LaFollette (1855–1925). Although losing to the Republican nominees Calvin Coolidge and Charles Dawes, the LaFollette–Wheeler ticket carried Wisconsin and 17 percent of the popular vote against Coolidge and Democrat nominee John W. Davis. A few months before his death at age 92, Wheeler shared this vignette from the 1924 race:

> To recall the events during the 1924 LaFollette–Wheeler Progressive Party campaign would take too long, but I did open the campaign on the Boston Commons. LaFollette and his friends felt that the man they had to beat was [Democrat Party nominee] John W. Davis. I disagreed with him and told him the man he had to beat was Calvin Coolidge, and I insisted that my first speech in the campaign would be my attack upon the Republican Party and the candidate, which I did in my opening speech, and I continued to do so throughout the campaign.

> LaFollette thought that we would be elected, but I never felt we would, and I told him that we would be lucky to get 5 million votes. We were given close to 5 million, but in some places our votes were not even counted.[9]

In an earlier chapter, I shared my story of calling on the telephone former Kansas Governor Alf M. Landon (1887–1987), the 1936 GOP presidential nominee vanquished by Franklin Roosevelt

---

9   April 5, 1974.

in his drive toward a second term. Landon wrote to me and offered these thoughts regarding his 1936 battle:

> I am sorry I do not have any campaign literature or materials to spare. I did not save it at the time, and am only now making a collection for my own grandchildren.

> I made three main issues in 1936 that are still hot ones: First, that inflation was like a whirlpool and, once we got sucked into it, it would keep getting bigger and bigger all the time. Second, the political corollary of a planned economy meant increased centralization of political power in the national government. Third, [we] need a long-range national land use policy.

> I made the usual "swing around the circle" as it was called then, in a special train from coast to coast. I had many visits with President Roosevelt.[10] [At age 84] I am feeling fit as a fiddle. I go horseback riding three or four mornings a week for between four and six miles.[11]

The man who helped crush Landon's presidential ambitions was Roosevelt's national campaign manager, James A. Farley (1888–1976). Before FDR's White House run, Farley managed the New York gubernatorial campaigns of Al Smith in 1922 (Smith became the 1928 Democrat presidential nominee), and Roosevelt in 1928 and 1930. Farley was a political dynamo. He revolutionized polling data and cobbled together the religious and ethnic coalitions that formed the base of the modern Democrat Party for generations.

---

10   December 12, 1974.

11   August 16, 1971.

ALF. M. LANDON

P.O. BOX 206   December 12, 1972   TOPEKA, KANSAS 66601

At my request, Landon wrote out and signed for me his presidential campaign slogan: "That leadership along the trail which we have loved long since, and lost awhile, has come to us again."

During Roosevelt's first two terms, Farley served simultaneously as the chairman of the Democrat National Committee as well as in FDR's cabinet as postmaster general. Considered a presidential dark horse candidate himself in the 1940 election cycle, Farley's and Roosevelt's relationship dissolved that year when Farley opposed FDR breaking the two-term tradition every previous president had respected.

Farley wrote and told me his side of the famous schism between the two former allies and longtime friends:

I disagreed with President Roosevelt on the third term and resigned as Postmaster General. He resented this very much and I only saw him on a few occasions after I retired as Postmaster General the last week in August 1940. I did support him openly in 1940 and 1944, although I did not make any speeches, but everyone knew that as a regular Democrat, I would support the Democratic candidate.

I was never a candidate for the presidency—there was no boom for me, but the Gallup Polls will show that I was always second to Mr. Hull [FDR's first Secretary of State] . . . I was for Secretary of State, Cordell Hull for president.[12]

Another leader left in the dust by the Roosevelt campaign juggernaut was Ohio Governor and U.S. Senator John W. Bricker (1893–1986), the 1944 GOP vice presidential running mate of New York Governor Thomas E. Dewey. Running for a fourth and final term, Roosevelt beat the Dewey–Bricker ticket (four years later, Dewey again stood as the GOP nominee and lost the presidency to Harry Truman). Bricker shared with me these observations on his 1944 campaign:

My name came before the 1944 Republican Convention originally as a candidate for the nomination for president. A combination of New York and California and other states that were subject largely to New York control prevented my having the number of delegates to be nominated. I did know most of the Republican leaders of the country and did accept at their insistence the nomination for vice president. I had no reaction [to my nomination] because I was advised beforehand how it would come out. I was willing to do what I could for the Party and what I believed to be in the best interest of the country. I therefore accepted nomination for the vice presidency and campaigned vigorously for the election.[13]

12   December 20, 1971.

13   June 21, 1972.

Mr. Dewey should have won in 1948, but the 1944 campaign was a very difficult one against Mr. Roosevelt in the middle of a war. We did carry Ohio for Mr. Dewey in 1944 and he lost it in 1948.

Mr. Roosevelt was a very appealing man. In fact, he invited me on his train when he visited Ohio rather than the Democratic candidate against whom I was running. We both later carried the state.[14]

Historians debate whether John F. Kennedy actually defeated Richard Nixon for the presidency in 1960. In the closest election in American history, official results showed Kennedy's victory margin was just 0.1 percent. With allegations of chicanery pouring out of Chicago and other key areas, Republican leaders nationwide demanded that Nixon contest the results.

Herbert G. Klein (1918–2009) was Nixon's campaign press secretary that year. He later served as press secretary for Nixon's 1962 race for governor of California, national communications manager for Nixon's presidential campaign of 1968, and White House communications director in the Nixon Administration. When I asked why Nixon chose ultimately not to contest the 1960 election, he shared the backstory, which he told me was unknown by most people:

On the Saturday following the 1960 election, I was in Key Biscayne with Nixon and Bob Finch and then-Col. James D. Hughes and our wives. The full impact of "officially" losing the election to Senator John Kennedy finally had settled in. [Nixon] was too depressed for conversation.

---

14   February 3, 1975.

We went to dinner at a local restaurant, and as we arrived the maître'd told me there was a call for Vice President Nixon. I took the call which was from former President Herbert Hoover. Joe Kennedy [JFK's father] had called him to find out if the Vice President would accept a call from Senator Kennedy [which led ultimately] to a meeting between the two. The former President gave me the President-elect's telephone number in Palm Beach.

I gave the message to Mr. Nixon and he immediately perked up and began discussing the problems of a country divided by a 50-50 vote. He then went to a public phone booth and called President Eisenhower in Augusta, Georgia. About this time the maître'd's phone rang and I picked it up, and it was John Kennedy. We had a conversation while Mr. Nixon talked to President Eisenhower. Senator Kennedy complimented me on my work. Five minutes later, Mr. Nixon called Senator Kennedy and arranged a meeting for the following Monday.

The Vice President then decided not to prolong the turmoil by challenging the election results. [Later, Nixon and Kennedy] met in Key Biscayne and made plans to preserve national unity between the future President and the new leader of the loyal opposition.[15]

In another of America's closest elections, Nixon came out on top when he squeaked by Hubert Humphrey in 1968 by a mere 0.7 percent. Humphrey's running mate that year, Senator Edmund S. Muskie (1914–1996), went on to serve as Secretary of State under President Jimmy Carter.

After he retired from politics, Muskie sent me a wonderful handwritten letter sharing the story of how Humphrey selected him for the second spot on the 1968 Democrat ticket:

15   December 3, 1991.

1968 Democrat vice presidential nominee Edmund Muskie and me, Washington, September 1975. (Author's collection)

Hubert first indicated his interest in a flight from Washington to Maine to attend the Maine Democratic Convention in May 1968. I was surprised and flattered but skeptical that political realities would permit him to choose a running mate from a small state like Maine.

I remained skeptical until the day after his own nomination in Chicago. He asked me to come to his room in the Conrad Hilton Hotel. The invitation convinced me that I was about to be selected—which of course proved to be the case.

As to my reaction, I was exhilarated and enthusiastic—notwithstanding the depressing events of the convention. We ended the campaign in the same spirit—and almost won! It was one of the greatest experiences of my life to be associated with Hubert Humphrey in such a venture![16]

16   December 9, 1982.

EDMUND S. MUSKIE

Dec 9, 1982

To James E. Rogan:

Thank you for your thoughtful letter!

Hubert first indicated his interest on a flight from Washington to Maine to attend the Maine Democratic Convention of May, 1968. I was surprised and flattered but skeptical that political realities would permit him to choose a running mate from a small state like Maine.

I remained skeptical until the day after his own nomination in Chicago. He asked me to come to his room

CHADBOURNE, PARKE, WHITESIDE & WOLFF
1101 VERMONT AVENUE, N. W., WASHINGTON, D. C. 20005
(202) 289-3000; TRT TELEX 140162

30 ROCKEFELLER PLAZA, NEW YORK, NEW YORK 10112
(212) 541-5800; WUI TELEX 620520; WU TELEX 645383

EDMUND S. MUSKIE

in the Conrad Hilton Hotel. The invitation convinced me that I was about to be selected, — which, of course, proved to be the case.

As to my reaction — I was exhilarated and enthusiastic — notwithstanding the depressing events of the Convention. We ended the campaign in the same spirit — and almost won! It was one of the great experience of my life — to be associated with Hubert Humphrey in such a venture! Sincerely

[signature]

CHADBOURNE, PARKE, WHITESIDE & WOLFF
1101 VERMONT AVENUE, N. W., WASHINGTON, D. C. 20005
(202) 289-3000: TRT TELEX 140162

30 ROCKEFELLER PLAZA, NEW YORK, NEW YORK 10112
(212) 541-5800: WUI TELEX 620520: WU TELEX 645363

Senator Edmund Muskie's letter to me describing how he became the 1968 Democrat vice presidential nominee, December 9, 1982. (Author's collection)

Another close election occurred in 1976 between President Gerald Ford and former Georgia Governor Jimmy Carter. Ford lost to Carter by only 2 percent. To his dying day, Ford blamed former Governor Ronald Reagan's GOP primary challenge for costing him the election.

Before he became president, Reagan wrote me several letters regarding his 1976 challenge to Ford. The final letter in the series included a curious denial of what he told me in the first letter. Two weeks after President Nixon resigned the presidency and Vice President Gerald Ford succeeded him, Reagan wrote me and suggested Ford had his support for a full term in 1976:

Since President Ford is our Party's new standard bearer who will undoubtedly run for re-election in 1976, I have no intention of challenging him for the nomination. It's never been more important for us to stand united; only so we can heal the wounds of Watergate and enhance our chances for an election victory. I am confident a Republican can win . . . in the next presidential election.[17]

A year later, things had changed. Now as a former governor, Reagan wrote me from his home in Pacific Palisades:

Dear Jim,

It was good to hear from you and I'm particularly grateful for your expression of support for my possible candidacy for national office. While the decision will be down the road a ways, the Committee which has recently been established in Washington will be a great aid to me in my assessment of who can best lead the Party to victory in '76 and lead the nation beyond that. If we use a scale from 1 to 10, I would say I'm an "8" in leaning toward seeking the nomination. I want to thank you for your kind offer of assistance if and when the time should come.[18]

17   August 22, 1974.

18   September 5, 1975.

After Reagan declared his candidacy against Ford in late 1975, I wrote Reagan at his private address and asked a few questions about the campaign. In one query, I quoted directly what he had written me in 1974 suggesting his support for Ford, and I asked him how he reconciled the abandonment of that pledge. I assumed that if Reagan made the statement to me privately, he had also made it to others, and that the press would grill him over it. Instead of getting an explanation, I got a denial. In a two-page letter dictated while on the campaign trail, he wrote:

First of all, I do not remember having made a statement pledging to support President Ford unequivocally. What I did say on several occasions was that I'd hoped and prayed that he'd do such a good job that my candidacy would not even be necessary and, as most Americans, I was sincere in giving President Ford my complete support when he took over the awesome duties of the Presidency. That was a year and a half ago. In the meantime, however, as all the public opinion polls have indicated, the rank and file of our party does not seem convinced that he is our party's best choice as standard bearer. My decision to challenge him for the nomination was only made after talking with people all over the country and being convinced that my candidacy would give them a voice in the coming primary elections.

Number 2: 1976 is an unusual year. President Ford was appointed to the job by a man who left office in disgrace. As a matter of fact, President Ford has never won or even run in a statewide election. I intend to run in almost all of the primary states, all of which I will try my best to win. How many victories are essential to my own campaign, I don't know.

Number 3: I'm not interested in the vice presidency nor am I interested in leading a third party ticket. If I get nominated, I will look for a running mate who shares my philosophy.

And, number 4: It's hard to say which of the Democrat contenders would be the most formidable but I do think Hubert Humphrey has the best chance of being nominated. I do feel he can be defeated by a Republican.[19]

My friend, former Massachusetts Governor Mike Dukakis, shared this comment regarding what it was like for him to stand before the cheering delegates as he accepted the Democrat presidential nomination in 1988:

> The Atlanta [Democrat National] Convention was a very special day for me, for Kitty and for our family. It was the culmination of over a year's work; thousands of hours of campaigning, and the coming together of so many of the people who put their hearts and souls into our primary effort. Would that we had done the same effective job in the final! Unfortunately, we peaked in Atlanta. But it was a great moment, one made even more poignant by the memories of my Dad, who would have been so proud of his son and of his adopted country.[20]

• • •

Within weeks of George McGovern's loss of the presidency to Richard Nixon in November 1972, the Watergate scandal started unraveling. In August 1974, Nixon resigned the presidency. A few leaders from that time shared their opinions with me on the unprecedented wound from which America sought to recover.

U.S. Senator Sam Ervin (1896–1985) served in the Senate from 1954 to 1974. He worked on two historic investigative committees: the hearings in 1954 that led to the downfall of Senator Joseph McCarthy, and—most notably—he chaired the Senate's "Watergate Committee," uncovering information that helped lead to Nixon's

---

19   January 14, 1976.

20   April 23, 1992.

resignation. After he retired from Congress, Ervin wrote me from his home in Morganton, North Carolina: "While the Watergate was a great tragedy, it eventually taught the American people that we have the wisest system of government on earth. It particularly shows the wisdom of the Founding Fathers in separating the powers of the President, the Congress, and the courts. When the president proved faithless to his constitutional obligations, the Congress and the courts remained faithful to theirs."[21]

The man Nixon defeated narrowly for the presidency in 1968, Hubert H. Humphrey (1911–1978), offered this insight in a letter dated just a few weeks after Nixon's resignation:

> I believe Mr. Nixon's resignation was in the best interests of the Nation. We must now turn to the duty of solving the difficult problems before us. The responsibility for governing, the task of rebuilding faith in government and confidence in our political institutions now belong to Gerald Ford and the Congress. I have pledged my full cooperation in achieving these goals.

> These have been difficult times for our country. We should take this time to reflect on the meaning of these events, but we as a Nation should not despair, because the Constitution has met and survived one of its greatest tests. We should have pride in our political system, and vow to preserve the traditions which have been upheld.[22]

Alf Landon, the 1936 GOP presidential nominee who addressed Nixon's nominating convention I attended in 1972, offered this terse assessment: "I said from the first that Watergate was a scandal that must be cleaned to the bone. It is—not only by President Nixon's resignation, but also the judicial proceedings covering all the parties

---

21   February 1, 1983.

22   September 24, 1974.

involved in that stupid and disgraceful criminal affair."[23]

Two days before Nixon resigned, the House and Senate Republican leadership—Senate GOP minority leader Hugh Scott, House GOP minority leader John Rhodes, and former GOP presidential nominee Barry Goldwater—trekked from the Capitol to the White House for a private meeting with Nixon. The press later reported that the trio demanded Nixon's resignation for the good of the country and the Republican Party. In a letter to me dated just three weeks after that historic meeting, Congressman Rhodes (1916–2003) discounted the media's version:

[T]he meeting of August 7 was set up at the President's request so that Senator Hugh Scott, Senator Barry Goldwater, and I could apprise him of the impeachment situation in the Congress. The meeting was relatively brief, as the President seemed to have a fairly accurate view of his own situation and only wanted us to confirm his impressions, which we did. At no point did we discuss the President's options. His decision to resign was one which he arrived at on his own.[24]

After Nixon signed his resignation letter and bade the White House staff goodbye on August 9, 1974, he boarded Air Force One for the lonely ride back to California. Accompanying him on that flight into exile was his White House press secretary, Ronald Ziegler (1939–2003). Almost two decades later, Ziegler wrote me and described that trip home and its aftermath:

I was one of the first men that President Nixon told that he had made the decision to resign his office. He said it was clear that he had lost the ability to lead the people of his country. Leadership in a democracy is grounded on freely received public support.

23 December 12, 1974.

24 August 28, 1974.

President Nixon knew that because of "Watergate" he had lost the ability to obtain or rally support for his presidency. He felt it was time to remove the turmoil surrounding this tragic episode from the agenda of the nation's leadership[.]

I flew out to San Clemente and into self-imposed exile, with President Nixon, in 1974. I did not know what to expect—how this man who had been disgraced, who had resigned from office, would deal with that circumstance. The first morning in San Clemente, I looked out the office window of what was called the Western White House, and saw former President Nixon walking across the compound from his home in a suit and tie. Not in a sport shirt, nor unshaven, not beleaguered, however, obviously feeling and showing the strain of the terrible position that he had placed himself in and the agony he felt because of it.

He began to use his mind in a disciplined way, focusing on his shortcomings, the mistakes of his administration, analyzing his own actions and the actions of other men. He talked about his achievements. He looked back—to learn from his shortcomings how he could strengthen himself, on a personal basis. He chose to survive and not to destroy himself. I learned from that experience that no matter how extensive an individual's humiliation or failure might be, that only they can destroy themselves. President Nixon clearly chose not to. Today he has written seven excellent books on foreign policy and on politics, is listened to as he speaks out from time to time on national and world affairs, and is living a quiet and healthy life in the East, enjoying his grandchildren.

I have always felt very fortunate to have had the opportunity to serve our Country in that capacity. It was also a privilege to be able to know a leader of our country on such a personal level. The President was always most considerate of and interested in my family and my own activities. The opportunities made available, knowledge gained and lessons learned have helped to shape my life both personally and professionally.[25]

• • •

A number of former Members of Congress wrote and shared recollections and advice for a budding young political aficionado.

E. L. Mecham (R-NM) (1912–2002) served as the 15th, 17th, and 19th governor of New Mexico. After he lost his bid for reelection in 1962, Senator Dennis Chavez died suddenly and Mecham appointed himself to the vacant Senate seat. Defeated for election to the term in 1964, he retired to New Mexico until President Nixon appointed him to the federal bench. Mecham shared this humorous anecdote—as well as a rare historical artifact for my collection:

> The only memento I have of my time in the Senate—two years—is a pen that was used by President Johnson to sign the legislation creating the [1964] Civil Rights Act. [Author's note: Senator Mecham gave me this historic pen. In 2000, I sent it to the Smithsonian's American History Museum in Washington, where it has remained on continuous display since.]
>
> I was a [Senate] peon at the time, being next to the last in seniority on the Republican side, and filling out the unexpired term of the late Senator Dennis Chavez with slight expectation by anyone of election. The Senate timetable was heavily burdened by the civil rights and federal aid to education legislation. I was also trying to mount an election campaign and spend as much time as possible in New Mexico without neglecting the Senate business, so I did miss out on quite a bit of the side play, significant and otherwise.

---

25   July 17, 1991.

Two of the more lasting memories are Ralph Yarborough's efforts to get a quorum for a subcommittee hearing to start consideration of the civil rights legislation. He would call a session with no quorum, get on the phone, send pages, and even go into the hall to try to find a subcommittee member to lure in. One such was Strom Thurmond who was resistant to Ralph's effort to pull him into the session. Strom decided the invitation had gone far enough so he offered to wrestle Ralph in the hall of the beautiful Old Senate Office Building, with the loser to abide by the wishes of the other. Ralph agreed and Strom then threw him in about three seconds. Ralph complained that Strom had a head start and wanted another fall. Strom agreed and quickly threw Ralph again, helped him up, brushed him off, and walked away.

The other was after the Supreme Court's opinion banning prayer in public schools. The rumor went around that it would be applied to the Senate. At the opening of the next [Senate session], after prayer, Dick Russell and Everett Dirksen, the [Democrat and Republican Party] leaders, went down on their knees in the well of the Senate chambers facing the Supreme Court Building and began to Salaam Oh Ye Mighty Supreme Court. [Here was] one time the Senate rule against cameras and recording was soundly abused.[26]

House Speaker John W. McCormack (D-MA) (1891–1980) served in Congress from 1928 until his retirement in 1971. I wrote him often, and he always replied in longhand with a steep right vertical slant to his penmanship. On a beautiful engraved vignette of the U.S. Capitol, McCormack penned for me his congressional philosophy: "Sometimes I think it might be well if we erect a large sign over Congress which contains this thought: 'Here the opinions

---

26   July 3, 1991.

of all Americans are heard and should be heard with equality.' As a result, the sense of their principles becomes the law of the land. And perhaps we should put it in more typical common language: 'Here your two cents does make a difference!'"[27]

I was a teenager when I met Senator Sam Ervin, the Senate Watergate Committee chairman, and I took a photograph of him addressing a college audience. Later, when I mailed the picture to him for his autograph, I mentioned that I hoped to go to law school one day. Ervin returned the photograph to this future lawyer with his advice inscribed on the border: "My father, who was an active practitioner at the North Carolina Bar for 65 years, gave me this sage advice: 'Salt down the facts; the law will keep.'"

"Salt down the facts...." Former Senator Sam Ervin, San Francisco, February 1975. (Photograph by the author)

---

27   August 30, 1973.

• • •

One letter in my archives came from an unlikely writer: James Earl Ray (1928–1998), the convicted assassin of Dr. Martin Luther King, Jr. Decades after King's murder, when I was a county prosecutor, I read an interview with Ray where he appeared to disclaim responsibility for the dastardly shooting. I wrote him at Brushy Mountain Prison in Tennessee and asked if he now denied responsibility for King's murder. I never expected a reply, but a couple of weeks later, a typed letter on a sheet of yellow legal paper arrived at my office bearing the bold signature of King's killer:

5 July 1988

Inmate #65477

In re to the MLK case, I've denies [sic] responsibility before the courts, and before the Congressional Committee that investigated the case. I don't deny or admit anything to the news media since I don't think I owe the media any explanations about anything. I know the newspapers quoted me as denying responsibility last April but that was their own words. Most everything (records), connected with the case have been classified, e.g., the Congressional Committee classified 185 cubic feet of its files following the investigation. . . .

I worked on a book about the case for five years then let an editor finish it up. I've enclosed a clipping about it in case you or anyone would be interested in it.[28] [Author's note: a few weeks later, a package came to my office from Brushy Mountain Prison. Ray had sent me an inscribed copy of his book on the Martin Luther King assassination. It remains the most macabre and peculiar volume in my library.]

---

28 July 5, 1988.

• • •

I'll end this chapter with a couple of favorites. One letter came from the legendary entertainer Bing Crosby (1903–1977). I grew up a fan of Crosby's records, movies, and television specials. My favorite Crosby vehicles were the classic *Road* films he did with partner Bob Hope (made between 1940 and 1962).

When I grew up in San Francisco, Crosby lived in a mansion in nearby Hillsborough. I saw him in concert twice. Near the end of his life, I wrote him a letter, told him I was a fan, and sent him a set of photographs I took of him and his family at their 1976 concert. He wrote me a delightful reply:

> Thanks for your letter. I am pleased to know you have been a longtime supporter of mine, and also of the work of my erstwhile partner, Mr. Hope. He's a very deserving lad, and I like to hear nice things said about him, because it encourages him in his work!
>
> Glad to know that you have some of my albums, also. You asked me what my favorite *Road* picture is. I guess I would have to say *The Road to Utopia*. Had some good songs in it, and I thought some of the gags—particularly the visual gags—were quite well conceived and executed.
>
> Also glad you liked *Going My Way* [Crosby received the Best Actor Oscar for his performance in that film]. That was a big boost for me and my career. Of course, the big thing that happened to me was Irving Berlin writing a song called *White Christmas*. This really has been a sustaining influence for me and for my work. I hope this finds you in good health and spirits.
>
> Always your friend,
>
> Bing

The final letter I'll share came from former U.S. Senator Ralph Yarborough (D-TX) (1903–1996). Some years after he left politics, and when I was a boy, he wrote me a longhand letter urging me to keep up my interest in politics and he gave me advice if I ever succeeded in my ambitions. "Never fear defeat," he said. "Never compromise yourself, serve always with the best interest of the people and the nation in mind, even if it means defeat . . . . Never do a dishonorable act."

The closing line of his letter has particular significance to me, and in its own way, it makes Yarborough's letter a relic of history. Twenty-five years after Yarborough penned advice for me, I stood in the chamber where he had served decades earlier and I read the end of his letter in my Clinton impeachment trial closing argument. My concluding words to the United States Senate and to a live worldwide television audience were these:

> From the time I was a little boy, it was my dream to serve one day in the Congress of the United States. My constituents fulfilled that dream for me two years ago. Today, I am a Republican in a district that is heavily Democrat. The pundits keep telling me that my stand on this issue puts my political fortunes in jeopardy. So be it. That revelation produces from me no flinching. There is a simple reason why: I know that in life, dreams come and dreams go, but conscience is forever. I can live with the concept of not serving in Congress. I cannot live with the idea of remaining in Congress at the expense of doing what I believe to be right.
>
> I was a teenager when a distinguished member of this body, the late Senator Ralph Yarborough of Texas, wrote and gave me this sage advice about elective office. He told me to put principle above politics, and to "put honor above incumbency."

I now return that sentiment to the body from which it came. Hold fast to it, senators, and in doing so, you will be faithful both to our Founders and to our heirs.

Senator Ralph Yarborough's letter to me (1975), which I referenced in my closing argument to the United States Senate in the impeachment trial of President Clinton, 1999. (Author's collection)

44

A Last Goodbye

The first famous person I ever saw in my life was Ronald Reagan. You may recall the earlier chapter in this book, *My Governor*, where I told the story of standing outside the gate of the San Francisco Opera House as he drove by and waved to me during the 25th anniversary of the signing of the United Nations Charter in 1970. Since he was my first encounter with fame and since he had such a profound impact on my life (personally and politically), I thought it appropriate to close this book of reminiscences with a final story about him.

•••

In a handwritten letter dated November 1994, former President Ronald Reagan informed the world that he suffered from Alzheimer's disease, an incurable neurological illness that depletes the brain cells. I suspected that he had it before the formal announcement. While a member of the State Assembly, Reagan's longtime press secretary and aide Lyn Nofziger campaigned for me in my Southern California district. As we ate a late evening dinner at a local Mexican restaurant, Lyn told me that he had dropped by Reagan's office that morning to see his old boss but that he would never return to see him again. Confused by the comment, I asked why.

"Because," he said, "he didn't know me. I had to keep telling him who I was. Something's wrong. I don't want to see him this way, so I won't be going back."

Shortly thereafter, lobbyist (and Reagan son-in-law) Dennis Revell visited my office in Sacramento. When I shared with him Lyn's disturbing observations, Dennis shook his head sadly and delivered a similar report about his father-in-law:

> Recently we had a family dinner when someone started talking about some major event of the Reagan presidency. He sat looking confused and interrupted by saying, "You're all talking about something like I should know what this is all about." At first, we thought he was kidding. Then it sunk in that there was something wrong.

> Maureen [Reagan's daughter] took his hand and said, "Dad, you were president of the United States. You served two terms in the White House."

> He looked dazed. "I was president?"

> Maureen led him to the window and pointed out the Secret Service agents stationed outside. "Dad, those are Secret Service agents. They guard you because you were president."

> "I was president?"

> A few minutes later, he was back to normal and engaged in the conversation as if nothing happened. That's when Nancy decided to call and make the doctor's appointment.

After the Alzheimer's announcement, Reagan maintained a public schedule at first, but the disease took its continuing toll. He made fewer visits to his Century City office and withdrew slowly from view.

Two years later, Republicans won a majority in the California State Assembly for the first time in nearly 30 years. The first official act of GOP Speaker Curt Pringle was to move Reagan's formal Capitol portrait from the basement to a place of honor at the entrance hall of the Assembly chamber. As the new majority leader, I authored a resolution honoring Reagan on the occasion of his 85th birthday. When I called Reagan's office to arrange having the framed scroll sent to him, I received a surprise invitation: would I like to come by and deliver it to the former president in person? The invitation came with a caveat. His aide told me that Reagan has "good days and bad days, and if it's a bad day you'll have to just drop it off with his secretary." I understood completely.

I had another reason for wanting to see Reagan one last time: to tell him how much I owed him personally. As I explained earlier, had Reagan not given me his speech notes when I waited three hours for him outside the Boundary Oak clubhouse in 1973, I would not have finished law school. This meant I never would have become a lawyer, a gang murder prosecutor, a judge, a state legislator, majority leader, and on my way to Congress in a few more months. I wanted to apologize for selling them to finance my education, but mostly I just wanted to say thank you.

I *needed* to say thank you.

• • •

When I mentioned later to Dennis Revell that I might see Reagan soon, he told me that his cognitive abilities are unpredictable. "It's like he's on a staircase. He goes along okay in a flat pattern and then there is a sudden big drop. Then he goes along okay at that level for a while until another big drop." He warned that the meeting might not happen.

• • •

The day before my scheduled meeting with Reagan, my Assembly colleague Tom Woods approached me on the chamber floor. He told me that his and his wife Alice's single greatest ambition was to shake hands with Ronald Reagan. He asked if they could accompany me. I didn't expect Reagan's staff to approve a group visit, but they granted permission for the additional visitors providing everybody understood that the meeting may or may not occur.

On March 21, 1996, accompanied by Tom and Alice, we drove to Reagan's office in Century City. An aide greeted us at the desk and brought us back to the suite outside Reagan's private office. Secret Service agents lingering in the hallways looked bored. Only a skeleton staff remained. Gone was the previous bustling activity in these suites. All was now quiet.

I chatted with an aide who told me that Reagan no longer made any public appearances. "He still visits the office occasionally, but only because the doctors think it's helpful if he's brought around familiar surroundings. He doesn't 'work' here anymore. About the only physical activity he gets is golfing now and then. We're all trying to keep his mind active."

As we talked, I saw a concerned look cross her face. "What are those?" she asked suspiciously while pointing to the leather-bound copies of Reagan's autobiography that both Tom and I carried. We told her we brought them in case Reagan was up to signing them for us. She explained quite firmly that when meeting Reagan *nobody* could ask him to sign anything. She said that these days, if Reagan signs something, they prefer to have him do it privately. The unspoken message was clear: they didn't want him embarrassed if he couldn't complete the task. She collected our books and said she would try to get them signed after our appointment.

• • •

When his aide invited us to enter Reagan's private office, Alice Woods walked through the door first. When she saw Reagan standing next to his desk—ramrod straight, graying hair, and wearing eyeglasses and two hearing aids—she gasped in excitement: "Oh, my goodness! It's him!" He shook our hands and greeted each of us with a sweet, slight smile. His voice, although hoarse, was still clearly identifiable as the one that moved a generation.

I told him that I had just become the first Republican majority leader of the California Assembly in 28 years—the first since he won election as governor in 1966—and that our inaugural act was to display his official portrait in an honored location in the Capitol. "That's wonderful," he replied. "I'm deeply touched by all you fellows have done." I handed him the framed birthday resolution. He took it and then studied it carefully. "Oh, my," he said. "It's beautiful."

"It's just something to add to your warehouse filled with these things that you've collected over the years, Mr. President."

He whispered repeatedly, "Thank you. Thank you. This is very beautiful."

Reagan took my arm and said he wanted to show us what he had displayed on the credenza and bookcase behind his desk. "This is my 'photo corner,'" he said as he pointed to signed portraits of German Chancellor Helmut Kohl, British Prime Minister Margaret Thatcher, Pope John Paul II, Japanese Emperor Hirohito, President Eisenhower and others. As we admired his impressive collection, Reagan said, "This way, you get in the photo all these—"

Here I am presenting President Reagan with a resolution from the California State Assembly recognizing his 85th birthday, Office of Ronald Reagan, Century City, March 23, 1996. (Author's collection)

His voice became still. He closed his eyes briefly and then he tried again to make his point while pointing to the framed pictures: "You know, these fellows here—"

He couldn't complete the sentence. I admired the photos aloud trying to ease him away from the awkward moment. Sensing his aide's growing angst, I thanked Reagan again and told him our caucus dedicated our 1994 victory to him, and that we planned to do the same in November when we retained a GOP majority. We shook his hand and said goodbye.

As I stepped from his office, I glanced back. There he stood, still straight and tall and with a sweet grandfatherly look on his face. I wanted to thank him. I wanted to tell him about those speech notes and about how they changed my life forever.

It wasn't to be. And I knew I would never see him again.

• • •

After we exited Reagan's office, his aide said she would go back and try to get our books signed. When she returned to his office and closed the door, I told Tom that she would probably sign them for him or else run them through the autopen machine. That wasn't a problem for either of us under the circumstances. I was wrong. She *was* having Reagan sign them personally, and the realization of it saddened me beyond words. From behind the door, I heard her voice as she gave directions to the great man:

"Mr. President, we'll have you sign these books for your two guests that just left. Sir, if you'll hold the pen—that's good. Now, on the first one write *To*—T—O. Now write *James*. J—A—M—E—S...."

And so it went for the next ten minutes as Reagan inscribed our books. My heart sank listening to her voice guide each of his pen stroke. Surprisingly, when she returned the books to us, his script (so familiar to me over the years) remained clear and strong.

Just before leaving, I ran into another longtime Reagan staffer, my old friend Peggy Grande. We chatted briefly, and then she stepped into Reagan's office carrying a folder with the presidential seal. She closed the door behind her, but I could hear her tell him in an elevated and slow voice, "Mr. President, I have some things for you to sign." The heartbreaking process began anew.

• • •

My 1973 Boundary Oak experience, where I received his coveted handwritten speech notes, was the first time I waited three hours for Ronald Reagan.

I waited three hours for him once more. It was on a hot, muggy afternoon in downtown Washington, more than 30 years later. At the first sight of the American and presidential flags leading his procession, I recalled Reagan's grimace, followed by a smile and an eye twinkle, when he handed over that stack of note cards to a glib kid in a Walnut Creek parking lot.

Our final goodbye: former President Reagan and me, Century City, March 23, 1996. (Author's collection)

Now, on this particular day, as I stood on Constitution Avenue with my family and watched his flag-draped casket and the riderless horse pass in front of me, I remembered what Ronald Reagan did for America and for the cause of freedom.

But mostly, I stood there and remembered what Ronald Reagan did for me.

Caisson with military honor guard carrying the body of former President Ronald Reagan to the Capitol Building, Washington, June 9, 2004. (Photograph by the author)

APPENDIX

This sheet bears some of the autographs I collected from various political leaders I met as a boy in the early 1970s. Many of their accompanying stories are included in this book. How many signatures can you identify? (Author's collection)

Engraved White House vignette signed for me by seven presidents of the United States: Richard Nixon ("RN"), Gerald R. Ford, Jimmy Carter, Ronald Reagan, George Bush, Bill Clinton, George W. Bush. (Author's collection)

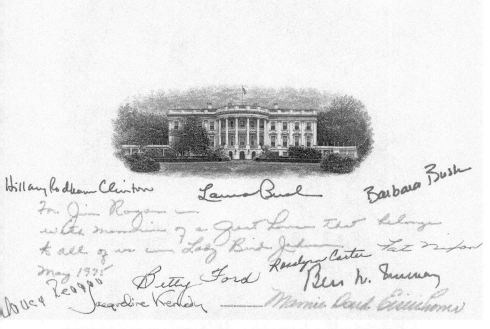

"WITH MEMORIES OF A GREAT HOUSE THAT
BELONGS TO ALL OF US."

I collected on this engraved vignette of the White House the signatures of 11 First Ladies of America—an unprecedented grouping: Bess Truman, Mamie Eisenhower, Jacqueline Kennedy, Lady Bird Johnson, Patricia Nixon, Betty Ford, Rosalynn Carter, Nancy Reagan, Barbara Bush, Hillary Clinton, and Laura Bush. (Author's collection)

To Jim Rogan – Happy Birthday!
Just keep celebrating your 39th!
Ronald Reagan

As I Remember Him: When I served as California Assembly Majority Leader, former President Ronald Reagan delivered to my office this special 39th birthday present in a leather folder, August 21, 1996. (Author's collection)

ACKNOWLEDGMENTS

Deepest thanks to WND Books and the crew who brought this project to life: founders Joseph and Elizabeth Farah, editorial director Geoffrey Stone, production coordinator Aryana Hendrawan, creative director Mark Karis, proofreader Thom Chittom, copyeditor Renee Chaves, typesetter Ashley Karis, marketing coordinators Michael Thompson and Amanda Prevette, and PR consultant Tamara Colbert.

Unending thanks to Speaker Newt Gingrich and my literary agent Jillian Manus, both of whom colluded years ago to make an author out of me, and who continue to give me more encouragement than I deserve.

My mother, Alice Rogan, was (in the words of a lifelong friend) "a tough old broad." She smoked two packs a day for over 60 years. The daughter of a longshoreman, she cursed like a sailor, lived off junk food, said whatever was on her mind, made it to almost 79, and she was gone in an instant without discomfort or fanfare. Had she lived a few months longer, she would have loved getting a copy of this book, and she wouldn't have cared what the rest of you thought about it. No son could have had a scrappier cheerleader in his corner. Life with you was never conventional, Mom, but it was rarely boring. Teri, Pat, John, your many grandchildren, and I miss you.

On those long-ago excursions to annoy famous people, I usually dragged someone along for the ride. My most consistent coconspirators were my junior high school classmates Dan Swanson and Roger Mahan, and my brother Pat. Dan is a senior partner at the law firm of Gibson Dunn and Crutcher in Los Angeles. Roger was a senior policy analyst for the Budget Committee of the U.S. House of Representatives; he died of cancer in 2018. My little brother is senior facilities director at Jones Lang Lasalle in Northern California. Thanks to each of you and, of course, if any of your memories conflict with mine, please keep your version to yourself.

Jim Dunbar, veteran KGO-San Francisco newsman and National Radio Hall of Fame inductee, died at age 89 in 2019. I'll always be grateful to him for letting a gaggle of kids hang out and meet his famous guests many decades ago instead of reporting us to the truant officers.

Now and then, a handful of friends read all or portions of the manuscript and gave me their input (or pointed out my unending trail of typographical and grammatical errors). Thanks to Ann Anooshian, Linda Bonar, Wayne Paugh, the Honorable Chris Evans, Trudy Kruse, Roger Mahan, the Honorable Chuck Poochigian, and the Honorable Scott Steiner.

Love and continued hugs to the three leading ladies in my life: Christine, Dana, and Claire. Once again, I'm through monopolizing the family computer for now.

I am always delighted to hear from readers. My website, www.jamesrogan.org, contains information on all of my books. If you wish, you can email me directly from the "Contact" tab. I read them all and (unless they're unduly obnoxious) I do my best to reply personally.

Until next time, thank you for reading my book. I hope you have enjoyed these stories of my misspent youth.

ORANGE COUNTY, CALIFORNIA,
JULY 8, 2021
WWW.JAMESROGAN.ORG